CONTENTS

INTRODUCTION

The seventies have the worst reputation of any decade in the twentieth century. Even the thirties are remembered as sweeping and tragic. In comparison, the economic crisis of the seventies, stagflation, seems positively goofy—certainly it lacks the depression's *Grapes of Wrath* poignancy, the drama of ruined farmers heading west in their overloaded jalopies. The seventies image of hard times? John Travolta in *Saturday Night Fever* gazing through a store window at platform shoes he can't afford and yelling at his father, "Would you just watch the hair? You know, I work on my hair a long time, and you just hit it."

In short, the seventies have become synonymous with mediocrity. It was a time when the economy slowed down rather than boomed or busted, happy-face buttons replaced clenched fists, and the cloying scent of strawberry incense hung over the land. Looking back in 1991, *Newsweek* made fun of the era's blandness, claiming that "it wasn't a decade of particularly widespread social action." If *Newsweek* said it, it must be true, right?

Wrong. While the seventies certainly produced its share of

1

Real-Life Seventies Nightmare

I'm thirteen, and I'm standing at a balcony in the Montgomery Mall, looking down at the waterfall with the tin seagulls and fiberglass rocks. Strangely, there is no handrail or fence around the balcony, nothing to keep people from falling off.

¶ Suddenly I realize I have on a terrible pair of jeans, the kind I've seen on other people and vowed never to wear. They're wide bell-bottoms made out of squares of denim sewn together for a patchwork effect. Orange stitching. Frizzy seams. Not only are the pants hideous, but they make my butt look fat. I want to die of shame. It's then that I begin to lean forward. In sickening slo-mo, I am falling off the ledge and down to my death on the fake rocks. And I'm glad.

dopey Top 40 hits, the decade was also a period of rapid, bewildering upheaval in social values. Many of the political ideas proposed in the sixties did not have repercussions for mainstream America until the early seventies—however, these changes tended to happen in homes and offices rather than in the streets. For instance, while feminism grew out of the sixties' civil rights movement, it was in the seventies that women demanded equality in the workplace. The first Earth Day was held in 1970. Civil rights came to mean more than the enfranchisement of blacks as a kaleidoscope of ethnic groups demanded power. Gay liberation, inaugurated with the Stonewall rebellion in 1969, grew to be such a powerful social force that the seventies are now synonymous with gay-influenced disco.

Moreover, the very structure of the family changed during the decade as the divorce rate climbed above 50 percent and open marriages, single-parent households, and swingers became commonplace. Meanwhile, "hipness" became a mainstream commodity, so much so that you could buy blacklight posters and beaded curtains—all the accoutrements of the teenage pot smoker's pad—at the Spencer gift shop in your local mall. In many ways, the quiet revolution of the seventies had far more effect on the way we live now than did the riots of the sixties.

Essayist Christopher Booker observed at the end of the seventies that "of all the decades of the Twentieth Century, it would be hard to pick out one with a less distinctive, less recognizable character." Yet, he asserted, "the Seventies were in fact the most important decade of the Twentieth Century" because it was the era in which we saw that "in our dizzying, upward flight, we have lost something of inestimable importance to us." For the first time, Americans had begun to understand the price of progress—that, for instance, the glory of splitting the atom would lead to the terrifying muddle of Three Mile Island.

So why has the decade come to seem like dead air? One reason, of course, is that the issues of the decade centered on private life, so they tended to occur beneath the surface and therefore to get less coverage in the news.

Another reason is demographics. The seventies saw a huge bulge in the number of people under twenty-five—the age group most obsessed with fads, fashion, hair, and root beer–flavored lip gloss. Worse yet, as legions of middle-aged people got divorced, many of them began slavishly following the fashions of the young. "The fads of the Seventies were no stupider than those of any other decade, but there were *more* of them," according to seventiesologist Candi Strecker, who publishes her own fanzine about the decade. "The Seventies' fads aren't what embarrass us; it's the knowledge that we took them so seriously." According to Strecker, we cringe when we look back on the decade because—with our Scott Baio haircuts and tube tops—we were fashion victims. The events of the seventies may not have been trivial, but our concerns were.

It was the beginning of the hipness-as-a-commodity era, when corporations began giving themselves makeovers to appeal to the new youth market. One ad with a caption reading "the real activists" showed a short-haired student bending over a desk. Who are the real activists? "They're the college students you don't hear much about these days. The young men and women who believe in action not violence. There are even some of their kind who are courageous enough to enter the world of business," read the ad copy for the Bendix Corporation. Other companies tried to cash in on youth by inventing a new, mellow kind of hipness that could be sold to people over twenty-five, too. In the late sixties, FM stations had pioneered free-form radio—stoned deejays who played endless space jams offered an alternative to the commercial jangle of AM radio. By 1970, pre-packaged rock and roll Muzak was coming to FM—a corporate version of revolution that everyone could enjoy. Consumption had been psychedelicized.

Everyone wanted to pose a rebel, a mystic, an antiestablishment type—even staid members of the power elite. Jimmy Carter took all of his cues from the counterculture: not only did he wear blue jeans and talk about God, but he portrayed himself as an outsider in the world of politics. He wanted the American people to see that he was in touch with those fundamental values we'd lost, like some kind of Euell Gibbons stalking through the Washington wilderness in search of the wild hickory nut of national restoration. But let's not forget that this simple farmer in blue jeans was a *member of the Trilateral Commission*, for Christ's sake.

As the president adopted what once had been the costume of the youth revolution, real-life activists became more and more invisible. The left wing—already dispersed, fragmented, and burned-out—began to seem irrelevant as the establishment itself became antiestablishment.

Painful Memory

My best friend had a crush on this guy who played guitar in a band called Tokyn (get it? the name could mean either tokin' or token, and it had a "y" in it just to give some heavy metal flair). The band played Steve Miller cover songs in people's backyards and we had to dance around for hours in our bare feet with our skirts billowing, in a desperate attempt to look like stoned hippie chicks rather than budding intellectuals bound for prestigious colleges.

"Manly, yes, but I like it too."

And people were all too eager to pronounce the sixties (that is, protests and riots) over. Historian Howard Zinn notes that "the press was full of articles with the theme, 'The movement is dead.' However, if one looked just a bit below the surface, there was massive evidence that ... people were on the move organizing.... In small towns and obscure places that had never seen such things before, there were tenants' organizations, antiutility committees, environmental groups, food cooperatives."

These radical blacks, feminists, environmentalists, and gays who were finding their voices all over the country may not have grabbed the attention of the news media, but they had turned the heads of sitcom writers. "Hip" fashion, music, and lifestyles had became a mainstream obsession, and TV was catering to a public that, on the one hand, voted Nixon into office and, on the other, had an insatiable appetite for braless hippie chicks clinging to revved-up choppers and well-muscled black thugs mouthing Marxist propaganda as they wasted honkies. The result was an endless stream of faux-hip, faux-political culture like "Get Christie Love," a series about a black undercover cop whose weapons are her karate chops and "ghetto" street smarts. Christie looks like she should be intoning revolutionary slogans and blowing up banks, but instead she works for The Man.

In the seventies, the media tended to embrace the counterculture's style but not its substance. Thus it created a bland version of hipness that even middle-aged Teamsters in Boise, Idaho, could emulate. Pop culture got the red out. It transformed those annoying radicals into cuddly Black Panthers and kooky, double knit–wearing feminists; it convinced Americans that Earth shoes had something to do with nature and that Studio 54 had nothing to do with homosexuality; it simultaneously popularized and undermined radicalism.

DON'T WORRY: THIS IS ONLY A NOSTALGIA BOOK. YOU WILL NOT BE CONFRONTED WITH ANY THREATENING NEW IDEAS.

OK, this is a nostalgia book, so why don't I just talk about "The Brady Bunch" and leave it at that? What's all this with the politics?

The seventies defy nostalgia—or perhaps they demand a new

kind of nostalgia, more ironic and self-aware. It's hard to get all choked up with longing for Watergate, Vietnam, the energy crisis, Kent State, the Iranian hostage crisis, or Jonestown. (Although compared to AIDS and the hole in the ozone layer, the crises of the seventies seem like laff riots.) While the fifties and sixties represented a period of unprecedented American wealth and optimism, by the seventies the boom had ended, the gas had run out, and the Great Society had stalled. Sonny Bono's song "Pammy's on a Bummer" seemed to speak for everyone: Americans had come down from the clean high of consumerism and now our trip had a paranoid edge to it. That is perhaps why so much nostalgia has focused on "The Brady Bunch"; many people would rather remember what was on TV in the seventies than what was actually going on in their lives.

(© 1994 DAN CLOWES)

There are other reasons why the decade is so difficult to idealize. Nostalgia is a form of escapism, and it's hard to escape into the seventies because they're so much like, well, now. Tom Wolfe noted at the end of the decade, "We are in that curious interlude of the twentieth century that Nietzsche foretold in the 1880s: the time of reevaluation, the devising of new values to replace the osteoporotic skeletons of the old." Along with the sweeping social changes of the seventies came new values and a new consensus reality, which we still live with today, only more so. (In the seventies, people's private lives and sexuality became a matter of open discussion; today they still are a matter of open discussion—ad nauseam, on "Oprah.")

Another problem: it's hard to get nostalgic about a decade that was itself so nostalgic. If you reminisce about your first date in 1975, chances are you were at a fifties sock hop, wearing a polyester poodle skirt and a scoop-neck T-shirt, while your escort had his long hippie hair greased back and his bell-bottom jeans rolled up to look more like James Dean. When you start getting nostalgic about the seventies' version of the fifties, you know things have spun out of control—instead of nostalgia you have ... *meta*nostalgia. And at some point in the future will we reminisce about the nineties' version of the seventies' version of the fifties? When will this madness end?

Between World War II and the 1970s, people tended to look forward to a future of technological marvels: rocket-powered cars would whisk us to fabulous vacation spots; computers would help housewives plan their shopping; a booming economy would wipe out poverty, offering a new egalitarianism of plenty. But by the seventies,

"Happy Days" rolled in on the wave of the fifties mania that followed *American Graffiti* (though the Ron-Howard-in-the-fifties concept was first introduced in an episode of "Love, American Style"). Originally the show had some of the "realistic" quality of the movie. The actors wear aggressively nerdy clothes, like rolled-up jeans and short-sleeve plaid shirts; Fonzie, the greaser, is a remote, scary presence; and characters constantly drop references to the larger fifties world, mentioning Eisenhower and Uncle Miltie.

¶ Slowly "Happy Days" ceased to make reference to the fifties at all and began to exist in its own hermetic universe. The beginning of the end was in the 1975–76 season, when Fonzie moved in over the Cunninghams' garage, thus transforming himself from dangerous JD to suburbanite wanna-be. Eventually he became such a loser that he taught high school shop class. A year after Fonzie moved in with the Cunninghams, the producers introduced a new, younger hunk—Scott Baio as Chachi, a character

it was clear that the future had arrived, and it wasn't so hot. Now, instead of projecting utopian fantasies into the near future, Americans began to mythologize the past. A 1970 *Newsweek* article reported that among toy manufacturers "space is a dirty word"; they had begun replacing no-longer-profitable space toys with "old-fashioned, pre-school toys."

Of course other decades had their nostalgia movements, but the nostalgia of the seventies was fundamentally different. The seventies' fifties become a full-fledged industry, a market segment, an imaginary past intended to help the bummed-out masses blot out the present. By listening to an oldies station, you could avoid ever having to hear disco or heavy metal; it could always be 1955 inside your car. By turning on the tube, you could retreat to Happy Days.

It was a strange time to grow up. The boys in my sixth-grade class would grease their hair before recess and then, with the soundtrack from *American Graffiti* pounding from someone's eight-track player, we'd dance the stroll out on the blacktop. The fifties represented a racy world of teen rituals, of well-defined gender roles and contact dancing. By the time I was in tenth grade, the fifties had changed entirely. Now it was a fluorescent-lit, numbingly bland setting for boring sitcoms. By then, many movies and TV shows about "the fifties" had nothing to do with the decade: they were set not in a different time period but in a parareality full of references to "Happy Days"—as if the TV show version of the fifties had become more authentic than the actual events of the decade (see sidebar). At the end of the decade, American punks created a new type of "nostalgia" by clipping pictures—usually of brainwashed-happy families or vapid-looking women—from 1950s *Life* magazines. For instance, the cover of the first Devo album showed an idiotic fifties man's face superimposed on a golf ball. To condemn American society one condemned not its present, but its nostalgic image of its past—showing the fifties' "innocence" as mindless absorption in consumerist fantasies.

But in mass media, the fifties stood for everything the seventies wasn't. A nostalgia book published in 1974, *The Happy Years*, finds the repression of the fifties goofy and charming: "We who came of age then ... are usually lumped together under the headings 'apathetic' or 'silent.' If we were 'bland' it was because we had simple, almost old-fashioned ideas of happiness." The book offers the comforting vision of the nation as one big fraternity, united. At times the nostalgia becomes almost threatening—"If we were black, we straightened our hair, if we were Jewish we straightened our noses"—as if to suggest that angry minorities were spoilsports who refused to participate in fifties fun.

In fact, *The Happy Years* is something of a groundbreaker, one of the first books ever to nostalgize a decade. Just as the book finds a touching lack of sophistication and hipness in the fifties, I find these qualities in the book itself—which reads like nothing so much as a gushy popular history with full-page black-and-white photos, a format that now seems strangely one-dimensional and coherent. Later nostalgia (like 1980s books about the sixties) would use spot illustrations, trivia questions, and top-ten lists—that is, short spurts of language intercut with graphics to turn history into sound bites, little blips removed from the flow of time. In the nineties, popular style mixes and matches eras; the average MTV clone might wear seventies combat boots with a fifties greasy 'do, a forties rayon shirt, and a peace sign pendant. History has become hip-hop, all bits and pieces and references and attitudes scratched together.

The fragmentation of history started in the seventies. "We are fast losing the sense of historical continuity, the sense of belonging to a succession of generations originating in the past and stretching into the future," observes Christopher Lasch in his 1979 book *The Culture of Narcissism*. While it has long been convenient to slice time up into decades, to turn these ten-year periods into units of style, our understanding of history would never be the same after the seventies, when our past was turned into a series of cutesy, dopey fashion movements that had seemingly happened on some other planet. The people in those old photos weren't us. We sneered at their innocence.

When did this fragmentation, or "decade-ization," of history really begin? Though its seeds were in the early seventies' nostalgia for the fifties, I believe it started in the late seventies, when pop culture began to face the difficult task of making the sixties safe for nostalgia. If the sixties were to be safe, time needed to be fragmented, so that events less than ten years old would seem as remote as the Middle Ages.

The Return of the Mod Squad, a 1979 TV movie, perfectly accomplished this task. The show opens with shots of the squad living their separate, straight, late-seventies lives. A frightfully puffy Pete, in a Botany 500–style three-piece suit, has taken over his father's business;

who seemed to have been transported straight from the seventies into the faux-fifties of the show. Chachi wore his hair blow-dried into "wings" and had an updated, sensitive-man friendship with Joanie. Toward the end of the show, Joanie turned seventies, too. She began to refer to cute guys as "hunks," part of her liberated-woman attitude toward men. In the last seasons, "Happy Days" became nostalgic not for the fifties—it almost dispensed with the fifties setting entirely—but for its own early episodes, with flashbacks and inside jokes. So in a sense, it became early-seventies nostalgia masquerading as fifties nostalgia.

Fonzie, who had started as a minor character, became its star at the peak of the show. He was nothing less than a fad—kids across the country were sticking up their thumbs and proclaiming "aaayyh!" —leading other series to try to cash in on his popularity. The result was that the fifties became synonymous with Fonzie. Instead of Ike, the cold war, and loafers (those symbols of the clean-cut era), the fifties now came to mean streetwise Italian-Americans with greased hair ▶

7

and gum-chewing girlfriends.

¶ For instance, Laverne and Shirley (who first appeared as dates on "Happy Days") lived in a camped-up working-class world of factory jobs, beer joints, and bowling alleys. Their show, in turn, spawned Lenny and Squiggy, the nutty JDs who put out their own album and went on a real-life concert tour. Lenny and Squiggy were anti-Fonzies: greasers who aspired to being high-toned rather than cool.

¶ By the time "Sha Na Na" aired in 1977, the TV-ization of the fifties was complete. The denizens of the variety show existed in a strange nether-fifties, in which guests from the wrong era might show up. It was a 1950s in which everyone, regardless of cultural heritage (including the one black Sha Na Na member, Denny Greene), acted like an Italian JD from Queens. The costumes also defied logic—instead of leather, these greasers wore silk, disco-influenced jackets, and even those piano keyboard scarves that were so popular in the late seventies.

¶ The same year, Donny and Marie guest-starred on the

Julie is a rich suburban housewife. Only Linc, a teacher, has retained any traces of hipness—his Afro has swelled to new heights. (Also, he has adopted a son, Todd Bridges, shuttled from his other foster home on "Diff'rent Strokes.") Though it's been only seven years, Pete and Julie seem to have retained none of the finger-on-the-pulse-of-the-youth-scene hipness that made them such valuable assets to the squad.

Weirdest of all, the villain in the show—a typical TV movie assassin—leaves two clues: a headband made of flowers and a peace sign. Everyone immediately understands that these clues refer to "the sixties" and that therefore the Mod Squad must be called back on duty; meanwhile, the fact that the squad actually quit (that is, got cancelled) in 1972 is never mentioned. Not only are the sixties reduced to a few stark symbols, but this revisionist history lumps the early seventies in with the sixties, to make the recent past seem more remote.

Things really get bizarre when Julie goes to visit an ex–drug runner, Richie, whom she used to know in "the sixties." Richie, now a drug casualty in a catatonic state, is kept in a soundproof room filled with cheesy psychedelic lights, antiwar posters, candles, beads. According to Richie's father, "the only time he's not agitated or even violent is when he's around things from the past.... But I couldn't take him back to the past, so I brought the past to him." Since the father is played by Tom Bosley (Mr. Cunningham) and his son's name is Richie, the show lurches into TV parareality, becoming a nightmarish version of "Happy Days." One can only wonder if, in the real "Happy Days," Mr. Cunningham had created an elaborate fifties setting to keep *his* son Richie sane.

At the end of *The Return of the Mod Squad*, it turns out that Tom Bosley is in fact the villain; he lures Julie into Richie's padded cell, forces her to wear a beaded Cher-like version of a hippie costume, and injects her with PCP.

While *The Return of the Mod Squad* is a blatant attempt to cash in on viewers' nostalgia for the sixties (and early seventies), it also implicitly threatens viewers with the dangers of trying to revive the sixties. One could end up like Richie, pathetically out of fashion in his cracked glasses and army jacket, locked away from the present in the padded cell of memory. Or like Julie, one could be forced to wear unfashionable clothes while freaking out on an unfashionable drug. Most important, the show infers that the counterculture died with the decade; it implies that radical politics are motivated by nostalgia (the antiwar posters in Richie's cell are there for atmosphere, not as political messages); and it threatens viewers with the consequences of seeing the demonstrations of the sixties as part of a continuous tradition of dissent in the country, one that lives on in the present.

By the eighties, this message had migrated from cheesy TV shows into the political arena. Protestors against U.S. policy in Central America were ridiculed as nutty retro-fashion enthusiasts longing for the sixties. Meanwhile, Reagan rode to power on a wave of longing for a past as gooily comforting as a plate of mashed potatoes. But it was during the seventies that politics began to speak the language of nostalgia, a pastiche of the past.

If nostalgia has become inherently political, then we need a new kind of popular history: guerrilla nostalgia.

loathsome "Brady Bunch Hour." In a fifties segment too weird to be believed, the Bradys head for a roller rink and affect Italian accents as they perform jazzed-up rollerboogie versions of oldies hits. Just when you think it can't get any worse, Donny Osmond shows up, calling himself "the Don," riding a motorcycle, and otherwise pretending to be the Fonz. This is TV at its most self-referential.

There is no cultural pattern these days, nothing ever to be nostalgic about. At least that has been the myth: we agreed not to have the Seventies because we'd been had by the Sixties. Too much hype.... We need a time-out, a period of nondefinition. And we got it in the seventies.... The seventies—the Nixon years—now seem as if someone had erased the tape of artifacts and clichés, leaving a gap.
—Howard Junker, *Esquire*, 1977

Ray Bolger, Susan Dey,
and David Cassidy
goofing around in a
generational clash on a
"Partridge Family"
episode aptly titled "The
Forty Year Itch."
(THE BETTMAN ARCHIVE)

TELE*V*ISION

TV CULTURE

The 1968 presidential campaign was the first to be waged primarily through TV ads and paid spots; by 1980, politicians played almost exclusively to TV audiences. In the sixties, TV shows like "Bewitched" and "I Dream of Jeannie" were set in a fantasy world, far removed from troubling reality; by the early seventies, shows like "All in the Family" were taking on some of the most difficult issues of the day—so much so that Archie's racist language, Maude's abortion, Mary's status as a single working woman became a part of the American debate over changing social values. Even high-brow culture—which seemed immune to TV's influence—yielded after the founding of the Corporation for Public Broadcasting in 1967 and shows like "Masterpiece Theatre" wooed intellectuals to the tube. By the mid-seventies, television finally edged out the written word once and for all when *TV Guide* became the best-selling magazine on the stands.

If the decade is remembered for anything, it should be as the

11

time when TV came into its own, vanquishing all other forms of American culture.

RELEVANCE, SITCOM STYLE

In 1968, the Tet offensive and the Chicago riots presented a unique problem to the creators of TV's comedies and dramas. If people watching the news saw a South Vietnamese police chief (in American military gear) shoot a suspected Vietcong at point-blank range, with blood spurting out of the dead man's head after he collapsed to the ground, wouldn't the upbeat hit shows of the season seem, well, a little off-key? For instance, how could you juxtapose "Family Affair" (in which a stuffy Englishman catered to the whims of spoiled American children) with America's impending defeat by a third world nation? How would the crime-free, innocent America of "Mayberry R.F.D." look next to news footage about the assassination of Robert Kennedy?

Clearly, TV shows had to be revamped to reflect increasingly explicit news programs and the depressing realities of the early seventies. In the jargon of the industry, shows had to become "relevant" if they were not to appear hopelessly out of touch. So, in what was perhaps the most radical about-face of TV history, all three networks scrambled to change their programming. As Erik Barnouw points out in *Tube of Plenty*, five years after the 1968–69 season, every hit show had been replaced—most of them by fare like "All in the Family" that would have been considered too controversial only a few years before. Not just the shows but the very fabric of TV reality had changed. (Strangely, the politicization of prime-time shows occurred just as Nixon was intimidating the press into silence about Cambodia and the Watergate break-in.)

Serious dramas, particularly those about lawyers, seemed to be the most obvious candidates for the relevance makeover, perhaps because TV attorneys like Perry Mason had already established themselves as sober yet liberal presences. However, the resulting shows—outlandish, pathetic stabs at hipness like "Storefront Lawyers" (1970), "The Young Lawyers" (1970), and "Adam's Rib" (1973)—didn't just tackle serious issues, they wrestled them to the ground and beat them senseless. For instance, the short-lived "Adam's Rib"—an update of the Hepburn-Tracy movie—debuted with an episode in which junior law

partners Adam Bonner and wife Amanda have an argument; Amanda believes that while a man is free to pick up a woman in a singles bar, a woman who tries to turn the tables risks being arrested for prostitution. The two decide to settle this burning question by making a bet, and Amanda heads for the nearest fern bar, tape recorder in hand; she chats up an undercover cop, gets arrested, and lands in jail.

The next day, she pronounces to her husband (in a world-weary, I've-been-there-and-back voice), "It sure is lousy—the clink. It's never quiet. Not even for a second." (This might seem somewhat of an understatement about the cruelties of the American penal system, coming a few years after the Attica riots, in which forty-three people died.) Because of her bummer night in jail, Amanda is too tired to defend herself in court, and Adam steps in to save her. Ostensibly, "Adam's Rib" champions women as the equals of men. In practice, Amanda is less Gloria Steinem than she is Lucille Ball; seemingly undistracted by her case load, she spends her energy on cooking up kooky schemes to humiliate her husband.

Relevance just didn't work in serious shows—they came off as didactic, wooden, and, strangely, less real than ever. But sitcoms proved to be the perfect vehicle for relevance. In 1970, CBS debuted "The Mary Tyler Moore Show." Unlike Julia of the eponymous 1968 show, Mary is not a widow, nor does she have a steady boyfriend. Instead she is a sexually liberated, independent woman succeeding in a male-dominated field. (The show's earliest outlines described Mary Richards as a divorcée—still a taboo subject. But since CBS execs worried that the audience would hate Mary for "divorcing" Dick Van Dyke, she was changed to a never-married.) "The Mary Tyler Moore Show" also broke ground by presenting a nonnuclear family; Mary's gang is made up of friends, neighbors, and coworkers, reflecting the informal communities that single people were establishing at the time.

"All in the Family" (1971), not just relevant, but excruciatingly real, broke every TV rule. Archie Bunker used taboo words like *nigger*, while characters argued about impotence, abortion, and interracial marriage. The controversial show became an immediate hit: Norman Lear had discovered a formula he would repeat in countless spinoffs, like "Maude," "Good Times," and "The Jeffersons." Instead of preaching to the audience (à la "Adam's Rib"), Lear brought up issues and let the audience draw their own conclusions—which they did. Conservatives and leftists alike saw in "All in the Family" a reflection of their

13

own values, according to a 1974 study of audiences' reactions to the show. Some saw Archie as a right-on social critic, voicing the working-class, white frustrations that they were afraid to express; others took the sitcom as Lear intended it, laughing at Archie's paranoid rants.

Not only did the show bring together the fragmented, alienated population of 1971 America, but it framed political debate in a new way. The same year that Archie Bunker first kicked Mike out of his armchair, Abbie Hoffman published "a handbook of survival and warfare for the citizens of Woodstock Nation." A how-to guide for making bombs, street fighting, and shoplifting, *Steal This Book* billed itself as "a manual of survival in the prison that is Amerika." While Hoffman's views may have been a bit extreme, his continual use of the metaphor of war to describe American life was common: in the early seventies, there was much talk of how the Vietnam War had "come home" to be waged not in a remote jungle but between the U.S. government and its people. After Kent State and Attica, it had become quite clear that Americans could gun each other down; people feared that all-out war might erupt at any moment, in the form of either armed revolution or martial law. In this climate, "All in the Family" was a brilliant stroke. It made the rift in American society seem safe. The arguments between Mike and Archie are not only humorous but harmless: underneath it all, the two men love each other.

The relevant sitcom became the predominant TV form of the time. In addition to "All in the Family" and "The Mary Tyler Moore Show," the top-rated shows of 1973–74 included "M*A*S*H," "Maude," and "Sanford and Son." These programs gave Americans a nonthreatening theater where new social values—proposed by the women's movement, the civil rights movement, and the sexual revolution—could be explored and laughed at. In effect, the relevant sitcom was a powerful form of propaganda used to train people to live in a post–civil rights society.

THE OTHER KIND OF RELEVANCE

One of the ironies of relevant TV was that it arose just as advertising was becoming a sophisticated science. The Nielsen rating service had begun to slice its audience by age group, gender, and buying power, allowing advertisers to pick and choose their viewers. As TV historian Erik

Barnouw points out, "by the early 1970s, this demographic information began to dominate trade talk"; "Gunsmoke," for instance, was cancelled not because of its ratings, but because its elderly viewers did not spend enough money. TV shows, then, were becoming vehicles through which to deliver the choicest consumers to advertisers.

Who were these consumers? Young adults, teenagers, children—the very group most likely to be seduced away from TV by the counterculture. Some shows strove to grab a young audience by adding a superficial "relevance" to the same old "My Three Sons" or "Father Knows Best" format—dressing up the sitcom family in groovy threads and having them occasionally refer to now issues.

For instance, "The Partridge Family," with its suburbanized version of hipness, offered a youth culture for the whole family. On the surface, the show appeared to be "with it." After all, it portrayed a rock group, a family headed by a woman, and life in a painted bus. But the show's brilliance was in its presentation of a cleaned-up counterculture. The generation gap? It doesn't exist in this rock and roll family. Vietnam? Never heard of it. Divorce? Mr. Partridge—like the unlamented former spouses of "The Brady Bunch"—was conveniently dead. Sex and drugs? The Partridge kids are too busy thinking up nutty schemes to get into real trouble.

In the pilot episode, the Partridges perform for the first time (in Vegas!). Afflicted by stage fright, they freeze up, until Mrs. Partridge advises her kids to close their eyes and pretend they're practicing at home. "The Partridge Family" wore the velveteen suit of hipness while simultaneously telling us to shut our eyes to the disturbing realities of the day.

The show prompted dozens of spin-off products, including a series of Partridge family mystery books in which the rock stars chase down Scooby Doo–esque ghosts. In one of these books, *The Haunted Hall*, the character Laurie uses the word *relevant* revealingly, as a metaphor for "hip" rather than for "pertinent":

> The Larkland Rock Festival now promised to be the thrill of [Laurie's] lifetime. Something she could really put in the diary she always kept, no matter what. After all, it was important that she register her ideas and thoughts so that one day she could look back and remember things exactly as they had been. Especially things that were really relevant.

Das Love Boat

What made "The Love Boat" such a strange show? Watch it repeatedly and you'll notice that there's a weird atmosphere aboard the *Pacific Princess*, a feeling of false cheer, as if something terrible has just happened, something so horrible that Captain Stubing, Julie, Gopher, and Isaac must hide the truth not only from the passengers romping on the Aloha Deck but also from us, the TV audience.

What made the show seem so ominous? One day it came to me, a revelation: "The Love Boat" is a disaster movie without the disaster.

Consider the actors. Disaster movies tended to bulk up their enormous casts with the same type of second-rate stars who appeared on "The Love Boat" (Dick Van Patten, for instance, wins a spot in the cheeseball hall of fame for doing time in both *Westworld* and a "Love Boat" episode). And both the movies and the show are structured in the same way: rather than a single story line, they weave together several (usually three) subplots.

Finally, almost all disaster movies are set in a high-tech luxury spot, such as a ▶

cruise ship, plane, skyscraper, or resort. The plot is usually the same, too: because of the negligence of the crew, technology goes berserk, plunging innocent revelers into a nightmarish fight for survival.

"The Love Boat" has the same ostentatious setting, the same crew's-responsibility-to-the-passengers theme. The difference is that on the TV show, technology never fails; the crew never loses control.

¶ Disaster movies reflect the widespread mistrust of government in the early seventies, when the Nixon administration built its own towering inferno—the Vietnam War. Meanwhile, "The Love Boat" (which first aired in 1977) sums up the mood of the late seventies. Captain Stubing, like Carter, may have control of his ship, but just barely. He seems to be more caught up in his nutty antics than he is in captaining. Disaster lurks, but it's outside the frame of the show, never to be mentioned: the energy crisis, Three Mile Island, Billygate, Jonestown, Love Canal.

Later Laurie gushes about a cute guy: "It's just that he seems so alive. So aware of his existence. So relevant."

Laurie here acts as a mouthpiece for the unseen policy makers of TV. "Relevant" has lost its political meaning in shows like "The Partridge Family," "The Mod Squad," "Getting Together," and "Get Christie Love" as burning issues became lite TV fare. For instance, in one episode of "The Partridge Family," the Partridges are helped out by cheery and subservient Black Panthers. The faux-relevant shows, rather than bringing reality to TV, succeeded in just the opposite: they made social issues seem like sitcoms.

FEAR OF ADVERTISING

In the sixties, Marshall McLuhan proposed that television was essentially different from other media. At the time, McLuhan seemed like a hip-talking, nutty Canadian academician whose views were to be discussed at grad school parties rather than taken up by advertisers. But by the early seventies, neurological researchers had measured TV viewers' brain waves and backed up McLuhan's medium-is-the-message thesis. "The response to print [advertisement] may be fairly described as active and composed primarily of fast brain waves," said one researcher, quoted in *Newsweek* in 1970. "The response to television might be fairly described as passive and composed primarily of slow brain waves." Advertisers, then, began to see TV as a magical link to consumers' subconscious. It was during the seventies that TV advertising developed into a science of riding the public's slow brain waves and commercials became increasingly impressionistic—precursors of today's sexy swirl of images.

Viewers, of course, were aware that their subconscious was under attack. One book captured public attention by "exposing" the methods by which TV, magazines, and pop songs control our minds. *Subliminal Seduction*—a pop science book that did for advertising what *Chariots of the Gods* did for UFOs—warns of airbrushing techniques and other subliminal cues used to hide secret messages in ads. In a follow-up book, *Media Sexploitation*, Wilson Bryan Key finds subliminals even on the surface of food.

Ritz crackers ... offer purchasers much more than merely a crunchy eating experience. Take half a dozen crackers out of the box and line them up on the table, face upward. Now relax, and let your eyes linger on each cracker—one at a time. Do not strain to see the surface, however. Usually in about ten seconds, you will perceive the message. Embedded on both sides of the cracker is a mosaic of SEXes [that is, the word *sex* is baked into the cracker dough].

The book shows several more examples of "sex" imbeds; the author, in order to aid untrained eyes, has scrawled "sex" all over magazine ads, a politician's poster, and even a *New York Times* photograph of an American helicopter lifting off as Vietnamese people cling to its landing skids.

Key's paranoia reflects an American fear of the media during the seventies; it was the era in which TV's full potential as a tool of social and political control was finally being tapped. Key warns: "A secret technology has existed and been in widespread use for years which modifies behavior invisibly, channels basic value systems, and manages human motives in the interest of special power structures." Though he's speaking about advertisements, his words had wider implications in the post-Watergate climate, especially after a Senate report revealed that in the fifties, the CIA had used LSD to control the minds of American citizens.

But by the seventies, the brainwashing drug of choice was TV. "We have watched so much television that we have come to expect life to be as clear and neatly packaged as the prime-time shows," said cultural critic Jeffrey Schrank in 1977. "The medium of television has so taken over the country that it has become our *only* mass medium."

THE PRESIDENTIAL AD

Nixon revolutionized the political use of TV. Given to paranoid hatred of the press anyway, he'd learned from the 1952 Checkers speech that his success depended on direct, emotional appeals to a TV audience—once he lost control of his televised image (as in his debates with Ken-

nedy), he might come off as shifty-eyed and haggard. So Nixon's 1968 campaign was built around commercials, a TV image he could shape.

The cover of Joe McGinniss's famous book about the campaign, *The Selling of the President 1968*, pictures Nixon's face on a pack of cigarettes—suggesting that his campaign relied on the traditional, thirty-second ads used for other products. Actually, the focus of Nixon's pitch were his "man in the arena" spots, hour-long segments in which he responded to the questions of (carefully screened) citizens. The segments mimicked news programs but were staged to filter out disturbing facts. As a result, Nixon's ad team more or less invented a new form: the infomercial. They had created advertising artfully designed not to look like advertising.

This suited the new environment of TV. In the seventies, credibility became all-important—perhaps because TV had become so slick, it no longer seemed believable. Advertisers' appeals now came hidden in a soothing package of "realness"; candid camera–like commercials featured ordinary people engaged in intimate conversations. For instance, one Right Guard deodorant ad mimicked a man-on-the-street news broadcast, with "average" people confiding their wetness problems to an unseen interviewer (one of the men on the street was John Amos, the father on "Good Times").

Other commercials adopted an even more subtle language. "Youth is more interested in buying an experience than a physical product," *Newsweek* observed prophetically in 1970. By late in the decade, advertising had become so oblique that the product barely mattered. Instead commercials sold a melange of style.

The message of these "lifestyle ads" (as advertising historians Edwin Diamond and Stephen Bates call them) was not that the product would solve a need, but that it would catapult you into a fabulous new life. For instance, in one car ad, Ricardo Montalban's exotic accent and his reference to "Corinthian leather" suggested that he was really selling European chic.

The Carter-Ford campaign of 1976 was the first to copy the "fake realness" of TV's most sophisticated ads and the first to fully exploit TV's visual dimension. Nixon's "man in the arena" spots, while groundbreaking, still featured the candidate on a podium, arguing his ideas. In Carter's lifestyle advertising, the would-be president argued his position with symbols rather than words.

In one paid spot, Carter roamed peanut fields in his blue jeans, talking (via a voice-over) about his closeness to the land. As he walks, the candidate reaches down and uproots certain plants, shaking them off and then throwing them back to the ground. How does he know which plants to uproot? Is he pulling them up because they're weeds or because they're inferior peanut vines? We, the citified TV viewer, have no idea what the hell Carter's doing; his decisiveness as he rips plants from the ground proves his knowledge of the land, more so than the voice-over.

The message of the ad is contained in its form rather than its content; the cheap, low-budget video look of the footage suggests that Carter is being filmed unawares, that what we are seeing is the private life of a real person. The implied message is one of authenticity, similar to Carter's Watergate-inspired promise to the American people, "I would not tell a lie."

Ford's ad team likewise tried to speak in the language of images, but with all the subtlety of a boisterous Pepsi commercial. One ad tries to make the president look folksy by picturing him seated in a living room, wearing a sweater and speaking to a group of kids. "If you have people working together and feeling good about one another, then you can work on the other problems," Ford says as the camera pans on a white girl in a sweater vest and polyester shirt, and then on a black boy wearing a junior-size leisure suit. The music swells as canned singers pick up the theme in a jingle: "feelin' good about America ... feelin' good about me." Today the ad looks pathetically dated. The folksy Ford seems stiff; the children in their Sunday best, nervous; and the feel-good message, saccharine. Nonetheless, the ad differed radically from past political spots in that it sold a mood rather than an idea.

By 1980, the image had become everything. An actor who'd once hawked hand soap on a TV commercial was now selling himself. And news show pundits now tended to focus on the image as much as the man, the media strategies as much as the issues. In a little more than a decade, the campaign had been transformed from a tentative attempt to capture voters via TV to a slick show choreographed to the tempo of the tube.

TV OR NOT TV

Something happened to reality in the seventies: it was replaced by TV. Media critic Mark Crispin Miller notes that "TV [seemed] strange" throughout the sixties—it had little to do with people's real lives. However, by the seventies, TV "was no longer a mere stain or imposition on some preexistent cultural environment, but had itself become the environment."

How did TV triumph? It edged out all other media, widening its scope to contain both the swankiest and the sleaziest that Western culture had to offer.

"Masterpiece Theatre" achieved a cult following with gossipy yet good-for-you shows like "Upstairs, Downstairs" that lent a new respectability to couch potatoism. Not only did PBS offer guilt-free TV, it also gave off an aura of classiness. Think of the opening sequence of "Masterpiece Theatre": a camera roves over an expensive study, perhaps in a rich British person's private home. The camera catches glimpses of leather-bound books, a mahogany table, and rich fabric as the classical theme trumpets. By the end of the seventies, commercials began to mimic the "refined" images of "Masterpiece Theatre," its use of bits and pieces of high culture to set a mood. In fact, highbrow culture became a lowbrow craze, with people plunking down money for anything that seemed French (bags labeled "Le Bag," cars labeled "Le Car") and wearing designer names on their butts.

Meanwhile, for the chic set, the lowbrow world of TV had become the ultimate thrill. "It's hard to say why, exactly, but all of a sudden a lot of fancy people are admitting they watch television," pronounced *Vogue* in 1975. "TV has become the latest 'in' perversion."

So popular was the tube that it began to edge out Hollywood, too. The TV movie, a form created in the mid-sixties, became a weeknight staple in the seventies. Unlike its big-screen equivalent, the TV movie was designed to be disposable, to "educate" viewers about a trendy new topic—like religious cults in *Can Ellen Be Saved*? and alcoholism in *The Morning After* (Dick Van Dyke with the d.t.'s!)—and then to be forgotten.

If it took two hours to address as complex a problem as alcoholism on TV, how long would it take to cover genocide? Nine and a half pious hours (*Holocaust*, 1978). The miniseries, a late-seventies genre, proved that given enough consecutive nights, even the darkest corners of the human psyche could be examined on TV. Hannah Arendt said that evil is banal, but I don't think what she had in mind was Robert Reed—dressed as an old-timey doctor—mouthing racist theories in the second episode of *Roots*. The miniseries helped to turn TV viewing into pageantry; shows became national events. The final episode of *Roots* drew more viewers than any program before it in history. These massive "watch-ins" were the seventies' answer to Woodstock.

Infotainment, yet another seventies innovation, brought to TV the lite-news stories that had once been the domain of *People, Life, Time,* and *Newsweek.* In 1976, a San Francisco station aired a "news" show called "Evening Magazine"; two years later, the syndicated "PM Magazine" spread the format to stations all over the country, with canned spots introduced by local anchorpeople—mustached men and bubbly blonds. Stories focused on such crucial issues as what it's like to ride in a hot-air balloon. The news-show-without-any-news reached full flower in 1981, when "Entertainment Tonight" aired daily to report on behind-the-scenes sitcom gossip and TV stars' birthdays. Shows like "ET" did more than just ignore hard news; by refusing to recognize anything that did not happen on TV or in mainstream movies, they ignored real life.

So while early-seventies TV shows sought to document reality, late-seventies TV sought to contain it. "Real People" (1979) was the ultimate expression of this new sensibility. The show introduced us to twin-brother midgets, a guy who claimed to keep 144,000 people (shrunk to one-inch tall) in his basement, a millionaire homeless man, a husband and wife who both planned to get sex-change operations. The clips were followed by in-studio gab among the show's hosts, who subtly ridiculed each week's batch of real people. The implied message: either you adopt the all-pervasive values of TV (consumerism, conformity) or you become a modern carnival geek, gawked at by a national audience. Rather than being a "real person," the show taught us how to be a fake person, the hosts serving as role models. They were grown-up versions of the cruel, popular kids in high school—Sarah Purcell flirted with the doltish Skip Stephenson as Byron Allen (who was younger and also the token black) tried hard to keep his place in the clique.

Self-Referential TV

With the proliferation of spin-offs in the early seventies, a strange thing happened to TV reality. Every sitcom became merely a corner of a larger TV world, an alternate universe that seemed to have developed a life of its own. Because actors like Sherman Hemsley (George Jefferson) had the same identities on two or more shows, you began to feel that *all* actors should retain their original sitcom identities. For example, when you see Robert Reed guest-starring on "Medical Center" as a transvestite, you can't help feeling that Mike Brady has run amok and ditched his Southern California TV family for a new life. Likewise, seeing this episode of "Medical Center" forever changes subsequent viewings of "The Brady Bunch."

¶ With increasing frequency, TV writers acknowledged the interwoven reality of all shows, allowing actors to "become" their previous selves, if only for a moment. (OK, so not all of the following examples happened in the seventies. So sue me.)

LIFE IMITATES TV

Self-help books, malls, pop swamis, Top 40 stations—all the cultural effluvium of the me decade mimicked the short attention span sensibility of TV. This may be why, despite the sweeping social changes of the decade, the seventies are now remembered for the bad blow-dried hair and Qiana jumpsuits, as a time of stifling dullness. Radical lifestyle changes of the time were trivialized and exploited by pop culture—T-shirts that proclaimed their wearer a "Foxy Lady" or a "Bitch," feathered roach clips for sale in your local mall, "Black Is Beautiful" cloth patches to sew onto your jeans. Movements like women's lib and the sexual revolution became *products*. For instance, one ad for the Singer Collection of Ethnic Fabrics proclaimed "Love Thy Neighbor" over a picture of a black model with her arm on the shoulder of a white one—achieving racial harmony had become as easy as buying the right fabric.

It was perhaps the stunning array of disposable, faddish products designed to do nothing but help the buyer feel hip that characterized the seventies. Pop social scientist Alvin Toffler theorizes that social change had begun to happen so quickly that we were all experiencing culture shock *in our own culture*. "Engineered fads are not new to history," he says in *Future Shock* (1970). "But never before have they come fleeting across the consciousness in such rapid-fire profusion, and never has there been such smooth coordination between those who originate the fad, mass media eager to popularize it, and companies geared for its instantaneous exploitation."

Is it any wonder that so many of us got caught without our mood rings on, wore the wrong kind of jeans, and generally felt like losers in the seventies? Why, when we look back at those old pictures, we seem like fashion victims, with our feathered hair and tube tops? Madison Avenue had just discovered youth culture; it came out with so many funky, outlandish products, and at such a dizzying pace, that no one could hope to keep up.

No wonder those of us who grew up in the seventies are now obsessed with pop culture. We spent our formative years chasing fads; our social status depended on whether our bell-bottoms dragged in just the right way under the heels of our Olaf Daughters clogs and whether we knew every word to "Run, Joey, Run." We suffered under TV culture's tyranny of grooviness.

At the same time that we feverishly chased after these fads—

throwing out hiking boots to replace them with Candie's high heels, for example—we also believed that history had stopped, rock and roll was dead, and nothing was happening.

According to seventiesologist Strecker, it was growing up under the shadow of the sixties that made us so depressed. "TV and *Life* magazine showed kids [of the early seventies] all the wild stuff the bigger kids were getting away with, and tantalizingly promised that someday we would have that same freedom to misbehave." But by the time we were old enough, "all that was left was decline" and we were "blamed by [the generation ahead of us] for 'not following through with the promise of the Sixties.' " Hanging out in mall parking lots, barfing at heavy metal concerts, getting wasted on quaaludes—when we tried to be rebellious, it just came off as tacky.

How could we ever live up to the mythologized sixties, especially when our elders, the baby boomers, tended to grab all the media attention? While we were in high school, they were off swinging in singles bars and discoing down at Studio 54. The same TV cameras that had captured them at Woodstock now followed them as they experimented with Est. Whatever the baby boomers got enthused about, the media proclaimed as the new trend. This may be one reason why the seventies have gotten such a bad rep: because our culture is boomer biased, America remembers the disco decade from the boomers' point of view—as the embarrassing period of their early adulthood. The seventies is seen as a dead time between the sixties and the eighties, because *that is how the boomers experienced it.* They waited out the decade drinking Perrier at the blond wood table of a singles spot.

Our generation has always lived under the shadow of the boomers. We are like the neglected sisters and brothers of an adored older child; our media "parents" gush about the activities of the sixties generation but seldom notice us. (Until the recent interest in twenty-somethings, that is.) After we spent our childhood watching teenagers disrupt society simply by sitting down in the street, it was awfully annoying when we couldn't seem to get any attention—not even by spray painting "Led Zep" all over the walls of our high schools or by performing stoned satanic rituals out in the woods.

● Robin Williams first appeared as Mork in an episode of "Happy Days" (February 1978). As Mork babbles at Richie in the staid Cunningham living room, he's interrupted by the TV set—you can't see what's on the set, but you hear the familiar "Andy Griffith Show" whistling theme song. Mork points at the TV and says something like, "I love that kid Opie." Years before, of course, Richie (Ron Howard) played Opie.

● In one episode of "The Love Boat," Carol Brady (Florence Henderson) and Mike Brady (Robert Reed) both appear as guest stars. The catch is, they're in different subplots. They don't even recognize each other, except for one brief moment when they exchange a significant glance. Like reincarnated souls, they seem to retain only the most fleeting memories of their past lives. I've said it before and I'll say it again: there's an undertone of horror, of pathos, in the perky world of the *Pacific Princess.*

● In one episode of "Batman," the Skipper (Alan Hale) plays a cook named Gilligan.

23

- In an episode of "The Fall Guy," Lee Majors approaches a bar where Isaac (Ted Lange) is performing his "Love Boat" job. The Fall Guy says something like, "Didn't you miss your boat?" Isaac (whose memory of his past life seems to have been erased) looks up quizzically.

- Byron Stewart (Warren Coolidge on "The White Shadow") plays an orderly in the "St. Elsewhere" hospital. Everyone in the hospital keeps mistaking him for a basketball player, even his former teammate Salami (Timothy Van Patten).

- In one episode of "The A-Team," Dirk Benedict (Starbuck on "Battlestar Galactica") is walking through a Hollywood set and does a double take when he sees someone dressed in a Cylon outfit.

POLITICIZING THE ELECTRONIC PACIFIER

To grow up in the seventies was to be profoundly alienated—always the ones watching TV, but never the teenagers who got to appear on TV as demonstrators, radicals, hippies, and drug casualties.

It was especially frustrating because in many ways, we were the first kids raised by the tube; as divorce skyrocketed and more and more women began seeking careers, many of us were left alone a lot with the electronic baby-sitter. And to accommodate stressed-out parents, the networks scrambled to create programming that kids could watch without supervision.

In the fifties, TV naysayers, clucking about rotting minds, recommended that children be kept from tuning in altogether. But by the seventies, everyone recognized that kids and TV went together like Cap'n Crunch and vitamin-enriched milk. A 1968 Kerner Commission report revealed that the average cartoon was essentially one act of violence after another; the seventies solution was not to get kids away from TV, but to provide cleaned-up programming. Networks began dropping action cartoons like the "Herculoids" and replacing them with new, nonviolent fare. (This may be one reason for the sudden proliferation of cartoon rock bands—the Archies, the Groovie Goulies, Josie and the Pussycats, the Osmonds. They might have kicked ass on their balloonlike cartoon guitars, but at least they weren't killing anyone.)

At the same time that they endorsed pacifism, cartoons became politicized in other ways, too. For instance, the updated Yogi Bear had more important things to do than steal picnic baskets; he was trying to undermine Mr. Bigot and Mr. Pollution. So while three-year-olds no longer had to see as many cartoon characters hitting each other with frying pans, they now had to grapple with issues like the destruction of the planet.

While the networks were carrying out the pacification of the cartoon world, PBS was pioneering "educational" TV. Shows like "Sesame Street" (1969) used the language of commercials (quick cuts, jingles, repetition) to teach preschoolers how to recognize letters. By the early seventies, the networks were copying this style to cram knowledge into the heads of their Saturday morning audiences. "Multiplication Rock" and "Schoolhouse Rock"—three-minute lessons that appeared between cartoons—mimicked not just the style, but the shallowness of advertising. As Gary H. Grossman points out in *Saturday Morning TV*, the educational spots were "not to be confused with the highly instructive vignettes in [Sesame Street].... Schoolhouse Rock and its imitators [dealt] with issues as complicated as women's suffrage so quickly that even Susan B. Anthony would be hard pressed to absorb the video accounts of her exploits."

I couldn't agree more. I still remember being confused by one "Schoolhouse Rock" segment about the role of conjunctions in sentences. Little train cars labeled "and" and "but" scooted around, linking together other trains (were the long trains supposed to be clauses?). All of this was set to a groovy rock song with a chorus that went, "Conjunction junction, what's your function?" I had no idea that this segment was supposed to be about grammar; instead I thought it was some sort of bizarre commentary on "Petticoat Junction."

If the networks' educational segments didn't do a very good job of teaching us about math or history, they did a great job of training us to be consumers. The educational portion of Saturday morning came in between the shows; these blurbs looked and sounded just like commercials. Thus, the networks taught us to pay attention to ads and to treat them as "educational," as sources of unbiased information.

But of course our real education came from prime-time TV—an especially twisted experience for those of us who grew up in the heyday of relevant programming. We learned what hip was not from our older sisters and brothers, but from Greg Brady, Linc, Sarah T. the teen alcoholic, Shaggy, and the Bugaloos.

My personal TV summer of love was in 1971, when everyone I knew seemed to live on the hazy edge between reality and Partridge family–induced fantasies. The eight-track player in our family car wheezed out The Partridge Family's "Up To Date" every time we drove. And my seven-year-old sister, left at the barbershop by herself, got her hair cut just like David Cassidy's—that peculiar shag with two lumps on top of the head. My best friend's room was plastered with posters of David, the kind that teen magazines described as kissable.

But I never watched the show for David's sex appeal. I loved "The Partridge Family" because it gave me my first taste of revolution,

rock and roll, and outrageous matching pantsuits. Sitting on the sofa Friday nights, eating Nilla wafers and freaking freely with Keith, Danny, and Laurie as they jammed in their garage was my Woodstock.

We eight-year-olds all thought that wearing ragged clothing, hanging out in parks, and taking LSD was just what one *did* when one became a teenager. But by the time we were thirteen, all of that was out of fashion. So instead we tried to emulate the singles scene by hanging out at the roller rink, sometimes gliding around on our Adidas-style skates to the beat of "Disco Duck." The girls stood in clumps, each wearing an identical outfit: scoop-neck T-shirt, tight bell-bottom jeans, and a big comb in our back pockets. Now the candy-colored hippie utopia of gyrating bodies and outdoor rock and roll seemed like a TV show we could barely remember; rebellion had become just something else you could buy in the mall. And so we shopped.

Not only were we alienated from youth culture, but we were also cut off from each other. In 1970, Toffler saw society breaking up into endless cliques, a trend he called the "subcult explosion." People were creating their own minicultures centered around low-rider cars, wine making, or macrame. Toffler saw people's tendency to immerse themselves in subcults as a response to the high-tech age, a filter to help make sense of an overwhelming barrage of information.

The same subcult explosion was happening in suburban high schools—though you defined yourself by your favorite band rather than by your favorite pastime. If you liked Yes, that meant you got high at lunch and hung out in the art room drawing dragons; if you liked the Stones, then you were majorly into partying; if it was Tull, you were a shy, awkward guy with long greasy hair, skinny legs, and hiking boots; if it was Heart, you were a heavily made-up girl with a smoker's hack laugh and a penchant for Boone's Farm wine. As in the grown-up world, the preteen social scene had split into a plethora of culture-specific cliques. It was no longer good enough to be a freak, as it had been in the sixties. Now the freaks divided themselves by allegiances to bands, beer brands, or car makes. We may have thought we were defining ourselves as individuals, but what we were really doing was consuming. No coincidence that instead of tie-dyed T-shirts, kids began to wear shirts with ads on them: Jack Daniels, Dannon yogurt, Budweiser, Chevy. We understood ourselves through advertising and—ultimately—television.

The Boy in the Plastic Bubble, a TV movie that achieved cultish popularity among teens when it aired in 1976, perfectly expressed our alienation from each other and the world. (The movie was coproduced by Aaron "Everything This Man Does Is Genius" Spelling, the guy who captured the mood of nineties teens with "Beverly Hills 90210.")

The movie stars a puffy, pre–*Saturday Night Fever* John Travolta as Tod, the boy born without any immunities. He lives in an elaborate germ-free environment with plastic walls; it looks something like a Habitrail cage (this comparison is made rather heavy-handedly, with closeups of Tod's pet mouse running on its see-through plastic treadmill). To keep up with school, Tod tunes in via a monitor—he watches the class on a TV and his schoolmates can see him on a TV set at the front of their room.

Being trapped in a plastic bubble is the ultimate seventies teen nightmare of unhipness and social failure. When Tod wants to hang out at a picnic given by his groovy neighbor Gina, his parents have to tote him there in a plastic crib, then stand by watching him in case his minienvironment fails. If having to go everywhere with his parents isn't bad enough, Tod has been isolated from his peers for so long that he has no idea how to act cool.

When Gina rides up on her horse (because no teen TV movie is complete without a girl on a horse), Tod says from his bubble, "I love to watch you ride."

"Do you always talk like that?" Gina mocks. " 'I love this. I love that.'?"

"But I do, I really do," Tod says.

"But you shouldn't tell people," Gina answers. "Because people will think you're dumb."

There you have it. The fundamental rule of seventies teendom: never act sincere.

Another crucial scene occurs when Tod, now wearing a space suit that filters his air, first attends school in person. He tags after Gina and her friends when they go out into the middle of the football field to get stoned. Tod watches as the other kids take tokes and burst into giggles. Then he pronounces, "I know what that's like.... What I do is stare at an object for a long time, any object, right? Then I let myself sink deeper and deeper inside my brain until I find this center place I like.... Have you guys ever heard of out-of-body travel?... I do it all the time."

If you were a teen in the seventies, *you had to get high*. That

meant that if you were stuck in a plastic bubble, you had no choice but to stare at your flashing disco light until you believed that you were traveling to other planets. For teens, all social functions centered around the need to *escape the seventies*, either by playing fantasy games like Dungeons and Dragons, or by pretending for all you were worth that you were a hippie and it was really the sixties, or by doing bong hits until you were drooling on the shag carpet.

In a way, we were all (those who grew up in the suburbs, any-way) the boy in the plastic bubble. We watched the exploits of hip teenagers on TV, but no matter how we lost ourselves in the riot of rock concerts or in secret pot smoke–scented cubbies of our friends' attics, our lives never seemed as cool as theirs. We tried to buy the products that would get us there—just the right bong or beaded curtain—but it never seemed to work. It was the plastic screen of TV culture that kept us from experiencing anything directly. Tod relates to the world like it's something on TV. At the beginning of the movie, he communi-cates with his classmates by watching a monitor; even one-to-one he speaks through an intercom, looks through vinyl, and kisses through plastic. To grow up in the seventies was to live inside the plastic bubble of the TV tube and consumer culture.

At the end of the movie, Tod simply walks out of his habitat into the germ-filled real world. Who among us wouldn't have liked to similarly escape from our plastic prisons into a reality unmediated by consumer products, malls, and TV shows? And so, many of us tried to go back to nature. Which leads me to the next chapter.

EARTH

*A*fter the publication of *Silent Spring* in 1962, Americans began to see themselves as custodians of nature; everything from bugs to bogs now seemed fragile enough to require human protection. But the environment didn't become a big issue until 1969—and then suddenly no other crusade seemed as important.

Why the short-lived, furious interest in environmentalism from 1969 through 1971? Maybe because pollution had little to do with Vietnam, a subject that many Americans preferred not to think about after the My Lai massacre. With the country in danger of breaking apart over the war, ecology seemed like an issue that could paste all of the angry factions back together—after all, everyone from Ronald Reagan to Ralph Nader agreed that *something* had to be done about pollution.

What Americans wanted in 1969 was an end to controversy. Nixon had virtually won the presidency on the reconciliation platform. He was "out to unite the nation again as he promised with every remark," Norman Mailer observed. In fact, what Nixon intended was not to stop the war but to take it out of sight. Once in power, the new

administration bashed the press for its negative take on Vietnam: Nixon insisted that the media had lost touch with the conservative "silent majority" and Agnew embarked on a speaking tour in which he denounced the press's "instant analysis and querulous criticism." The cowed press complied, giving little coverage to the invasion of Cambodia.

So what was the press reporting on, if not Vietnam? The same year that the largest demonstration in American history (a mobilization to stop the war) received no live network coverage, a media blitz focused attention on threatened species and habitats. For the embattled media, ecology was a safe topic—which may explain why so many papers were quick to dub the seventies "the decade of the environment."

Not to say that much good didn't come of the ecology craze. Legislation like the National Environmental Policy and Endangered Species Acts and the creation of the Environmental Protection Agency would forever change the government's role vis-à-vis the land. But when the Earth Day fervor died down sometime around 1971, ecology had become—for the masses—little more than a fashion movement. In the darkest night of the energy crisis, most people wished they'd never heard of the environment. *American Graffiti*—which celebrated the car culture of the early sixties—became a huge hit; it portrayed America as a nation of teenagers cruising in classic cars, drunk on cheap beer and plentiful gas. Hard-hit drivers wanted to return not to a technology-free Garden of Eden but to the revved-up, chrome-plated, red leatherette abundance of the postwar period.

HOW CUTE WAS MY VALLEY

And another thing: Americans hungered for liteness. Nothing had been lite in the late sixties. For instance, if you wanted to distract yourself with a play, you might end up at a Living Theater performance in which people wailed "I can't smoke marijuana" and then groped each other; and when you switched on the TV, you might be subjected to now-generation undercover cops like the Mod Squad and the Rookies arguing politics with hippie outlaws. Americans weary of all the controversy found that there was no escape, because entertain-

ment had suddenly become politicized, too. Even romance seemed to be dead, since the sexual revolution had stripped away the dance of courtship; after Masters and Johnson, sex was science.

The cuteness backlash began just as the decade turned. In February of 1970, *Love Story* hit the stands (it had the largest paperback first-print run ever). A flood of mushy products followed: Hallmark gift books, posters of sunsets with inspirational messages, cheesy paintings of children with big eyes, happy-face buttons.

Earth Day—April 22, 1970—the heady high point of the ecology movement, was as much a product of the new, mushy sensibility as it was of the countercultural revolution. In contrast to the angry protests of 1968, Earth Day was characterized by a saccharine sentimentality. Yes, some overenthusiastic protestors burned cars, but in general the New York demonstration was a peaceful, spring day be-in. The city virtually shut down (cars were banned from Fourteenth Street and Fifth Avenue), so the NBC camera crew had to cover the event from a horse-drawn carriage. If that wasn't cute enough, millions of schoolchildren all over the country took part by working on cleaning up their communities—and no doubt by drawing pictures of happy-face suns.

Of course, back in 1970, it was easier to be hopeful about saving the earth. That, along with the mushy sensibility of the time, may explain why the seventies ecology movement was so different from today's environmentalism.

Even the words imply different things. *Ecology* connotes the connection among living organisms—*cute* organisms like baby seals with tears dripping from their big black eyes. Seventies ecology was about saving endangered species and local beauty spots, picking up litter and cleaning the air; if you were sensitive, it was about feeling kind of weepy when you thought about the plight of the earth; and if you were *really* sensitive, it was about writing Rod McKuen-inspired poetry about trees and leaves and rain and more trees.

The word *environmentalism*, on the other hand, is not cute. It reminds us that we are trapped in the midst of problems from which there is no escape—problems like the hole in the ozone layer that elude our control. We no longer see ourselves as custodians of nature so much as victims of the natural forces that we have thrown out of balance. That is perhaps why, in retrospect, many of the ecological concerns of the seventies seem so nutty and off-target.

EARTH

Actor John Travolta dominates the globe.

31

DUKES OF HAZARD: WHAT PEOPLE WORRIED ABOUT IN THE EARLY SEVENTIES

The earth wasn't beyond repair: it was sort of like a basement rec room filled with partying teenagers who throw cigarette butts on the floor, nick the wood paneling, and crank the volume up to ten. The solution, of course, was to scream down the stairs, "You kids clean up—and turn off that stereo."

Somehow America had become loud, crowded, and dirty. These aesthetic complaints gained more attention in the early decade than did festering problems like the country's growing dependence on nuclear power.

Noise Pollution. Those who sounded off against noise insisted that you weren't safe even in your own home: "The modern kitchen, with its array of washing machines, garbage-disposal units and blenders, often rivals the street corner as a source of unwanted sound," according to *Newsweek* in 1970.

Partly the hysteria was based on a report issued by the EPA that found that noise posed a threat to 40 million people. Most frightening for seventies swingers was the study's claim that loud noise could impair sexual performance. Though concern might have been somewhat valid, the noise pollution scare also may have been an excuse for squares to condemn the "clamor of rock music," as *Newsweek* called that danger to ear drums.

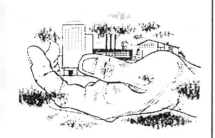

Visual Pollution. If loud noise could ruin your sex life, what about loud wallpaper? The *Better Homes and Gardens* column "Environment YES, Hysteria NO" (which amusingly reflects that period's mainstream, don't-rock-the-boat ecology) tackled the visual pollution problem in 1970. Our "commercial districts ... are jungles of clashing colors," worried the columnist. Other visual villains were "drab, ill-designed housing," dune buggies, and billboards. (The magazine didn't mention its own ill-conceived interiors, including avocado-colored love seats that even the Brady family might have snubbed.)

Litter. It wasn't large corporations dumping dioxins into the water supply, it was *you:* that tinfoil gum wrapper, that pop-top, that cigarette butt you dropped. Antilitter hysterics saw the planet as a messy room; our only problem was how to get everything into the trash can. *Better Homes and Gardens* suggested that science would soon solve this problem: "Pneumatic tubes will whisk garbage to central collection plants" was the magazine's perky solution. While some worried that—what with airtight, poisonous landfills—simply moving the garbage around was no solution, most were content to blame a polluted planet on litterbugs.

One of the worst pieces of propaganda was a public service announcement created by the Advertising Council, a commercial that plagued my childhood with guilt. In the commercial (as I remember it), a carload of partying people speeds down the highway; they throw a bunch of bottles out the window; their trash lands right at someone's feet; the camera then pans up the man's body and we see he's a Native American; a close-up of his face shows a tear rolling down his cheek. Seemingly the Indian doesn't mind the highway that cuts through his land or the cars that pollute his pristine sky. No, it's those bottles and wrappers on the side of the road that have prompted his silent crying. The commercial used to send me into paroxysms of guilt when I was a kid—after politically charged American history classes in elementary school, I was already painfully aware of my passive role in stealing land from Native Americans. The ad cleverly capitalized on this guilt, but at the same time it implied that we could right our wrongs toward Native Americans simply by refraining from pitching Coke bottles out our car windows.

The Bald Eagle. Nowadays a bald Eagle may mean an aging member of the group that recorded "Hotel California." In the seventies, however, the bald eagle was a bird, most famous for its threatened existence. In the bicentennial year, *Natural History* magazine lamented that "the bald eagle is acquiring a doleful new role as a symbol of Americans' destruction of their own natural heritage." Now here was an environmental cause that both hard hats and hippies could get behind: everyone worried about DDT's effect on the eagle—and the national embarrassment that would ensue if the bird became extinct.

Bruce Dern, Superstar?

Now he's known primarily as the father of Laura Dern, but once upon a time, Bruce was considered one of the hottest actors in Hollywood. Renowned for his ability to play psychos, he made his reputation in more than a hundred TV shows and numerous sleazy films, like *The Incredible Two-Headed Transplant* (in which he ate a baby).

Merely the presence of Mr. Dern in a movie assures that it will be either a horrendously overacted exposé of the now generation or a mainstream film with some kind of unintended weird vibe to it.

Dern studied method acting under Lee Strasberg in order to learn how to emote. And boy could he emote. With his husky voice and glittering eyes, Dern radiated barely contained madness; he was the consummate Guy on the Edge.

Maybe that's why he always got the same kind of roles. For instance, he has only a few seconds on-screen in Hitchcock's *Marnie* (1964), but they're crucial. As Marnie remembers the incident that has driven her mad, who should be at the ▶

center of the scene but Dern? He's the sailor who was killed by her prostitute mother.

¶ In *Psych-Out* (1968), Dern plays a sackcloth-clad hippie who proclaims, "God is in the flame" and lights himself on fire, much to the dismay of his deaf and dumb sister, who's on STP.

¶ In 1967's *The Trip*, he costarred as Peter Fonda's "baby-sitter," guiding Fonda through an acid trip. Fonda freaks out, and with Dern for his guide, who can blame him? The same year, he scored a lead role in American International Pictures' *The Cycle Savages*, in which he rode around on a chopper and dispensed LSD to underage girls.

¶ The seventies was Dern's decade. Suddenly he was getting large roles in movies that had nothing to do with bad acid trips or topless hippie chicks—including such respectable productions as *Coming Home* and *King of Marvin Gardens*. In 1975, *Time* magazine speculated whether Dern would become a big-name star: "There is a human time bomb ticking away in Hollywood. He is called Bruce Dern."

34

Also threatened with extinction was Senator Tom Eagleton, McGovern's 1972 running mate. In the course of the 1972 campaign, it came out that Eagleton (who was not bald) had undergone shock treatment. He was then dropped from the ticket. On the whole, the bird came through the seventies much better than did the senator.

SPACESHIP EARTH

If any film sums up the weltanschauung of early-seventies ecology, it has to be *Silent Running* (1971). The movie takes place on board a space freighter that carries the last of Earth's plants and animals, which of course are housed in huge geodesic domes. Four crew members man the freighter; three of them can't wait to return to sterile Earth. The fourth, played by Bruce Dern (see sidebar), wanders around in a burlap Jesus robe, eats only food he grows himself, and wears his hair long and straggly. Like Shakespeare's mad Ophelia, he sings ditties to himself—only Dern intones park service jingles.

We learn that Earth is doing just fine without its forests: the temperature's an even seventy-five and there's little disease or poverty. So when Dern's shipmates ask him what he has against the enclosed mall that the planet has become, Dern answers, "There's no more beauty."

Predictably, faceless bureaucrats order the crew to destroy the forests and return home, and Dern murders his shipmates to save the trees. After that, Dern is the only actor on-screen as the movie veers way off into outer space. In fact, with endless scenes of Dern emoting, talking to himself, and following his own mad logic, the movie begins to resemble some sort of unhinged Beckett one-act.

Campier than the geodesic domes that house the forests or the white plastic interior of the spaceship is the soundtrack of Joan Baez songs that swell at every dramatic moment. Also of note are the robots that make whimpering sounds, which become Dern's only companions. Director Douglas Trumbull, who created special effects for *2001: A Space Odyssey*, makes his robots more cutesy than the doomed bunnies in the forest. (Fact: Trumbull created his two-limbed, knee-high drones by putting amputees in robot costumes. A few years later, *Star Wars* would copy these cute robots with the whistling R2D2.)

What does this say about early-seventies environmentalism? First of all, the movie is set in space, which had become, oddly, the vantage point for those who wanted to save the earth. At about the same time that *Silent Running* was made, *The Whole Earth Catalogue* chose as its symbol a picture of our planet as seen from space; this symbol of the "whole earth," it was hoped, would make us more aware of our common fate.

The movie also reveals the naivete of the era. While in *Silent Running* the earth stays an even 75 degrees without any vegetation, most people are all too aware nowadays that the planet would be more likely to average about 125 degrees if plants weren't around to help stave off the greenhouse effect. But for mainstream ecologists back in the seventies, grass was little more than Earth's shag carpet and mountain views its wallpaper. In fact, designers used huge color photos of mountainscapes and forests to turn nature into wallpaper—literally.

Also characteristic of the seventies is the movie's paranoia, pitting an individual against a society gone wrong. In *Futureworld*, two reporters try to expose an amusement park that is replacing world leaders with androids (not a bad idea, actually); and in *The Poseidon Adventure*, those who survive do so because they ignore the instructions of ship officials. But Dern is not your typical disaster movie victim; after murdering three people and raving about the taste of fresh cantaloupe, he's hardly a sympathetic hero—or an advertisement for ecology. Rather, the film resembles *Billy Jack* in its moral haziness: in both movies, a violent hero battles a lunatic establishment—all in the name of pacifism, of course.

Dern's environmental vigilante may seem too campy to be true, but in the seventies, life had a way of imitating low-budget movies. A few years after *Silent Running* appeared, Manson gal Squeaky Fromme tried to gun down President Ford in a wacky bid to save the earth. At her hearings, the freckle-faced "family" member spouted, "There is and are an army of young people and children who want to clean up this earth. . . . The important part is the redwood trees. We want to save them." And she told a reporter, "Cutting down redwood trees is like cutting down your arms and legs." Squeaky, a real-life version of the *Silent Running* ecology lunatic, seemed to relish the idea of chopping human limbs to save tree limbs.

Why did Dern suddenly do so well? Perhaps the answer has less to do with his talents than with the zeitgeist of the seventies, a period during which any psycho on a crazed mission to remake society could became a superstar (Spiro Agnew, the SLA, Jim Jones). Dern perfectly captured the mood of seventies madness. No run-of-the-mill nut who murders randomly, Dern instead played clever paranoids—guys who would do anything for the sake of their ill-conceived mission. His performances also may have touched a nerve because—with his asexual, panic-tinged megalomania—Dern resembled a hipper version of Richard Nixon.

Unfortunately, his timeliness in the seventies proved to be Dern's downfall. Hollywood's ticking time bomb fizzled in the eighties, when it was no longer fashionable to be psycho.

Carter: The Negative Heel

There are frightening parallels between the advertised images of Jimmy Carter and the Earth shoe. While the "natural look" had been popular since the late sixties, the Earth shoe pioneered a new sort of fashion statement: outright ugliness. "There was a time when the Earth negative heel shoe was the only shoe in the world with the heel lower than the toe. In those days the other people who made shoes just laughed at us," reads a 1975 ad. The Earth shoe billed itself as an outsider to the frivolous fashion industry, a piece of footwear so healthful that it made all other shoes seem ornamental.

¶ Likewise, Carter styled himself as an outsider to Washington power circles, a man of such purity that he lacked the flash of all other politicians. In his ads, as in those for the Earth shoe, he played up his victim-of-a-conspiracy image: "Are you going to let the Washington politicians keep one of our own out of the White House?" And his connection with nature: "My children will be the sixth generation on the same land." And his down-home honesty: "I'll

THE POLYESTER LUMBERJACK: ECOLOGICAL FASHION FADS

The essential contradiction of seventies fashion was one of form and content. The fabrics were as synthetic as could be, but the look was "Little House on the Prairie" smocks and child-of-nature overalls. The weirdest of the synthetic odes to the earth would have to be those shiny shirts made out of Lurex (or some other wonder fiber) with photographs of nature printed all over them. I begged for one of these when they came out sometime around 1976, and I actually got one—a clingy, itchy button-down with photos (yes, real photos) of waterfalls on it. The shirt shone like Mylar, the greens of the trees as iridescent as a beetle's back. Without meaning to be, the shirt had a bad-trip, psychedelic edge to it. I wore it to school once and then never again—I felt like some kind of shimmering, tree-and-waterfall-covered clown in it.

So many pieces of seventies fashion testified to this same ambivalence toward technology. For instance, a company called Arpeja made tops with the label "Organically Grown" sewn into the neck—but the shirts hardly looked like something you'd wear on a commune in Vermont. Instead they were skintight and "space dyed"—a futuristic term to describe those thin streaks of color that blended into one another for a blurry pastel effect. (This fabric design showed up on every knit item from sweaters to hats to vests in the seventies.)

Earth shoes, meanwhile, used science to help you return to nature. Anne Kalso, the appropriately dour inventor of the shoe, "saw footprints in the sand, and realized that with every footprint the body was designing the shoe." Then came her years of research; to read the ad copy, you'd think she had spent the whole time in a lab coat pouring fluids into test tubes and checking her oscilloscope readings until finally . . . the shoe.

And speaking of bulbous footwear, hiking boots were must-haves. For the complete just-in-from-the-campground look, you needed a flannel shirt over a T-shirt, scruffy jeans, a bandanna and a backpack.

Or, a slight twist on the hiking outfit was "The Waltons" look. In such a getup you could imagine yourself one of the decent working folk who rose with the sun every morning to toil with wholesome dignity out in the fields. *Esquire* called this the "Pepsi Proletariat" look in 1970.

According to the magazine, it "consists of overalls, flannel shirt, and heavy work boots, the traditional accoutrements of the working class. . . . To adopt the Pepsi Proletariat guise is to express one of the more euphoriant pipe dreams of the counterculture: the hope that a coalition may someday be fashioned out of workers and freaks."

ROLL YOUR OWN FASHION

Also big during the decade was do-it-yourself recycling of waste materials into high-fashion garments. *Seventeen*, for instance, urged its readers to make gypsy skirts out of sewn-together neckties and knickers out of old jeans.

The most outlandish and fervent do-it-yourselfer had to be Pop-Top Terp, the man who started the pop-top clothing craze and then named himself after it.

In 1970, you opened a soda or beer can by grabbing a ring and peeling back a triangle of aluminum. The resulting "pop-top" came free from the can and could be dropped onto the ground— preferably on an unspoiled beach or in a wooded glade. Millions of pop-tops polluted the country, and to judge from public outcry, they represented the number-one threat to the environment. In Jimmy Buffet's song "Margaritaville," he ruins a perfectly good flip-flop when he steps on one of the aluminum gizmos. Yes, pop-tops could become shards of death for those not equipped with proper footwear. (And who was?)

Just when it seemed America would drown under a silver sea of pop-tops, a fashion genius with a seventies flair for crafts came to the rescue. While others had thought to hook pop-tops into strings, Pop-Top Terp's breakthrough was to attach them sideways, too, into "chain mail." As with other avatars, Terp's genius lay less in his technological discovery than in its application. His first creation was a vest, but later there were chokers, hats, dresses, tunics, and accessories.

As documented in his 1975 book *Pop-Topping*, Terp made his fashion debut at a Tom Jones concert. "I *had* to have something really outstanding to wear," recalled Terp. Luckily for the course of history, the concert was delayed and Terp had time to show off his outfit. "Everyone was amazed. . . . They wanted to know if the pop-tops cut us, or whether they weren't a little too heavy to wear." Faster than you

never make a misleading statement."

In short, both the shoe and the president took the same advertising tack—in the spiritual mid-seventies, they offered us a vision of a world without artifice. The Earth shoe was a fashion item that pretended to be too good to care how it looked; Carter was a politician who pretended to be too pure to court the power elite. Nonfashion. Nonpolitics. It made sense back in the era when no one wanted to be associated with the establishment.

Up until the sixth grade, I went to one of those earnest religious day schools, the kind of place that had been unduly influenced by early-seventies sentimental Christianity of the *Godspell* variety. They taught us how to weave God's eyes out of Day-Glo-colored yarn. Also to say "I love you as a Christian"—which we girls used as ammunition against the boys. You'd go up to a boy and say, "I love you," wait to see his look of panic, then quickly add, "as a Christian" and burst out laughing.

¶ I was, like, queen of this school. For one thing, when it came to the SRA reading cards, I got up to the aqua ones while most of the other kids were still struggling with the brown ones. Best of all, when the Christmas play came around, I got to be Mary because I had the perfect hippie-style scraggly blond hair. The kid who played Joseph was black (for that multicultural effect). Jesus was a flashlight swaddled in toilet paper and lying in a doll's crib. I had a total crush on my stage husband, who was commonly acknowledged as the cutest boy in our

38

can say "what's new, pussycat?" pop-topping became the rage in a nation hungering for anything silvery, synthetic, and ecologically correct.

Terp appeared on TV game shows and in *Time* magazine. He even used his craft as therapy for troubled teens: "My work with Boys' Clubs has been especially satisfying, because in several instances problem children have taken new interest in creative activity.... Pop-topping has kept most of these boys off the streets, where they otherwise would have been, and out of the way of bad influences." One boy, he wrote, "not only achieved a sense of accomplishment, but had actually come to the point where he could effectively supervise the younger boys." What hoodlum would have time for robbery if he had to scavenge the street for the hundreds of pop-tops required to make a full-length tunic?

Then aluminum can manufacturers dealt a fatal blow to this indigenous American folk art: they invented the stay-on tab. A hush settled over the pop-top world, and then ... it was gone. Let's ask ourselves: were the benefits of the nondetachable tab worth what we lost as a nation? Sure, our parks are cleaner, but crime is on the rise as restless youths roam streets that are now barren of the aluminum slivers that once made their lives worth living.

DIET FOR A SMALL PLANET

In 1974—thanks to the politicization of consumers—the FDA required companies to list ingredients on packaging. People were especially concerned with the content of their food because what you *shouldn't* eat had become an obsession. Whereas in the optimistic postwar years, health-conscious eaters chomped down wonder foods, studies in the seventies were showing that everything from meat to saccharin could give you cancer, so the emphasis had shifted from what you should eat to what you shouldn't.

The most evil of foods, of course, was white sugar. In our house, the health-food craze hit around 1972 when Mom suddenly got hip to the sugar conspiracy. One day our shelves groaned with Hohos, Lucky Charms, Pop Tarts, and those subliminally embedded Ritz crackers; the next day, the only snack food in the house were these rock-hard molasses cookies that you had to suck on first so as not to break a tooth.

Enthusiastic hikers, my parents also sometimes kept a bag full of gorp (granola mixed with nuts and, "for energy," M&Ms) around, as if any minute we might be suddenly be called on to climb a perilous mountain pass. Because all other junk food had been purged from our shelves, the M&Ms were a coveted commodity, and many was the time when my father would storm into the kitchen saying, "Are you girls picking the M&Ms out of the gorp again?"

But while Americans were developing a taste for granola and yogurt, a gastronomical counterrevolution was also taking place. As noted by cultural critic Jeffrey Schrank, "Fifty corporations effectively control much of the food we eat.... The shopper is almost forced to choose among an increasing number of highly processed food combinations and must exert extra effort to purchase simple, natural foods." Schrank saw the health-food trend itself as a sign of how bad things had gotten: "The highly processed, additive-laden food is considered normal"; it was healthy food that was the anomaly.

Part of the trouble was that Americans *liked* high-tech, gimmicky food. We wanted to be eating whatever the astronauts were eating, even if Tang tasted like toxic waste. We wanted food that was entertaining: like Pop Rocks (the candy that exploded in your mouth and was rumored to be the death of Life cereal's little Mikey), Pringles (perfectly formed potato chips made by stamping a mush of vegetable matter and chemicals into identical chips and stacking them in tennis ball–like cans), and Koogle (peanut butter that came mixed with jelly or chocolate sauce). And with Bac-Os, Sugar Jets, Wink, Bugles, and Kix around, buckwheat bread seemed kind of boring.

Also, because working mothers and single-parent families had less time to cook, convenient (and highly processed) food had become a necessity. In the Decade of the Environment, McDonald's sales increased tenfold.

THE DEPARTMENT OF ENERGY

As the decade began, the ecology movement was much more concerned with wildlife conservation than with energy policy (though of

class. When he and I stood there with our flashlight baby Jesus—while all the kids who had to play donkeys and sheep and cows groveled at our feet—I felt that everything in my life had clicked into place. I was popular.

Then tragedy struck. My parents began to realize that the school was turning me into a mini Jesus freak. I had started gazing at people with this glazed look and saying, "I prayed for you today. Jesus is going to come wash out your heart with soap and water."

So the next year, 1973, I found myself at a new school. It was like going from *The Living Bible* to *Lord of the Flies*. My classmates never said "I love you as a Christian." Instead, whenever the teacher made one of his frequent disappearances, they slammed each other to the ground or kicked each other with their hard little athletic legs. The first week of school, I came home with a red welt on my face where someone had thrown a shoe at me. After that, I took to hiding between the door and the wall, trying to remain invisible in the midst of this progressive-education hell.

I was not alone in my ▶

misery. Watergate was in full swing—the adults were glued to the TV, watching men in suits argue. And suddenly there was this scary feeling that even as the government toppled, America was no longer the land of plenty. Inflation soared and the energy crisis hit. Gas had become as regulated a substance as liquor: you couldn't buy it on Sundays.

¶ The worst part was, even though everyone knew Nixon was evil, he still retained his supernatural powers, like some kind of crazy wizard locked in that White House, casting curses on this blighted land. It wasn't just speed limits he was tampering with, either, it was the very nature of time. In November, he decreed that America wouldn't "fall back" an hour for winter—we'd stay with the summer's daylight savings time in order to save energy.

¶ So the winter of the energy crisis, kids went to school in mornings that were like nighttime. When I woke up at 6:30, it was really 5:30 in the morning (non-1973 time). And when my family sat around the table for breakfast, it seemed more like we were eating a midnight snack. All of the

40

course the issues often overlapped). The early antinuke activists, for instance, tended to criticize reactors for the way they spewed hot water, killing off the wildlife in lakes and streams. It seems strange now that environmentalists worried about dying fish rather than, say, the rise of infant mortality in communities around the reactors or the risk of a meltdown. However, since the antinuclear movement's strongest weapon was the 1969 National Environmental Policy Act, all the fuss about fish made sense: the legislation was designed to protect local ecologies, so activists found that using the fish-kill complaint was the best way to shut down reactors.

But in the coldest days of the energy crisis of 1973–74, preserving fragile ecosystems began to seem like the least of America's worries. The crisis started during the Yom Kippur War, when the United States supplied military aid to Israel; the Arabs retaliated with an OPEC oil embargo. The effects of the embargo on Americans' day-to-day life were immediate and crippling—most notoriously, the long lines at gas stations. In 1979 (after civil war broke out in Iran and OPEC pumped up oil prices), people once again found themselves waiting in line; freaked-out drivers would fight, riot, even shoot, for gas. "These people are like animals foraging for food. If you can't give them gas, they'll threaten to beat you up, wreck your station, run you over with a car," said one Texaco dealer, quoted in a 1979 *Life* wrap-up of the decade. "We're all so busy at the pumps that somebody walked in and stole my adding machine and the leukemia-fund can." The sudden scramble for what had once been so plentiful and cheap seemed like a symbol of America's mediocrity, its transformation into a country that could be pinched by other world powers and circumscribed by scarcity.

People felt enraged and defeated by much more than just long lines. In the paranoid post-Watergate years, almost 50 percent of those polled said they believed the gas shortage had been fabricated so that oil companies could raise prices—not an unreasonable assumption, considering that these companies had enjoyed tremendous profits during the height of the energy crisis.

While Nixon coddled the oil interests, he enacted an energy conservation program aimed at getting the average citizen to turn the heat down, drive slowly, and use less light: The housewife who forgot to turn off the hall light was to blame, not the oil concerns that failed to invest in domestic wells or companies that gobbled energy to churn out products like happy-face toilet seat covers.

But hey, why force Americans to do without when you could rely on the magical, clean energy of the atom! Nixon's real solution to the energy crisis was not conservation or solar power; it was a new energy policy with a cheesy bicentennial name, Project Independence, that pushed nukes. The president so afraid of investigative reporter Jack Anderson had little fear or curiosity about the power of the atom. "All this business about breeder reactors and nuclear power is over my head," Nixon once blithely commented. "But it has always been fascinating to me that if a people are a great people, we must always explore the unknown." Nixon lobbied for relaxation of safety measures so that reactors could be built in a jiffy.

Meanwhile, the antinuclear movement was massing. In 1974, Karen Silkwood's car ran off the road as she was on her way to give the press information about the plutonium-reprocessing plant where she worked. The same year, the Atomic Energy Commission—which had just released a report about the high fallibility of reactor safeguards—was dissolved. In its place, the industry-oriented Nuclear Regulatory Commission took charge. The name change said much about the new attitude toward nuclear energy. The word *atomic* was a relic from the 1950s fetishism of the bomb. Cashing in on Americans' awe of the wonder weapon, companies used the word to sell products like Atomic Fireballs (those hot candies you can still find in some truck stops). One town in Idaho even named itself Atomic City. *Nuclear*, on the other hand, was a rather ominous scientific term for the same thing—no one would want to name their town Nuclear City. "Atomic" energy would power the fabulous cities of the 1950s future, giving us magical radioactive barbecues that never needed coals to heat up; but "nuclear" reactors were a complicated fact of the 1970s here and now. Atomic energy worked perfectly—the product of postwar American ingenuity. But "nuclear energy" had a depressing seventies ring to it, especially when you imagined slipshod engineers designing the radioactive equivalent of a Pacer or Gremlin.

For instance, a 1975 fire at a plant in Brown's Ferry, Alabama—which started when a technician, who was trying to find a leak, held a candle too close to some insulation—made many question the safety of other such plants. (The real question, of course, was why the

lights in the kitchen blazed and the windows, like black mirrors, reflected us as ghostly shapes. I used to imagine that the world outside had turned to tar, like some "Twilight Zone" episode where we were the last ones left on Earth, only we didn't know it yet. I cannot exactly express it, the horror of those black-windowed breakfasts. Here my parents were—my mother telling us to finish our oatmeal and my father reading the paper—as if they were trying to trick my sister and me into thinking everything was normal, that the sun was out instead of the stars.

At 7:30 (really 6:30—I was always subtracting an hour in my head), I walked the two blocks to my bus stop. When my mother hugged me good-bye, I could feel by the tightness of her grip how afraid she was to have me stand under the stars, alone, waiting for the bus. She made me carry a flashlight, which I clicked off as soon as she closed the door. I'd walk along between the pools of light cast by the streetlamps, which made the pavement scintillate with each of my steps. It was magical and scary. My mother had told me not to talk to any ▶

41

strangers in the dark, and I half expected some man to follow me or watch me from the shadows, but no one ever did.

¶When the bus came, it bore down on me with its headlights, groaned, and then swung open its hinged door to let me in. It would carry me to my day of hiding in the corner of the classroom. It would carry me to this senseless new school that existed inside this senseless world of oil rations, Watergate, and Vietnam.

¶I kept having the same nightmare that year. I dreamed that I stood at my bus stop in the crisp, frosty air of night, my breath coming out like cigarette smoke. Just standing there, I felt a thread of terror. When the bus came, it moved the way things do in dreams—appearing soundlessly from nowhere. It rolled up like a hearse and came to a stop in front of me, but the driver seemed not to see me. I pounded on the bus, I yelled, but he wouldn't open the door, for the night had turned to tar, muffling my voice. And then the bus started up again and pulled away. That was all—so ordinary and yet so terrible. Nineteen seventy-three—so ordinary and yet so terrible.

guy was using a candle. Couldn't they afford a flashlight?) With Ralph Nader's activism, the death of Karen Silkwood, and the controversy over several plants around the country (and, simultaneously, the U.S. withdrawal from Vietnam), nuclear power had become *the* liberal crusade. However, with the election of Jimmy Carter, who dumped Project Independence and de-emphasized nukes, it seemed that the movement might lose steam.

And then came Three Mile Island. The reactor core of the Pennsylvania plant threatened to melt down after the cooling system failed; instead it released radioactive gases. Much has been made of the uncanny way in which *The China Syndrome* predicted Three Mile Island. The movie, which premiered two weeks before the accident, depicted a similar near-meltdown. If that wasn't weird enough, a scientist in the movie explains that the China Syndrome could take out "an area the size of Pennsylvania." (No one ever talks about how the 1977 TV disaster movie *Red Alert* anticipated the accident *years* ahead of time.)

What's interesting about *The China Syndrome* is the way it tries to turn a nuclear accident into another Watergate. Jane Fonda stars as a typical late-seventies lite-news anchorwoman who happens to be doing a breezy story at a nuclear plant when the accident occurs—she then transforms herself into a classic investigative journalist hero. The plot of the movie tells the same old seventies tale: journalists battle corporate powers and government restrictions to get the story to the people—as if merely seeing a news show that reveals the truth about a nuclear plant can inoculate people from the deadly effects of radiation, as if a media barrage can save us from a meltdown! While the gripping movie may overemphasize the press's ability to galvanize the public, it does show the Nuclear Regulatory Commission as an arm of the industry, unfit to enforce safety regulations.

But the depressing reality was that the American public, already beset by a string of crises, found it hard to worry about a problem as invisible as radiation. Two weeks after Three Mile Island, 80 percent of those polled were still in favor of nuclear energy; more depressing, Three Mile Island only helped to confirm the worst fears of the environmental movement: no amount of safeguards could make a nuclear plant safe. For this writer (who attended antinuclear rallies as a bored high school student), there was an air of hopelessness.

While *The China Syndrome* eloquently sums up the corruption of the nuclear industry, another movie, *No Nukes*, inadvertently shows how depressing it was to be an activist after Three Mile Island. The film documents several concerts held to benefit an antinuclear group. On hand are some of the worst lite rockers of the decade, playing to one of those massive stoned audiences (a sea of pink faces and bandannas) typical of the post-hippie, middle-of-the-road music scene. The Doobie Brothers sing "What a Fool Believes" and James Taylor does "Your Smiling Face"—the frightening possibility of a melt-down seems absurd after you've been numbed by so much musical blandness.

Though 300,000 gathered at one demonstration several months after Three Mile Island, the antinuclear movement soon lost momentum. Reagan reversed Carter's energy policy, undoing in several swoops the work of the seventies antinuclear movement. Jane Fonda, once the movement's most flashy proponent, began making exercise videos in which she urged women to "feel the burn"—and she didn't mean the burn of radiation.

By the mid-eighties Americans could laugh off Three Mile Island as an averted disaster. But even as Reagan relaxed safety standards, the effects of radiation lingered in Harrisburg.

Although demonstrators had blocked the construction of more than a hundred reactors, pronuclear forces had the money and political clout to make nuclear energy seem like business as usual. By the mid-eighties, Three Mile Island Unit 1 was back in service.

EARTH

"Sometimes you feel like a nut."

43

Democratic presidential candidate Jimmy Carter munching on a BBQ chicken leg. With him is his brother Billy in Billy's service station.
(UPI/BETTMAN)

LABOR

I n the hopeful, booming sixties, it had seemed as if poverty could be wiped out. Terms like the "war on poverty" suggested that Washington technocrats finally would conquer society's oldest scourge.

Around 1969, things began to look a bit more complicated. As Barbara Ehrenreich observes, it was then that people in the professional class suddenly "discovered" that America didn't just have an urban underclass, it also had a mistreated and malcontent working class, many of whom were white.

One person who suddenly became aware of white angst was Harvard student James Fallows. In 1969, he went before the draft examiners and got himself disqualified on a medical technicality. But as he left his draft examination that day, he realized that it was class privilege, not his devout pacifism, that had saved him from having to go to war. "Even as the last of the Cambridge contingent [i.e., Harvard and MIT students] was throwing its urine and deliberately failing its color-blindness tests, buses from the next board began to arrive. These bore the boys from Chelsea, ... the white proles of Boston," Fallows recounted in a 1975 *Washington Monthly* article. "It had clearly never

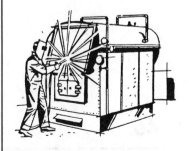

occurred to them that there might be a way around the draft. They walked through the examination lines like so many cattle off to slaughter." For Fallows, the Chelsea boys were passive (even stupid) victims of an unjust system.

They were not as passive as he thought. Resentment had begun to ripple through the white working class, and it would take some ugly forms in the seventies. Many felt betrayed by Great Society programs and civil rights legislation that seemed to favor minorities and the unemployed while passing over whites. Within a few years, the "white proles of Boston" would riot, throwing rocks and screaming insults at black children on buses bound for the South Boston high school.

Of course, the antibusing activists hardly represented the working class as a whole. Wage earners were a diverse lot and many of them had become newly infused with radical politics. Panther-inspired groups sprung up among black auto workers; women began wanting careers rather than just secretarial jobs; and young, long-haired workers were sneaking out of the factory at lunchtime to smoke doobers. But as the seventies dawned, attention focused on a decidedly un-Marxist segment of the working class: conservative white men. America may have suddenly begun paying attention to its Archie Bunkers because this group was drifting away from the Democratic party. Its defection would help conservatives to forge a new, populist right wing.

The same year that Fallows noticed the blue-collar boys headed for Vietnam, Nixon turned his attention to the working class. In November, as protesters were massing for a huge mobilization against the war, Nixon brilliantly discredited the peace movement. Out there in America, he announced in a televised speech, was a "silent majority" of average people who approved of the war and backed their president.

Fallows called them cattle. Nixon called them silent. While liberals and conservatives might not agree about what the working class wanted, both seemed convinced that (in contrast to students, civil rights activists, and feminists) wage earners would never put their anger into action.

THE MAJORITY: FROM SILENT TO MORAL IN JUST TEN YEARS

It's important to reiterate that the working class was much more than white, male, and conservative. But those who did fit the stereotype—perhaps emboldened by Nixon's nod—became increasingly vocal and visible. On May 8, 1970, when antiwar activists gathered in downtown New York to memorialize the dead at Kent State, a crowd of construction workers descended on the scene. Wielding the tools of their trade, they lashed out at the demonstrators in a working-class riot that oddly reversed the roles of the sixties. In New York that day, it was the construction workers, not the longhairs, who represented an enraged counterculture.

Backlash was becoming fashionable. In a 1970 movie, *Joe*, a machinist who spews insults about "niggers" and "queers" goes on a hippie-killing rampage. Perhaps the most disturbing thing about the movie was that *Newsweek* found it a fair portrayal of the working class. "The film, no mere easy put-down of the silent majority, is a realistic and disquieting vision of the U.S. predilection for violence," says a 1970 review, which also calls the movie "a close-up of the 'forgotten America,'" as if a movie that showed a hard hat offing hippies was some sort of documentary.

A year later, Archie Bunker appeared on the tube. His racist jibes were funny because he was powerless to put his hate politics into action. Archie seemed ridiculous and pitiful rather than dangerous because he lived in a sitcom world where the black guy next door was movin' on up and he wasn't.

But in the real world, Archie was much more than an obscure resident of Queens. He had become a symbol for conservative whites—so much so that he became a "candidate" for president. Some stores, billing themselves as "campaign headquarters," sold pro-Archie buttons, bumper stickers, and T-shirts with logos like "Another Meathead for Bunker."

In one of the most surreal episodes of "All in the Family," Archie decides to write a laudatory letter to President Nixon; he falls asleep and dreams that Nixon is reading the letter on TV. (For pure weirdness, however, this doesn't come close to "The Jeffersons" episode in which the dollar bill that hangs on the wall of George's dry-cleaning business begins talking.) The seventies saw a plethora of figures like Archie's

Van Halen Concert, Michigan

When she was a preteen, my friend Mimi moved from Cambridge, Massachusetts, to the Comstock, Michigan, area. She describes her sojourn in Michigan as the most classically seventies of her youth. In the lawless Midwest, stoned youths rode around on dirt bikes, set things on fire, and wore their hair in long, greasy strands down their backs. This is Mimi's story:

—On that early evening the parking lot was crowded with Bondo-caked fat-tired cars. I was oscillating between trying really hard not to do or say anything stupid and genuinely enjoying myself. From the backseat of Ellen Norris's Chevy II, I could see a line forming at the entrance to Wings Stadium, which was normally the home of the Kalamazoo Wings hockey team but which was presenting tonight only Van Halen. I thought maybe we should be getting in line, but I didn't want to suggest it, because Ellen and her boyfriend John were older and had been to rock concerts. The only other time I'd been to Wings ▶

47

"dream president," populists such as Anita Bryant, George Wallace, and Phyllis Schlafly who were unafraid to hint at the most impolite fantasies and fears of disempowered whites. These politicians tended to organize around single issues like gay schoolteachers, the ERA, busing, pornography, and affirmative action.

With antielitism in the air, right-wing guys cultivated a folksy demeanor and right-wing gals went for the crusading-housewife-who-ultimately-defers-to-her-husband look. Old-style conservatives were out, especially those swinging right-wingers who flirted with libertarianism. Now you needed to seem squeaky clean, like Jerry "Jesus-Was-Not-a-Pacifist" Falwell, who founded the Moral Majority Inc.

The new right wing depended on direct-mail fund-raising, rather than the old boy network, for its support. Because of post-Watergate reforms that put a cap on the amount of money one person could donate to a candidate, strength lay in numbers. Now money would come from huge mailing lists rather than a few wealthy backers. "The clout of the New Right is the result of their expertise in the field of direct-mail solicitation, an art they have been refining for years," conservative writer Alan Crawford noted in 1980.

The result was that if you got on the right mailing list, you might get a "personal" note from Anita Bryant with this impassioned appeal (as recorded by Crawford): "When the homosexuals burn the Holy Bible in public . . . how can I stand by silently. . . . I don't hate homosexuals! But as a mother I must protect my children from their evil influence. . . . Do you realize what they want? They want to recruit our school children under the protection of the laws of the land." Such carefully sculpted letters informed like-minded people about the dangers of baby killers, atheist school systems, spendthrift social programs, and Communists.

Reagan, of course, was the ultimate New Right politician—a TV populist with Moral Majority backing. His sweeping victory in 1980 attested to his success in wooing a working class that had increasingly become disenchanted with the Democrats' promises.

LUST FOR LOWBROW

It was not just in the realm of politics that the average guy suddenly became king—culturally, too, America seemed to be obsessed with its working class. Think how many fads of the late seventies celebrated "tacky" taste and blue-collar culture: vans, CB's, southern rock, trucker movies, denim clothing, the sudden fascination with rednecks both imaginary ("Dukes of Hazzard") and real (Billy Carter), heavy metal, *Saturday Night Fever*, tube tops, beer can collecting, Burt Reynolds.

And in many ways, the seventies nostalgia craze was also an excuse to revel in blue-collar culture. By putting heroes like brewery workers Laverne and Shirley back in time, TV made bowling alleys, pizza joints, and Italian-American accents seem exotic. Meanwhile, many of the late-seventies sitcoms were set in the numbing reality of dead-end jobs and chintzy houses. In shows like "Alice"; "Angie"; "One Day at a Time"; "Mary Hartman, Mary Hartman"; and "Flo" (why were they almost always named after a woman?), the sets were cheap and the lighting was depressing. It was sitcom vérité, depicting the American purgatory of malls, boring work, and shag-carpeted apartments.

Blue-collar culture had become interesting partly because it was disappearing. As the Steel Belt became the Rust Belt and as skilled laborers were replaced by automation, the guy in a hard hat with a belt full of tools was a dying breed—and with him went a distinct subculture. (The 1978 movie *Blue Collar* shows the auto plant as a social world in decay, a place where the Mafia-like union is in cahoots with the management.)

But the collapse of manufacturing was only part of the story. The real culprit was TV. By the seventies, watching TV was Americans' most time-consuming activity after work and sleep. With everyone glued to the tube, distinct class cultures had little chance of surviving.

Now to be "classy" you no longer had to have a Harvard degree. High culture had been reduced to a pastiche of French words, classical music riffs, and swanky brand names. You could wear a T-shirt proclaiming yourself "Classy" (with a rose underneath the glittery lettering), or show off "designer" labels like Jordache and C'est Bon on your butt. Class had become high camp.

And as Tom Wolfe notes, some skilled workers were beginning to earn more than executives; even those who didn't could use plastic to buy the upscale products of their dreams. "America's extraordinary boom began in the early 1940s, but it was not until the 1960s that the *new masses* began to regard it as a permanent condition," says Wolfe. "Only then did they spin out the credit line and start splurging." Blue-

John and Ellen were orange. I hoped they would think of me as orange, too. The weed was making my thoughts float like that, making me unsure of what was interesting enough to say out loud and what was not. It occurred to me that leaving the Chevy would be really complicated when my head was already so full of expressible and maybe inexpressible thoughts.

But a question was forming. Something about tickets. John had explained to me about how I didn't need one because of open seating, somehow.

"But how am I going to get through the gate?"

"When you get to the front of the line, I'll push you through," he said. "Then you gotta book and meet us at the pop stand. Never mind. It'll work."

Book. That was a Comstock word. Did they say that in Cambridge? Maybe they did, but not until eighth grade, which I was in now. Everyone here goofed on the way I talked, lampooned my speech as strange and formal, which made me feel good and bad at the same time. Partly I wanted ▶

49

not to draw attention to my oddness; I wanted to be a freak in the "peakin' and freakin'" sense, not in the "freak of nature" sense. But then I had my oddness for a fallback. ¶ I made a mental note of "book" and decided to work it into my repertoire, though even now I could see the smirks on my cousins' faces when I tried it out.

¶ My cousin Peter was at this moment knocking on John's window. John cranked it down and a billow of smoke escaped. ¶ "How's your scar, John?" A reference to John's most recent bonfire accident. John was obsessed with fires and burning things. Last fall, I'd taken over his paper delivery job—he was dealing now and didn't need the money—and he'd walked me through the route. At the last house, a decaying ranch style with a leaf-filled kiddie pool and two Big Wheels in the front yard, he showed me what to do to fuckers who hide when you try to collect. He pulled a can of lighter fluid out of his bag, drenched a *Kalamazoo Gazette*, crammed it into the mailbox, and torched it. In about two seconds,

collar workers were "outfitting their $12,000 RVs with so many microwave ovens and sauna booths, it was impossible to use the word 'proletarian' any longer with a straight face."

In short, the working class had been subsumed into the mishmash of suburban culture. By the late seventies, real Archie Bunkers would be less likely to wear work boots than Lacoste shirts and Adidas sneakers.

RUNNING OUT OF GAS

Perhaps nothing symbolized America's decline during the seventies as much as the tiny Japanese car. You might wear a "Fuck Iran" T-shirt with a picture of Mickey Mouse giving the finger, but that wouldn't change things: OPEC (and the American oil cartel) controlled our gas supplies.

For anyone used to driving a big ol' Galaxie 500, having to cram yourself into a small car was humiliating. It could be dangerous, too. The Ford Pinto's faulty transmission could slip from park into reverse, and this was one car you definitely didn't want to be in when it was rolling down a hill because it also tended to explode when hit from behind. And then there was the AMC Pacer, that dome-shaped car with bug-eyed headlights. This so-called economy car got about fifteen miles per gallon—but you probably didn't want to drive it around too much anyway, because the steering wheel could freeze up. With American production values at an all-time low, it made sense to swallow your national pride and buy a Toyota or a Datsun.

The longer the gas lines got, the more romantic those big American cars of yore started to seem. What began as a working-class subculture, car customizing, became a mainstream obsession that celebrated the decoration of gas guzzlers.

Vans, especially, became popular because they satisfied so many seventies needs at once. A pleasure dome on wheels, the van could be outfitted with a quadraphonic eight-track system, waterbed, shag carpeting, refrigerator, and beaded curtain—the swinger's version of an RV. It was the perfect place for indulging in sex or drugs, since you could see out through that little moon-shaped window but nobody could see in. (Bumper stickers added to the van's reputation with ditties like "Gas, grass or ass, no one rides free" and "If the van's

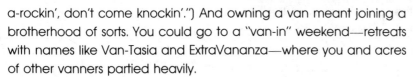

a-rockin', don't come knockin'.") And owning a van meant joining a brotherhood of sorts. You could go to a "van-in" weekend—retreats with names like Van-Tasia and ExtraVananza—where you and acres of other vanners partied heavily.

For an exhaustive catalogue of seventies car culture, see *Corvette Summer*. This 1978 movie chronicles a car customizer's (Mark Hamill) search for his stolen Corvette. The 'vette in question looks something like a giant candy apple red running shoe—the seventies dream car is an impractical confection, all airbrushed flames and fiberglass fins.

The boy's hunt for his 'vette turns into an odyssey through the car-customizing demimonde. Hitchhiking to Vegas, he gets picked up by a convoy of low-riders; the dialogue between the boy and the Hispanic driver reduces ethnic differences to car makes. The low-rider immediately guesses the boy's favorite kind of machine. "Corvette: anglo. Anglo: Corvette," he says.

THE TRUCKER THING

My friend Mike remembers taking a CB hell ride to Florida as a little kid in 1974. His dad had outfitted their puke-brown Valiant with a CB and, inspired by his high school mascot, had adopted the handle Brown Beaver. Little did he suspect that *beaver* was the suggestive CB synonym for *chick*. Mike began to realize that something was wrong when one of the truckers chortled over his "Ten-four, good buddy" response—and Mike's humiliation deepened when it dawned on him that his dad had named himself after female genitalia.

But Mike also remembers from that trip many alluring glimpses into the highway underworld of CB culture. When they pulled up at truckstops, they could hear prostitutes chatting with truckers. And they sped along at ninety miles per hour, protected from the police by a convoy of road rebels.

With CB's, even a workaday dad could fantasize that he lived the renegade existence of a trucker. The citizen band let motorists join in an impromptu rebellion against traffic cops and gas lines—against all of the frustrations that kept Americans from exercising their God-given right to drive fast.

The trucker became the most flashy antiestablishment hero of

John had run halfway up the street and I was still staring, transfixed by the flaming newspaper.

Now I listened to the latest fire story—something about an exploding car battery.

Peter grinned at me. "Enjoying the mary-joo-wanna cigarette?"

I opened my mouth and a tense little squeak came out. All at once I was anxious to leave the car, to have John push me past the guards, past Peter, past my awkwardness, into anonymity.

MEN at WORK

the late seventies. In the hit song "Convoy," C. W. McCall sang (or talked) about breaking speed limits as an epic deed: a guy named Rubber Duck leads a line of speeding trucks past barracades of "bears." Then a chorus of high-pitched women's voices urges the listener to join the revolution—to roll along with the convoy.

A wave of movies also cashed in on the CB craze. The mother of all trucker movies is, of course, *Smokey and the Bandit* (1977). A pair of millionaires (one played by Paul Williams!) hires a trucker named Bandit (Burt Reynolds) to smuggle a load of Coors across the South. Pursued by an ornery sheriff (Jackie Gleason) and other assorted cops, Bandit speeds around in a Trans-Am, clearing the way for his friend in an eighteen-wheeler. The (mostly fat, mostly idiotic) cops never have a chance. They keep crashing into each other and driving off bridges. And Bandit, folk hero that he is, gets help along the way from CB pals like a black undertaker and an old lady.

Other trucker movies followed. The 1978 *Convoy* turned the C. W. McCall hit into a film, starring Kris Kristofferson as the hero with the Rubber Duck handle. Again it's noble CB outlaws against obese cops. Weirder still was the 1977 *Breaker! Breaker!*, a Chuck Norris movie: lots of crashing eighteen-wheelers and hand-to-hand combat.

Then, of course, there was "The Dukes of Hazzard." Though the heroes drive a Dodge Charger, "General Lee," instead of a truck, the plot relies on the same old *Smokey and the Bandit* formula. The two hunks and their hunkette cousin constantly outwit and outdrive the fat lawman "Boss" Hogg.

The trucker genre portrayed the southern working-class male as both hero and villain, but seldom anything in between. On the one hand, he is the good trucker: a guy who respects blacks and women, can do a U-turn at sixty miles per hour, and seems happy with his lower-class lot. On the other hand, he is the bad cop: a Dixie version of Archie Bunker who eats like a pig, insults minorities, and abuses his authority.

The South had become a post-Watergate version of the Wild West—a new kind of frontier, terrorized not by outlaws but by its own sheriffs. To regain their freedom, ordinary people (that is, CB'ers) must dupe the corrupt lawmen who control the roads. In short, the trucker genre was one by-product of the right-wing populism of the late seventies. Is it any surprise that Reagan won the presidency a few years after *Smokey and the Bandit* became one of the largest-grossing movies of the decade? Reagan billed himself as a subdued version of Bandit: a good ol' boy who battled soft government officials in the name of laissez-faire economics.

Of course, pop culture's fascination with Dixie had a lot to do with Jimmy, too. The president embodied the corporate and slick New South, while the clan he brought with him into the White House seemed like geeks straight out of *Deliverance* (1972). The redneck cop stereotype may have been inspired by Jimmy's less-presentable relatives—in fact, Billy Carter actually *played* a redneck cop in a 1979 TV movie called *Flatbed Annie and Sweetiepie: Lady Truckers.*

THE TRUCKER-CHIMP THING

OK, admittedly, the idea of pairing truck drivers with primates did not exactly sweep the seventies—only a few movies and one TV show used this "Twilight Zone"-ish plot device. But if you think about it, the trucker-chimp genre was one of the most inspired of the decade. You've got your rough-and-tumble guy, riding alone in his truck cab. Maybe he finds it difficult to talk about his feelings with his buddies or his girlfriend. So who can he open up to? Who can he kiss and cuddle without losing his tough guy reputation? Who's a really good listener? That's where the chimp comes in.

The trucker-plus-pet thing may have started with *Smokey and the Bandit.* In that movie, a hound dog rides shotgun in an eighteen-wheeler with country singer Jerry Reed. Obviously, the movie's creators put the dog in to provide something for Reed to talk to besides his CB. But somehow, the hound just doesn't have much charisma—all he can do is sit there—and besides, he isn't grotesque enough. Those shortcomings would be amended a year later.

Clint Eastwood's *Every Which Way But Loose* (and its sequel, *Any Which Way You Can*) costars an orangutan who aids his master by leaning out the window to give the finger, fighting off bikers, and sometimes even by driving. An oft-dismissed movie, *Every Which Way But Loose* (1978) is a mind-bogglingly strange meditation on American manhood. Eastwood plays a no-'count pickup truck driver whose weak spot is a no-good woman. A hard man in every other way, Eastwood's

The doors opened right when we got in line. Everyone was shuffling forward, saying what songs they hoped Van Halen would play, what pyrotechnics they wanted to see, where they were going to hide their stash, what happened to you if you got busted, how to tell a narc. It occurred to me that maybe this wouldn't work, that I'd get turned back at the gate and have to walk the four miles back to my aunt's farm. I almost hoped for it. Maybe I wanted to jog along the break-down lane of Sprinkle Road, turn off toward Comstock, past the park, over the train tracks, along the creek, up Aunt Dorothy's long, rocky driveway, then cut through the pine woods from which I could see the light in the kitchen where Aunt Dorothy would be stirring her vodka and tomato juice with a chewed pencil and sifting through a box of library books, not wondering about her own kids or me, just inhaling her solitude the way I would be inhaling the piney air of the cool, dark slope next to the house. Suddenly we were almost to the door and John was handing me an ▶

character is oddly innocent and chivalric in love. Not so Clyde the orangutan. He gets it on in a zoo (first movie) and in a motel room (second movie) without any romantic fuss.

Instead of pitting the good trucker against the bad cop, *Every Which Way But Loose* brilliantly recognizes these characters as two sides of one person. Clint Eastwood and Clyde ride around like ego and id trapped inside the same truck cab. Interestingly, the makers of *Smokey and the Bandit III* also experimented with this idea. That film—originally titled *Smokey Is the Bandit*—would have starred Jackie Gleason as both the good guy and the bad guy.

The trucker-chimp concept hit TV in 1979 with the series "B.J. and the Bear." But what's the point of a truck-riding monkey in the prim world of prime time? You can't show the chimp getting it on with his old lady. He can't moon anyone. Poor Bear. Unable to give the finger, he was reduced to performing innocuous duties for his master, like changing the eight-track tapes.

TAKE THIS JOB AND SHOVE IT

"Youth culture" had become big business by the seventies as companies dressed up their products in the garb of revolution, sex, and drugs. "With careful marketing, such button-down corporations as American Express, Hamm's Brewing Co. and Arrow Shirts have scored solid gains in university communities," *Newsweek* announced in 1970. But the youth market also was expanding outside the college campus and into factories and fast-food restaurants.

Once college students had worn jeans to look more like manual laborers and farmhands; now working-class kids were donning jeans to look more like rich kids. Designer jeans were the ultimate irony—the traditional uniform of the working class given a rich-sounding name (like Studio 54 or Gloria Vanderbilt) and sold back to the working class.

College students had endorsed sex, drugs, and rock and roll as part of a drop-out lifestyle. But for blue-collar kids who had to show up at work on Monday, hippie hedonism meant something else entirely. You smoked pot not to become one with the universe but to get baked, fried, fucked up, buzzed. And free sex lost its Marxist connotations when high school kids got it on in vans and girls began advertising

their availability with shirts that said, "I'm a virgin" and then underneath, in tiny letters, "This is a very old T-shirt." Rock no longer was synonymous with the gentler values of the sixties: heavy metal acts like Blue Oyster Cult, Ted Nugent, and Aerosmith—wearing their umlauts like cheap cologne—brought macho posturing back into style. For the Clearasil-and-devil-worship crowd, Kiss made violence cool: they dubbed their fans the "Kiss army" and sang about the joys of firing off one's "love gun." A new radio format, album-oriented rock (later classic hits), was crafted for the average white guy, ages thirteen to twenty-five.

The cut-rate hippie culture of the seventies was a bohemianism that everyone could afford—unabashedly commercial and working-class oriented. My favorite store in the mall was Spencer Gifts, where you could buy beaded curtains, blacklight posters, fuzzy foot rugs, bubble gum candles, and those trippy lights made of swaying plastic fibers. "With your imagination, you can create a mood room as unique as you are," promised the store's ad. "And at a Spencer Gifts store, it'll fit your budget."

In short, when youth culture became mass culture, kicking out the jams no longer meant overthrowing capitalism. It meant getting as wasted as possible on Saturday night to blow off steam before you went back to work on Monday.

The ultimate in working-class hedonism was, of course, disco. What had started as a black, Latin, and gay subculture quickly became mainstream. For instance, those who couldn't get into Studio 54 could boogy the night away at clubs like L'Amour: "Both singles and couples abound in this straight, mostly white and heavily Italian disco. While people in Manhattan work hard at looking funky and outrageous, unisex and glamorous, in Brooklyn men work at looking like men and women work at looking like women," says a guidebook to the scene called *Nightdancin'*.

Disco habitués found in the pulsing palaces a fantasy world far from the frustrations of work. One secretary, whose disco name was Foxy Roxy, slept two hours every night so she could hang out in clubs like 24K, according to *Nightdancin'*.

In 1977, *Saturday Night Fever* helped to further turn disco into a pastime for working-class ethnics. Italian-American Tony Manero works at a hardware store and lives with his parents. In real life, he's nothing, but when he gets on the dance floor at 2001 Odyssey . . . well, then he's a guy to reckon with. Tony is a tragic figure—so charmed by

55

Qiana shirts, platform boots, and flashy glamour that he's trapped in an otherwise joyless world.

A short-lived TV series called "Makin' It" (perhaps the most suggestive title ever given to a TV show) further elaborates on this theme. A blatant ripoff of *Saturday Night Fever* (with Ellen Travolta as Mom and Bee Gees music), the show centers around the travails of Billy Manucci, who's torn about whether to be a star on the dance floor or a college graduate. The 1979 show also portrays disco as a working-class trap that keeps young Italian-Americans from moving up the social ladder.

DISCO SUCKS?

Even at the height of its popularity, disco was an embarrassment—especially as searing, outrageous hits like "You Sexy Thing" and "Love to Love You Baby" became lost in the mainstream mishmash of Dolly Parton's "Baby I'm Burnin'," Rod Stewart's "Da Ya Think I'm Sexy," and disco remakes of "Baby Face" and Beethoven's Fifth. That's when the backlash began.

FM stations began launching "disco sucks" campaigns and the slogan "Death to disco" appeared on high school walls as heavy metal fans and punks lashed out against the slick music. Many have called the antidisco movement racist or homophobic—and certainly such prejudices played a part in the backlash against shaking booty. But by the late seventies, disco meant John Travolta.

As Tom Wolfe puts it, "The discotheque is the 1970s quotidian and commercial ritualization of what used to be known as a homosexual rout, a fact that generally has not been laid on Mom & Dad & Buddy & Sis as they drive the Bonneville over to the mall to take disco lessons so they'll be ready for Vesper Disco nights at the church."

I believe the "disco sucks" movement was aimed as much at the ethnic working class as it was at blacks or gays. White high school boys may have yelled "Death to disco" the loudest, but the people who engineered the movement tended to be the sixties-generation deejays who controlled the airwaves.

Middle-class baby boomers accustomed to having their own music blasted on album-oriented rock stations were aghast when somebody else's songs became popular. Vita Miezitis, who later wrote the disco handbook *Nightdancin'*, remembers having a personal crisis after her favorite station turned disco: "I cried and walked about clutching Joni Mitchell and Rolling Stones albums to my chest all morning. I hated disco music.... I thought people who went to discos to dance to that dumb disco beat were stupid mindless morons.... Where had the Sixties gone? What had the world come to that disco had been conceived?" Where once rock had been an alternative form of high culture, disco seemed commercialized, crass, and, let's admit it, lower class.

I remember being vaguely aware that when my high school peers said disco sucked, they meant the Bee Gees, not Funkadelic or even the Village People (the latter two bands were so weird that most of us couldn't tell whether we should risk liking them or not). Hating disco was simply our first, tentative step toward hating the seventies. By "disco" we meant the whole bland, clean package of cut-rate chic mainstream culture. Unfortunately, we also meant the Tony Maneros who took Top 40 disco at face value.

The backlash against disco was part of a larger, middle-class revulsion toward the Saturday night fever of working-class rebellion. "There's a nasty tinge of elitism in the claim that the Sixties was the true locus of sex, drugs and rock 'n' roll. In the Sixties, nice, white, well-off college-student types played with free love and LSD," claims seventies-ologist Candi Strecker. "When the common people got their hands on sex, drugs and rock 'n' roll, the magic seemed to wear off them. The Seventies fulfillment of the Sixties revolution was unattractive blue-collar teenagers puking Quaaludes at the Grand Funk Railroad concert. The Woodstockers who made that scene possible would really rather dissociate themselves from it."

With that in mind, you can only wonder why the seventies has become the decade everyone laughs at—a time that supposedly epitomizes the nadir in fashion. Maybe it's because the seventies, more than any other postwar decade, reveled in the culture of the common denominator. And now, when tastemakers look back, they cringe at rollerboogie, CB's, and "Three's Company" because these are relics of a time when everyone—no matter their socioeconomic status—longed to be part of the freewheeling working class.

Singer Anita Bryant, a television huckster for the Florida Citrus Industry, is seen pouring orange juice for board members of "Save Our Children" before a meeting in her Miami Beach home. The group was seeking repeal of Dade County's new ordinance barring discrimination against homosexuals. Anita's stance was clear: "Gays" are a danger to Miami's youth.
(UPI/BETTMAN)

WAR

U.S. troops did not leave Vietnam until the fall of Saigon in 1975; but for most Americans in the seventies, the war seemed to have ended long before that. As historian Godfrey Hodgson notes, "By the spring of 1969 the war was over, because you didn't see it on the tube any more."

What had happened? How did the most controversial issue of the sixties suddenly become invisible as the decade turned?

You can blame it on happy-face buttons, "Have A Nice Day" bumper stickers, and a lot of pot smoking—that fuzzy, feel-good mood that took hold as people tried to ignore the unpleasant realities of the time. But most of the credit for America's uncanny ability to wage a war without noticing it should go to Nixon.

This was the man who had a special podium built—by the designer of "The Dating Game" set—for the 1972 Republican Convention so that none of the speakers would appear to be taller than he was (according to journalist Joe Spear). This was the man who called on his supporters at the convention to pretend to erupt into unplanned "Nixon Now" demonstrations. This was the man who used Sammy Davis,

Jr., as a political prop, hugging the entertainer on stage at a rally as if to say, I, too, can embrace a black man.

Nixon waged the war with the same showmanship, the same eye toward TV that he had displayed at the 1972 convention. Early in his presidency, he announced a new "Vietnamization" plan, which called for increasing reliance on South Vietnamese soldiers to fight on the ground while Americans bombed from above. The idea was to make the war more palatable back home by incurring fewer American casualties. Unlike the atrocities that had shocked the public in the late sixties, Nixon's war was impersonal and technological, and therefore it seemed less real.

At the same time, Nixon staged distracting PR events. His most impressively orchestrated media show took place not in Indochina but in China. Certainly the president's trip to the communist superpower helped to forge a cautious détente between East and West. But more to the point, it made good TV. Arriving in the country during American prime time, Nixon embarked on a round of diplomatic dinners and visits to historic monuments that made Barbie's dream vacation look like a drive to the supermarket. Vietnam? What's that?

Nixon was the perfect president for a country in deep denial. Americans, after all, were exhausted by a war that had dragged on inconclusively for almost ten years (and had been waged covertly for much longer).

Like the president, pop culture tried to gloss over the war. The most obvious thing you can say about the Vietnam of TV shows and movies was that it didn't exist. Sure, "M*A*S*H" may have depicted war as an absurd struggle waged by an insane bureaucracy, but the sitcom was set in Korea. While the show seemed to be commenting on Vietnam, its rebel heroes never had to confront the far-more-troubling issues of the contemporary war. Worse, "M*A*S*H" created a new myth about Vietnam: the show taught us that misfits like Hawkeye were really in charge of the military while career soldiers like Frank Burns had no power. Of course, in real life, the opposite was true.

"M*A*S*H" comforted viewers with the idea that even if the U.S. government napalmed Vietnamese peasants, Americans were essentially decent people. We were Hawkeyes (those who cared only about healing victims of the war) rather than Burnses (those who identified with the objectives of the war). In fact, "M*A*S*H" almost never showed Americans dropping bombs or firing mortars; instead the be-

Chemicals

leaguered doctors were constantly suffering hits from an anonymous enemy. War had become an impersonal force, a natural disaster, waged, seemingly, by no one, and American soldiers were its victims.

Of course, "M*A*S*H" was the exception: few shows mentioned war at all—or its vets, many of whom had become the most outspoken antiwar activists. (It was not until the eighties that the deranged Vietnam vet made regular appearances on shows like "The A Team." Characters who were vets on seventies shows, like Chico in "Chico and The Man," seldom made a big deal about it.)

But while it ignored vets, the media began celebrating a very different type of soldier. The anointed heroes of Vietnam were those who literally had disappeared: the missing in action.

PRISONERS OF HYPE

Nixon had one and so did Bill Cosby. Sonny and Cher each had one. My best friend Anne had one, too, as did her teenage hippie sister. They were POW/MIA bracelets, those circlets of steel that bore the name of a missing soldier. You were supposed to wear it until your guy came home or, more likely, his remains were found.

I begged to have one, but my mother wouldn't let me. She'd gotten the idea that if I slipped and fell, the sharp edges of the metal bracelet would slit my wrist and I'd bleed to death, a ten-year-old victim of the war machine. Also, Mom wasn't sure about what kind of statement I'd be making—did wearing the bracelet mean you were a hippie pacifist or a jingoist warmonger?

Actually, it all depended on which elementary school you went to. My friend Danny remembers conservative kids—like boys who still wore *undershirts*, for God's sake—sporting the bracelets as a no-American-is-free-until-all-Americans-are-free statement. But my friend Diane says that in her elementary school, the freaks wore POW/MIA bracelets. In fact, she—a budding socialist—had one, too, though it wasn't exactly opposition to U.S. imperialism that inspired her to wear it.

"It was '71 or '72," reminisces Diane. "My best friend Laura Amelse went to visit her dad in the hospital and this nurse gave her a form to get a bracelet. I got mine because Laura had one, and she was so cool. She came from this really hip family with young, liberal

"Vietnamization."

"Death to the fascist insect that preys upon the people!"

parents. A few years later, her older sister had an affair with Jimmy Buffet. You see? So I had to have a bracelet.

"My soldier was Thomas Kolstad. They found his remains in '76 or '77. I still have the clipping somewhere. But even when they found him, I didn't take off the bracelet. I mean, I literally never took it off, even though it turned my wrist gross colors and it was itchy—but, hey, that was my sacrifice. What else could a little kid do about the war?

"I finally took the bracelet off in tenth grade when this boy I had a crush on, Jim Rosenberg, said, 'You're still wearing that?' When I first got the bracelet, I thought it was such a hip, subversive thing, but when he said that, I realized it was just an elementary school thing. Unfortunately, even when I took the bracelet off, Jim Rosenberg only liked me as a friend."

Looking back, it's no wonder that we kids were confused about whether wearing the bracelet made you a hawk or a dove. Both sides used prisoners of war and missing soldiers as symbols for their causes.

In the mid- and late sixties, it was the peace movement that was most supportive to the families of POWs. The left-leaning Committee of Liaison with Families of Servicemen Detained in North Vietnam set up a system under which prisoners could be tracked and their letters sent back home. During this same period, the military establishment tended to give POW families the brush off. According to one report issued by the Center for POW Studies, "From 1964 until May of 1969 the general guidance to the families [of POWs] by the United States Government was to say as little as possible."

But in 1969, as Nixon tried to promote an unpopular war, the administration showed a sudden interest in the welfare of the prisoners. Freeing the POWs, rather than winning the war, became a reason for escalating the bombing of North Vietnam.

Though we in elementary school may have thought it terribly subversive, the POW/MIA bracelet was actually a promotional toy used to whip up public anger at North Vietnam and therefore to continue the war. Created by the Victory in Vietnam Association as a sort of antipeace sign, the bracelets were simply one part of an elaborate propaganda campaign designed to remythologize the war, as H. Bruce Franklin points out in a 1991 *Atlantic Monthly* article. In fact, the very term *POW/MIA* itself was devised in 1973 to stir up ire against the Vietnamese, according to Franklin: never before had the missing in action (most of whom were presumed to have died in combat) been lumped together with prisoners of war. The implication was that every missing soldier might be wasting away in a prison somewhere, even years after the war was over.

Meanwhile, other soldiers hardly fit so well with Nixon's PR effort. In 1971, a group of protesting veterans—fenced off from the Capitol by fearful authorities—tossed their medals away. Some recited atrocities they'd seen in Vietnam before they flung their Purple Hearts or Silver Stars over the fence. This ritual brilliantly dramatized their point—that in Vietnam, true heroism had been impossible.

The liberal show *M*A*S*H* and the Nixon administration had one thing in common: both celebrated the most pitiful victims of the war. Meanwhile, those soldiers who'd killed under orders came to symbolize the inhumane and fruitless U.S.-backed war, and they became the "crazy" vets of popular imagination. It was easier to believe that the atrocities of Vietnam occurred because soldiers in places like My Lai and My Khe had gone over the edge than to see these events as part of a larger U.S. policy.

WAR IS PEACE

Protesters against Vietnam often spoke of "bringing the war home"—that is, using disturbing images or violent acts to make the war real for complacent Americans, a line of thought that led some factions to attempt bombings they hoped would shut down the war machine. While peaceful activists found it hard to grab media attention in the seventies, violent groups had no such trouble. For instance, in March 1970, three Weatherpeople died when their bomb factory blew up, making for dramatic news stories and ensuring that the public would never again picture antiwar activists as flower-strewing hippies.

Weirdly, just as peace protesters were getting stereotyped as violent nuts, they were themselves becoming victims of violence. In May 1970 at Kent State, the National Guard shot down four students who'd been peacefully protesting Vietnam; ten days later, police gunned down two students who were demonstrating at Jackson State, a southern black college. Still, it didn't matter who had been the victims and who the aggressor, for the peace movement had become associated in pop culture with violence, and for many, Kent State was further proof that those who spoke out against the war were themselves warlike.

In a 1971 episode of "The Mod Squad," students take over a campus building. As the cool student activists run around boarding up windows and taking hostages, one nerdy little guy in elevator shoes keeps getting left out—they even forget to save him an armband! Once the students have secured the building, their Greg Brady–esque leader leans out a window to address the people gathered below. "Students and faculty of City College: Welcome to the revolution!" he pontificates, and throws firecrackers into the crowd. "Hear that sound, Dean?" he says. "That's the sound of war.... That's just what you're going to get if our demands aren't met."

But suddenly the firecracker blasts turn into real gunshots. Students and police take cover; a few fall, wounded. Someone is shooting from another window. Who could it be? Why it's the nerdy guy, now wearing an old army jacket and carrying a rifle. "I told you you'd need me," he snivels to the other students. "It's like you told [the dean]. We're in a war."

"The Mod Squad" episode retells Kent State as pop mythology. In the TV version of the tragedy, a student (rather than the police) guns down innocent people. And on TV, the activist chooses violence not to defend his ideals but as a desperate bid for popularity.

THE PEACE VIGILANTE

Pop culture was full of characters who embodied America's ambivalence about pacifism—heroes, as well as villains, seemed muddled about morality. The early seventies superstar kicked butt in the name of nonviolence, love, meditation, Buddhism, whales, and multiculturalism. The new hero embodied the contradictory desires of America: we wanted peace but we also wanted revenge.

Consider the difference between the sixties hippie hero and his seventies equivalent. In 1969, the outlaw adventurers in *Easy Rider* refused to fight their redneck tormentors; a few years later, the left-wing hero was a killing machine, a hipper Dirty Harry. Push him too far and he'd stop quoting Gandhi and start kicking ass.

Billy Jack, of course, was the ultimate peace vigilante. The 1971 film opens as evil establishment types herd beautiful mustangs into a pen; Billy Jack appears out of nowhere, accompanied by the tenuous tinkling of mystical bells, to stop the shooting. We learn that Billy is a "half-breed" and a "war hero who hated the war," a man with an itchy trigger finger and a mean karate foot. His mission: to defend multiethnic children who attend the Freedom School on the Indian reservation.

In one scene, some of the students go into an ice-cream store, only to be harassed by local bigots. Billy Jack comes to the kids' rescue, first stroking the head of a Native American child and then saying in a dangerously calm voice, "The kids at the school tell me that I'm supposed to control my violent temper and be passive and nonviolent like they are. . . . But I just go BERSERK." With this he erupts into a righteous frenzy, pitching a bad white guy through a plate-glass window.

One of the strangest plot elements in the movie is Billy's apprenticeship to a Native American wise man, whom we glimpse only for a moment. It's as if the shaman has been stuffed into the script just to make sure the movie covered all of the politically correct bases, but no one really wanted him there—because wouldn't any mystic worth his salt object to Billy's passionate violence? The shaman never complains about Billy's temper or does anything but sit there looking venerable. Instead it's Jean, the woman who runs the Freedom School, who nags Billy to control himself.

As much as the movie tries to be about Indians and rednecks and improvisational drama groups, it's really about Billy and Jean— alias Tom Laughlin and his wife Delores Taylor. The duo produced, directed, wrote, starred in, and distributed the movie, foisting on the public their own paranoid vision of an America in which the forces of groovy and of ungroovy were about to erupt into all-out war.

The public loved it. The independent movie became the surprise hit of 1971, perhaps because it paired bloody fight scenes with preachy antiwar songs. Or maybe its appeal was its hopelessly earnest vibe. For Laughlin and Taylor, *Billy Jack* wasn't just a movie, it was their own legend: the couple had themselves run a progressive school. Twenty years later, Laughlin ran for president in the 1992 election. He still seemed confused about his identity: "I'm not an actor. I'm Billy Jack," he told the *Washington Post*.

The couple's 1974 sequel, *The Trial of Billy Jack*, went even farther over the top. Seventiesologist Candi Strecker praises the movie for being so stridently self-righteous that for the modern viewer, it

The Overarching Role of Denim

They started the decade patched, frayed, and faded, and they ended it starched, sequined, and designer labeled. Along the way, blue jeans adorned everyone from Paul Williams to President Carter. Denim was so popular that just wearing jeans was not enough for the desperate-to-be-hip seventies consumer. Zenith made a denim-covered TV set. A cologne dubbed Blue Jeans came in a denim box with an "Indian" stitched belt. Enterprising teenage girls made purses out of their old jeans (when the purse was full, it looked like they were carrying around someone's butt). AMC's 1973 Gremlin was upholstered with denim. Denim: the perfect fashion statement for a nation whose social fabric also had become fashionably frayed.

65

Remember those Saturday mornings of yore, watching cartoons and chomping down a cereal that was more than 50 percent sugar, preferably with chalky marshmallow bits that turned slimy in your mouth? Lucky Charms sufficed, Cocoa Puffs would do, but you were really in luck if you could get your mom to buy you one of the General Mills monster cereals. ¶ In 1971, Franken Berry (a strawberry Frankenstein monster) and Count Chocula (a chocolate vampire) exploded on the cereal commercial scene. Like Casper the Ghost, they were sensitive spooks. They acted scary in the beginning of the commercial but could be terrified into teeth-chattering convulsions by a little boy. Unfortunately, Franken Berry had to be pulled because "parents were aghast when the strawberry coloring turned their kids' stools bloody red," according to *Flake*, a cereal collectors' magazine. ¶ In 1972, General Mills added two more spooks: Boo Berry, a blue ghost; and the all-but-forgotten Fruit

seems like brilliant satire: "One unforgettable image from *Trial* is the scene where a one-armed child from the Freedom School is shown learning to play a guitar with his hook. Of course it's a twisted bit of inspirational hokum, but if you saw it on 'Twin Peaks' you'd say, 'That David Lynch is a genius!' "

THE PEACE SIGN AS A WEAPON

The same year *Billy Jack* came out, another movie took the violence-in-the-name-of-nonviolence idea to its ultimate extreme. In *The Peace Killers*, bikers threaten to overrun a hippie commune. At first the hippies passively resist their tormentors, but after numerous plot twists, they finally decide to fight. Using a knife sharpener, they turn their plowshares into swords (well, not exactly swords, but eye-poking-out devices). They also sharpen the edges of their metal peace medallions, turning them into impromptu Ninja stars. A melee ensues, involving endless shots of peace sign bloodletting. By the end of the movie, you can't see a peace sign without expecting someone to use it to slice through skin.

However, the most shocking image comes earlier in the movie. When the bikers decide to torture the commune leader (a whiny pacifist with a Jesus complex), he gets a dose of his own ideology. The bikers string him up on the giant peace sign that hangs over the commune's entrance. This is *actual crucifixion on a peace sign*! The symbolism is so dopey and yet so profound. As an image it crystallized the early-seventies attitude toward pacifism: if you try to resist violence, you'll end up an ineffective, effeminate martyr. Better to kill with your peace sign than to be crucified on it.

EVERYBODY WAS KUNG FU FIGHTING

CAINE: [Read in bad Chinese accent with lots of pauses between words.] I merely want some water from your well. A bowl of porridge is all I ask.

RANCHER: [Adopt a twangy western accent.] Get out of here you dirty chink so I can rape that widow.

CAINE: I do not want to fight you, but if I must, I will do it in slow motion.

That, in essence, is the plot of every episode of "Kung Fu," the Buddhist-fugitive-in-the-Wild-West series that ran from 1972 to 1975.

Like *Billy Jack*'s Laughlin, David Carradine of "Kung Fu" seemed to have a weak grasp of the difference between his on-screen persona and himself. Living in a shack in the hills and rumored to trip on acid, Carradine claimed to be "possessed by the spirit" of the late Bruce Lee. Like *Billy Jack*, "Kung Fu" was a surprise hit—one that also helped to turn martial arts into a pop cult craze.

Karate, kung fu, and jujitsu seemed to be everywhere in the seventies. First of all, there were the songs: "Kung Fu Man," performed by Ultrafunk and featuring Mr. Superbad, Freddy Mack; the Kalifornia Kid's "Kung Fu Fighting"; Roberta Kelly's "The Return of Kung Fu"; and Curtis Mayfield's "Kung Fu," among others. Then there were the reclusive celebrities who worked out in white karate suits—Elvis being the foremost. Imagine him in Vegas, fat and sweaty, performing "Suspicious Minds" as he does air karate chops. This was martial arts in the late seventies—no longer a rigorous discipline that called for sublimation of the ego, but instead a decadent and showy athletic hobby that could be part of any bad dude's lifestyle.

Karate was everywhere. Miss Piggy expressed her anger with a loud "Hiii-yaaaa" and a chop of her hand. Richie Cunningham—way ahead of fifties fashion—took karate lessons from Arnold (Pat Morita). And in *Saturday Night Fever*, Tony (John Travolta) prepared for a night of disco by gazing at his poster of Bruce Lee and then practicing some chops in the mirror.

Martial arts were the perfect obsession for a country consumed with regret about Vietnam. The Asian traditions seemed to promise not only a mystical source of strength but the mental discipline to know when to use it. If you practiced a martial art, you could congratulate yourself both for your awesome ability to mete out death-dealing blows and for having the Taoist restraint to use your powers only for good reasons. Presumably, like Kwai Chang Caine in "Kung Fu," you wouldn't erupt into violence unless you had to protect a widow, a child, or maybe a cute pet. The martial arts, then, represented the moral use of violence—something Americans desperately wanted to believe in.

From Billy Jack to Caine, the heroes of the early seventies were men who busted heads in the name of peace. Perhaps that was because Nixon—using buzzwords like *peace with honor* and *pacifica-*

Brute, a werewolf who hawked a green-and-pink cereal that was more than 65 percent sugar.

But just when the monster cereals seemed to be all a breakfast lover could ask for, a pall fell over the land. Throughout the fifties and sixties, cartoon characters had pitched nutritionally deficient cereals to kids and it had seemed like innocent fun. But in the early seventies, a new awareness of health food and consumer politics changed all that. Our Day-Glo-colored heroes—like the General Mills monsters—were accused of being nothing more than pushers, trying to get us kids hooked on the White Lady, refined sugar. Attacks on such commercials resulted in a 1974 code that regulated advertising aimed at children. The postcode ads might have been more responsible, but they weren't as much fun. Now commercials for sugared cereals had to show their products as simply one component of a square meal, or use a phrase like "With toast, juice, and milk it's part of a nutritious breakfast." Which explains my confusion at the time, because who has room to eat both toast *and* ▶

cereal? Also, the prospect of downing a tall glass of orange juice after swilling a bowl full of marshmallows is disgusting, even to a kid. Count Chocula and Boo Berry have survived the slings and arrows of the health-food curmudgeons, but sadly, with the wooden stake of nutritional awareness driven through his heart, Fruit Brute disappeared in 1977.

"Yes, Master Po."

tion, along with his fabrication of a Cambodian "cry for help"—had created an enduring myth about American aggression. We liked to believe that instead of entering the conflict to pursue our own political goals, we had come on a mission of mercy. Instead of escalating the war, we were restoring peace.

Vietnam had mystified the reasons for American aggression. And so Americans turned to mysticism to help justify violence. Thus, every peace vigilante had a spiritual guide: Billy Jack was advised by his Native American seer and Caine was taught the arts of fighting by Master Po. These mystics blessed violence.

As the seventies wore on, Americans would crave such blessings all the more. Certainly, the moral morass of Vietnam contributed to the rise of a mass religious revival that would come to be known as New Age.

RACE

In the late sixties, J. Edgar Hoover declared the Black Panthers the number-one threat to American internal security, and the FBI launched a counterintelligence movement that helped to destroy the group. By the early seventies, most militant black leaders were out of commission, either in jail or dead.

No wonder so many of the black activists who'd survived the late sixties were committed to a new strategy: electoralism. At the dawn of the decade, African-American leaders shared a sense of disillusionment not just with militarism but with their old ally, the Democratic party, and hoped for the formation of a distinct political party. In 1972, activists and community leaders met in Gary, Indiana, for the Black Political Convention, where Mayor Richard Hatcher opened with a hopeful prediction: "The Seventies will be the decade of an independent black political thrust. Its destiny depends on us here at Gary."

The seventies didn't exactly turn out as Hatcher had expected. Blacks not only remained close to the Democratic party, they became its most crucial voting block. In the 1976 election, the largest black turnout ever pushed key states to Carter's side. The black vote was a

"Bugs Bunny," "Roadrunner," "Porky Pig," "Tom and Jerry"—these were the staples of other generations' Saturday mornings. Old-style cartoon characters lived in their tightly bounded worlds, blindly pursuing their own Sisyphean aims (for instance, the coyote's doomed attempts to catch the roadrunner). These cat-and-mouse cartoons, with their limited plots, required only that children be familiar with a few details of the natural world: barnyards, mouse holes, trees. ¶ Until the seventies, that is. Rather than assuming that kids knew what it was like to go out-of-doors, seventies cartoons required that children have little knowledge of nature and a vast knowledge of prime-time TV shows. Instead of using animals, cartoons like "The Partridge Family: 2200 A.D." took prime-time personalities and threw them into the fantastic world of animation. These cartoon spin-offs tended to be shameless copies of the original (like "The Barkleys," which replaced "All in the Family's" human characters

deciding factor in that contest, as social historian Manning Marable has pointed out. Of course, political clout works both ways: by the end of the decade, the number of African-American elected officials had more than tripled.

But while some blacks shot up the social ladder, most sank ever lower. The 1968 Kerner Commission had "warned of the development of 'two nations, one black and one white,'" says Marable. "Instead, within the black community we are observing a unique class phenomenon—the evolution of at least two distinctly different communities." Some blacks became entrepreneurs, professors, and buppies, but most languished in cities that decayed as whites fled for the suburbs.

If the black vote was decisive in 1976, it was hardly so in 1980. Now it was whites—sick of Carter, sick of the hostage crisis, sick of the seventies—who swung the vote to Reagan. The backlash against civil rights legislation, which had begun in the seventies with antibusing protests and Allan Bakke, would become public policy under the new president.

GUESS WHO'S COMING TO DINNER, SUCKA

The most visible black leaders of the late sixties were militants; in the seventies, the most prominent blacks were those—like Shirley Chisholm, Hatcher, Jesse Jackson, and Maynard Jackson—who were willing to work within the system. Just the opposite shift happened in pop culture.

In the sixties, on-screen black people tended to be soft-spoken and middle of the road. Sidney Poitier appeared in movies like *Guess Who's Coming to Dinner* as an elegant, cultivated guy who patiently breaks down barriers by proving himself worthy to join white society. On TV, Diahann Carroll played Julia, a widowed nurse who seemed to be unaffected by discrimination. Making an appointment for a job interview, she informs her future employer that she's a "Negro." "Have you always been a Negro, or are you just trying to be fashionable?" he chortles. Black women may have been one of the lowest-paid groups in the work force, but you'd never know it from Julia's apartment and her kicky conservative suits. You would never know from late-sixties TV that armed African-Americans were policing their own neighborhoods and black auto workers were bringing radical politics to their unions.

Looking back, it seems amazing that pop culture took so long to clean up and sell the black rebel. (By the time the hip-talking revolutionary, wearing wraparound shades and a beret, had become a familiar sight on the movie screen, many real-life Panthers, like Huey Newton, had dropped their militant rhetoric.) Besides a political style, the Panthers, like the hippies, had invented a whole new way of dressing and talking, a new kind of cool that was eminently marketable. H. Rap Brown, for instance, expressed much more than contempt for the white power structure. His political writing was also an outrageous jeremiad, full of quirky insights and shock-value poetry. "My first contact with white america was . . . when a white doctor pulled me from between my mother's legs and slapped my wet ass," he writes in his 1969 book *Die Nigger Die!*

It only remained for someone to translate the beat of black anger into a saleable product. That person was Melvin Van Peebles, more or less the father of blaxploitation (and undeniably the father of Mario Van Peebles). In 1967, Van Peebles made a movie about a fling between a black soldier and a white woman, released in America as *The Story of a Three Day Pass* to some acclaim. Columbia Pictures then hired him to direct *Watermelon Man* in 1970, a comedy about a bigoted insurance agent who wakes up one day with black skin. To play the character as a white man, Godfrey Cambridge wore a blow-dried wig and a layer of white powder on his face—looking neither black nor white but more like an Asian guy with a really bad perm. It was a minstrel show in reverse, a black man putting on whiteface for laughs—and absolutely the wrong movie for the humorless Van Peebles to direct. What starts out as a comedy does a tailspin at the end, when Godfrey Cambridge joins a paramilitary group in order to ready himself for the black revolutionary takeover of America. One can only wonder what Van Peebles would have done if the studio had handed him *The Nutty Professor*.

Too much of an oddball for Hollywood, Van Peebles found his niche when he struck out on his own to write, direct, and star in *Sweet Sweetback's Baadasssss Song* (1971). The hero, Sweetback, ends up on the wrong side of the law when he defends a brother who's being beat up by police. From then on, the movie becomes a rambling chase scene, with shots of Sweetback running (and wearing a truly fly

with pooches), but geared down for a preschool audience.

So here's a summary of the cartoons that reflected the new sensibility of Saturday mornings of the seventies, when TV made new shows by simply combining bits and pieces of old ones, anticipating the cut-together, highly referential style of postmodernism:

The "Addams Family" and "Star Trek" cartoons were no-nonsense copies of the originals, using many of the original actors' voices, but "The New Adventures of Batman" added a superhero mouse, Batmite. The cartoon "Brady Bunch" lived in a treehouse, played rock and roll, and wore even groovier clothes than in real life (especially Jan's op-art shirt). "Baggy Pants and the Nitwits" combined the seemingly uncombine-able: Baggy Pants was a cat version of Charlie Chaplin while the Nitwits were Ruth Buzzi and Arte Johnson reprising their roles on "Laugh-In." "The Buford Files" was like "The Rockford Files" and "The Andy Griffith Show" put together—the bloodhound Buford was a southern old boy (Jim Nabors's voice) whose cohorts were a sheriff and his dumb deputy. ▶

71

"Emergency Plus Four" added kid interest by giving the crew of NBC's "Emergency" paramedic team four young helpers. In "Jeannie," the magical slave belongs to a high school–age surfer rather than an astronaut. "My Favorite Martians" added another extraterrestrial and a space dog to the Bill Bixby classic. "The Oddball Couple" replaced Felix with a fussy cat and Oscar with a messy dog. In "Return to the Planet of the Apes," Bill, Judy, and Jeff explore the chimp-filled world of the future; also spaced out were Moe, Larry, and Curly, who had become "The Robonic Stooges."

¶ Meanwhile in the past, "These Are the Days" capitalized on the popularity of "The Waltons" with the antics of a turn-of-the-century family.

¶ Most unrelentingly seventies cartoon: "The C. B. Bears" was based on "Charlie's Angels," except that—get this—the angels were three trucker bears named Hustle, Bump, and Boogie.

¶ Cartoon spin-offs of other cartoons: "The Godzilla/Globetrotters Adventure Hour," "Sabrina and the Groovie Goolies" (the teenage witch got together

velveteen vest) superimposed over shots of the ghetto while a free-jazz soundtrack plays endlessly. Sweetback got his nickname because he's so good at using his thang, and use his thang he does, to get out of every scrape imaginable—like the best scene in the movie, where Sweetback meets up with a gang of bikers. They threaten to make him fight a duel with a baaad dude. When the dude turns out to be a chick, Sweetback "duels" her on the floor, naked, and when she flails her legs and moans with pleasure . . . he wins!

Van Peebles was the kind of eccentric who could have become prominent only in the early seventies, the era of "relevant" entertainment. Like Tom Laughlin (who wrote, directed, produced, and starred in *Billy Jack*), the strident Van Peebles seemed only vaguely aware that there was any difference between himself and his on-screen alter ego. He had a dotted line tattooed around his neck with an inscription underneath it: "Cut on the dotted line—if you can." "In the last year a lot of people have tried," he told *Life* magazine shortly after his movie came out.

Director-actors like Laughlin and Van Peebles took the kung fu and the soft-core-porn movie, respectively, and turned them into statements. Because the directors seemed to be telling their own stories, seemed to be putting their real lives on the screen, these exploitation films became political polemics. Never mind that both Laughlin and Van Peebles had fabricated personas for themselves. Never mind that both films strain our credibility, to say the least. (In the final scene of *Billy Jack*, Billy is led off to jail through a line of fifteen-year-old white kids raising the "black power" salute. How self-righteous can you get? Meanwhile, every single time a policeman walks onto the set of *Sweetback*, you know he's going to bust open the head of an innocent black man.)

Still, Van Peebles was much more in touch with reality than was Laughlin. For all the braggadocio and swagger of *Sweetback*, it was the first movie to turn black anger into pop-culture myth and the first to reimagine the black male. Sweetback may be the stereotypical stud, but he also is outraged at what has happened to his people and unafraid to stand up to The Man. Blacks fighting back—it was an idea that proved wildly marketable. Shot for about $500,000, *Sweetback* grossed twenty times that figure in its first year. Part of the reason the film did so well was that it captured a market that was wide open. Blacks, though never seriously courted as a market by Hollywood, were avid consumers—in the late sixties, they were spending more per person on seeing movies than were whites.

WHO'S THE BLACK DICK THAT'S A SEX MACHINE FOR ALL THE CHICKS?

But Van Peebles didn't quite catch Hollywood sleeping. MGM had been working on its own way to woo black audiences, though its first effort was much less strident. *Shaft*, crafted for both white and black audiences, was a weird amalgam of James Brown and James Bond. Director Gordon Parks, Sr. (like Van Peebles, a black wunderkind who had written, directed, and produced his own film, *The Learning Tree*, in 1969) saw the movie as nothing more than entertainment. *Shaft* is not about black anger, it's about clothes, guns, foxy chicks, and snappy comebacks. For instance, when asked where he's going, Shaft replies, "To get laid. Where are you going?" In fact, the only time Shaft seems mad at white society is when he can get a cool one-liner out of it. When his lady asks, "Got problems, baby?" he deadpans, "Yeah, I got a couple of 'em. I was born black and I was born poor."

Though plotwise nothing but a conventional detective story, *Shaft* created a new look and sound for the black movie. (Visually, *Sweetback* seems like a cross between a sixties drug movie and a "Sesame Street" filmstrip about urban neighborhoods.) *Shaft* was among the flood of early-seventies movies that recycled the most tired Hollywood formulas by giving them a new, funky look. *Blacula* livened up the vampire story; *Mahogany* was a black version of *A Star Is Born*; and *Black Godfather* was a ripoff of *The Godfather*. *Shaft* and its ilk were very much like the "race" movies of the twenties and thirties, which put black cowboys on the range and gangsters in Harlem.

However, other blaxploitation films—the ones descended from *Sweetback*—abandoned formulaic plots for a provocative new theme. The most interesting blaxploitation films all posed pretty much the same question: how can the black male assert himself as a free individual without getting killed? In *Superfly*, a coke dealer tries to make one final score so he can give up his business forever, but the white drug syndicate refuses to let him out. In *The Mack*, the pimp hero refuses to join the mob and pays the price.

The blaxploitation hero was not always a pimp or a dealer. In

with a monster rock band), "Josie and the Pussycats in Outer Space," "Pebbles and Bamm Bamm" (the Flintstones kids grew into teenagers and, like all cartoon teenagers, were in a rock band; the voice of Bamm Bamm was supplied by child-actor-gone-psycho Jay North), "Scooby and Scrappy-Doo," "The U.S. of Archie" (a bicentennial version of "The Archie Show"), and "Yogi's Space Race."

Not based on other TV shows but weird anyway: "The Adventures of Gulliver," a Hanna-Barbera cartoon inspired by the Jonathan Swift novel, turned the Lilliputians into seven dwarf-like characters; I confused Gulliver with Gilligan and thought this show was somehow really about the shipwreck of the *Minnow*. "I Am the Greatest: The Adventures of Muhammad Ali"—need I say more? The animated antics of Mr. Sting Like a Bee. And "Will the Real Jerry Lewis Please Sit Down?" recycled the nutty professor as a cartoon character.

73

an obscure movie called *The Spook Who Sat by the Door*, the protagonist is a token black hired by the CIA. After putting the aptly named hero, Freeman, through rigorous intellectual and physical training—all of which he aces—the agency prevents him from becoming a spy. Instead Freeman is sent to a back room to operate the Xerox machine. Disgusted, he leaves and organizes a black revolutionary group, using his training to turn street youths into a crack team that can outwit the CIA itself.

In the best scene of the movie, the revolutionaries take a break from their strategizing to goof around. They act out bits from horrible old plantation movies, making fun of the banjos and the "Yes, Massas" and the down-on-one-knee speeches. At this moment, politics and filmmaking dovetail. We the audience are forced into awareness of how director Ivan Dixon has tried to reverse the stereotypes that run through film history. When his revolutionaries camp it up as Uncle Toms, we get a sense of exactly how deadly movie images can be—or how freeing. The hero in *Spook* uses white society against itself; likewise, the director twists images from white films into parodies of themselves.

EIGHT MOTIFS THAT MAKE A BLAXPLOITATION MOVIE

Isaac Hayes doing what he did best in *Three Tough Guys.*
(UPI/BETTMAN)

The Montage Sex Scene. A black PI spends his day busting heads, so when he comes home to his lady, he wants to relax with some Muzak-like jazz on the hi-fi, a snifter full of cognac, and a spliced-together sex scene. You know what I mean. The camera shows the couple in bed and then closes in for shots of a mouth open in ecstasy, fingernails digging into a back, as that smooooooth music drones on.

Cut to the next morning, when the phone rings and our hero sits up in bed, revealing a pair of awesome pecs. With one last kiss, he's out the door. The black PI may be suave as hell, but he's definitely not boyfriend material.

Revolutionaries. The early-seventies film screen was full of cut-rate Malcolm X's sporting back-to-Africa colors and clenched-fist patches on their jeans jackets.

Unfortunately, blaxploitation tended to celebrate flashy hoods rather than outspoken leaders. In *Superfly*, for instance, when community activists ask a dope dealer for some funds, he gives a coke-addled speech about killing honkies: "You go get you a gun. And all those black folks you keep doing so much talking about get guns and come back ready to go down and I'll be right down in front killing Whitey. Until you can do that you go sing your marching songs somewhere else."

The faux-Panthers added a dash of radical chic to any scene, but since they didn't drive white Cadillacs or have waterbeds, why make a movie about them?

Jocks.   Remember the early-seventies obsession with football—the Superbowl, "Monday Night Football," et al.? My little sister used to stuff the shoulders of her sweater with toilet paper and pretend to be playing defense for the Redskins. One day, Jim Brown came to my junior high school to promote literacy and instead of going to lunch, I followed him around, hoping he'd drop something. Eventually he did: a styrofoam cup with the dregs of some coffee in it. I tried to sell the cup to my sister for fifty cents, telling her that it would give her "Brown power." She didn't buy it.

But a lot of football fans did, and a jock's name boosted film sales. In two movies, Jim Brown starred as a detective named Slaughter—which was what he did during much of his time on-screen. Brown was not the only football star to make the crossover. Fred Williamson's film career started out respectably, but he soon ended up in the blaxploitation ghetto as well, most notably in *Black Caesar*.

Then there was karate-black-belt-turned-actor Jim Kelly. He never played football, but he was in a Bruce Lee movie once. At the height of the blaxploitation craze, this was enough to land him his own movie, *Black Belt Jones*.

Meanwhile, Rosey Grier had to be the weirdest of all the jock stars. Walking the line between machismo and sensitive-guyhood, Grier launched a media crusade to convince men to take up needlepoint. After all, the massive Grier had mastered the art of purl stitching, and he certainly wasn't a sissy. He even published a book full of needlepoint patterns for guys (lots of footballs and golf clubs). At the peak of his sensitivity, he appeared on TV to sing a song aimed at boys: "It's All Right to Cry."

Grier also starred in *The Thing with Two Heads*, a movie about a black convict who has the head of a white scientist grafted onto his

Shaftmania

When actor Richard Roundtree traveled to Ethiopia to film *Shaft in Africa*, he found a country full of beautiful traditions —markets stocked with lions' teeth and masks, wine made from honey, men plucking the one-stringed masenca, according to *Ebony* magazine. He also found a country that had gone *Shaft* crazy. Most Africans seemed to recognize Roundtree —especially as he walked by Shaft's Bar and Grill in downtown Addis Ababa. Roundtree's fame even earned him an audience with Emperor Haile Selassie, during which the Rasta messiah asked Roundtree, "Are you sure you're only 30?"

Yes, after filming *Shaft* and its sequels, model-turned-actor Roundtree seemed wise beyond his years. Or maybe world-weary. Or maybe just tired of playing the same character over and over. Anyway, that's how he appears in the "Shaft" TV series—the erstwhile hour-long show that ran during the 1973–74 season.

The TV show was weird, but of all the *Shaft* spin-off products, the strangest has ▶

75

to be the books. In *Shaft Among the Jews*, the big guy overcomes the notorious tension between blacks and Jews to help out some jewel dealers. And then there's *Shaft's Carnival of Killers*. Best paragraph: "Shaft felt mean, miserable and tight. He hadn't been able to unwind his big black body or the mind that made it move—not with beds, broads or booze."

shoulder. The two heads fight for control of Grier's body. Complex metaphor for racism or shameless exploitation of a black football star? You decide.

Paranoia. After the FBI launched its COINTELPRO campaign against the Panthers, blacks certainly were right to worry that they were being conspired against. But some paranoia went beyond the pale. In *Three the Hard Way*, a Nazilike scientist invents a potion that kills black people while leaving whites unharmed. This one is a must-see for all AIDS-was-planted-in-Africa-by-the-CIA conspiracy buffs.

White Villains. You're doing a little hustling, making some bread, and suddenly The Man leans on you. I'm not talking The Man as in the white power elite or as in Jack Albertson of "Chico and The Man"; I'm talking mashed potato–faced Mafia thugs and racist cops, drug kingpins and their mealy mouthed, business-suited henchmen—the honky in all of his most unflattering guises. I'm also talking The Man as in Ed McMahon. He appears in *Slaughter's Big Rip-Off* as one of the most smarmy white guys ever. It's as if years of being Johnny's sycophantic sidekick, of intoning "I did not know that, sir," has pushed McMahon over the edge. In *Rip-Off*, he plays a crime boss who coolly surveys his victims from behind aviator-shaped mirrored shades and who slaps friends on the back only moments before he has them rubbed out.

The Soundtrack. The best musical scene of any blaxploitation film has to be in *Superfly*, when the hero goes to a nightclub and stumbles on Curtis Mayfield performing "Pusherman." Mayfield looks—in glasses and a sports jacket—less like a pusher than a nerdy professor from some northeastern college's Afro-Am studies department.

The blaxploitation soundtrack was not just background music—it elaborated on the action and commented on the characters. Often such songs became as popular, if not more so, than the movies themselves.

After Isaac Hayes won a Grammy for his work on *Shaft*, it's no wonder he decided to do more than just write soundtracks. Now he wanted to star in his own movies. Poor Isaac. He looked great in those floor-length Jesus robes on his album covers, but he never seemed baaaad enough to play dudes like Truck Turner.

Pimps. For a pure pimp extravaganza, you've got to see *The Mack*. Ostensibly, it's a story of one man's bid to make it big in the underworld without losing his soul; what it's really about is clothes, hair, and cars. As such, the movie takes liberties, shall we say, with the realities of urban life. Our hero, Goldie, hangs out at a special beauty parlor that caters to men of leisure. Later he attends the Players' Ball, a grand function where pimps parade around in their finest. The scene calls for more white rabbit–fur trim and velveteen suits than you can shake a walking stick at.

Max Julien, who plays Goldie, started out as a hippie in drug films like *Psych-Out*. You can only wonder if Julien took too much acid along the way after you see the weirdest vignette in *The Mack*. Goldie, who seems to have bought his own planetarium, stands at the controls making constellations appear and disappear as his 'ho's gaze up at the domed ceiling, transfixed. Godlike, Goldie explains to them their place in the universe. Does this pimp have style or what?

Former-football-player-turned-actor Jim Brown and his fiancée Diane Stanley attending the premiere of the film *Three the Hard Way*. (UPI/BETTMAN)

Antonio Fargas. From *Foxy Brown* to *Shaft* to *Cleopatra Jones*, the whiny-voiced actor with the hooded eyes, Antonio Fargas, played bit parts in several blaxploitation classics. Fargas especially stands out against the ex-jock actors who populated the action movies; their acting was merely wooden, his was a model of over-the-top campiness. *Shaft* never worked as a TV show (actor Richard Roundtree seemed bored with the cleaned-up script); instead it was Fargas who singlehandedly brought the look and sound of 'sploitation to the small screen in his weekly bit part on "Starsky and Hutch." Even though Fargas's character, Huggy Bear, was a restaurateur rather than a pimp or a player, he still strutted and street talked for all he was worth. No one knew Huggy Bear's real name, "including his bank and his employees," according to a 1975 novelization of the TV show. "He signed the paychecks 'Huggy Bear.' He was a tall, lean black man with close-cropped hair and elfin eyes. Usually he was a rather sporty dresser, given to loud checks and colorful bow ties." In the midst of the white-boy cop show, Fargas was a one-man blaxploitation movie.

In 1977, NBC aired a special, Fargas-centric episode of "Starsky and Hutch" called "Huggy Bear and Turkey"—it was intended to be a pilot for a new detective show starring the flamboyant informant. Can you imagine how intoxicatingly terrible and strange a weekly show about Huggy Bear would have been? Watching a show like that would

"Dyn-o-mite!!!"

77

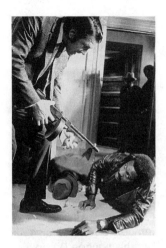

After a shoot-out in which he is wounded, Richard Roundtree (as Shaft) is threatened by another hoodlum.

have been the TV equivalent of guzzling down cherry cough syrup mixed with Colt .45. Unfortunately, it was not to be.

WAS BLAXPLOITATION BAD OR JUST BAAAAD?

As a boy, trumpeter Wynton Marsalis must have watched too many movies like *Hell Up in Harlem* and *The Mack*. Under the influence of blaxploitation, Marsalis imagined himself to be "Wimp the Pimp" and dreamed of growing up to hustle fast women, says jazz writer Stanley Crouch in a 1991 *Details* article. Luckily, Marsalis didn't stick with his plan, but one can imagine that other kids may not have easily shaken off blaxploitation's spell.

Black parents and leaders were understandably worried about the influence of a genre that celebrated kicking ass and selling superfly. "We must insist that our children are not constantly exposed to a steady diet of so-called black movies that glorify black males as pimps, dope pushers, gangsters and super males," protested *The Crisis* in 1973. Crouch blames the blaxploitation movie for starting a harmful trend in black culture—the "cult of the hood" that resurfaced in rap music.

(This writer, by the way, worked as Stanley Crouch's assistant when she was a young pup at the *Village Voice*. While Mr. Crouch never directly expressed his views on blaxploitation to her, he often expressed his dismay at her Xeroxing and collating skills.)

Dangerous as the blaxploitation genre may have been, it also was a boon to blacks in the industry. The most famous blaxploitation films, *Superfly* and *Shaft*, were both directed by black photographers (Gordon Parks, Jr., and Gordon Parks, Sr.). Max Julien wrote *Cleopatra Jones*, and Michael Schultz directed the classic *Cooley High* and *Car Wash*.

With the rise of the genre, actors who'd been able to land roles only as sidekicks or slaves became superstars, while others found themselves able to put together enough money to produce and direct their own films.

One such actor was Ivan Dixon, now known for playing the token black guy in late-sixties episodes of "Hogan's Heroes." In the seventies, Dixon proved himself capable of much more than kissing up to Hogan and interpreting Morse code signals; he directed several TV shows and two films, including *The Spook Who Sat by the Door* (1973), discussed earlier. Years before the Senate investigations revealed how deeply the FBI had infiltrated the Black Panthers, *Spook* showed the CIA and black activists as intimately intertwined, the two flip sides of a divided, racist country. Unfortunately, the film was so poorly distributed by United Artists that it more or less vanished without fanfare.

In addition, the blaxploitation genre, with its waa-waa soundtracks and ultrawide lapels, helped to create a new style—one that white Americans were eager to imitate.

I WANT TO BE BLACK

"How do you respond to a white female, with a tinge of color in her cheeks and a new frizzled hairdo that she considers a bush, who comes up to you and remarks, 'Look at me! I'm starting to look more and more like you-all,' " Linda G. Morris asked in *The Crisis* in 1976.

Whites had begun to appropriate black style as never before. Of course, much that we consider uniquely American—from the word *hip* to the cakewalk contests at high school fairs, from the banjo to many of our jokes—originated in Africa. The African-ness of our culture attests to a long history of cross-fertilization, or to put it less politely, of whites impersonating blacks (from the minstrel show to the "Amos 'n' Andy" show) in order to make fun of them.

But suddenly in the seventies, whites began to experience their lack of "blackness" as a deficit. As the traditional family fell apart and America increasingly became a nation of nomadic singles, people longed for a kind of tradition, closeness, and community that they couldn't find at the mall. Often white people imagined that black people had that. It's interesting that *Roots*—which started a genealogy craze among people whose ancestors had come from Moscow and Manchester, too—was about African lineage. Blacks symbolized rootedness in the midst of a rootless culture.

Seeking to be hip, radical chic, or just trendy, whites copied everything from African-American fashions to the subtlest gestures. "A white professional golfer sinks a winning birdie putt on the 18th hole on the last day of the tournament and raises his hand in a clinched

The Other Mr. T

Everyone knows who Mr. T is—the beefy black guy with weird facial hair who cozied up to Nancy Reagan and urged kids to stay in school. Ah, but you're thinking of the eighties Mr. T. In 1976, Mr. T. was a Japanese nerd (Pat Morita) who clashed with his freewheeling Midwestern nanny in the sitcom "Mr. T. and Tina." The show didn't last long, but what can you expect from a spin-off of "Welcome Back, Kotter"?

"What you talkin' 'bout, Willis?"

79

fist salute: didn't black Olympic track stars Tommie Smith and John Carlos get in trouble for that back in 1968?" asks Louie Robinson in *Ebony*. "And people who may have been pleasantly surprised to hear President Lyndon B. Johnson in his drive for civil rights legislation of the mid Sixties declare a la Martin Luther King, 'We shall overcome,' were less enthused a few years later when Nixonion bureaucrats in crewcuts and Brooks Brothers suits slapped palms and exclaimed: 'Right-on, Baby!' "

Of course, when it comes to summing up the intentions and desires of a culture, the first place to look is the head—not what's in it, but what's on top of it. To judge from seventies hairstyles, Caucasians would rather have been anything but. By the later episodes of "The Brady Bunch," TV dad Mike had gone from a Bill Bixby–type buzz with 'burns to a Sly Stone 'fro, and his eldest sons were not far behind. (Greg even used the word *funky* once.) Stevie Wonder sported cornrows, but then so did Bo Derek.

And let's not forget clothes. An early-seventies *Esquire* article celebrates "flash," that particular sartorial style invented by downtown drug dealers. "His name is Jimmy. He is thirty, built like a halfback, and has a trim moustache and moderate afro. He reached under his soft-brown sweater-shirt which was worn outside his slim, brown, custom-made trousers, and from a specially tailored pocket he pulled out a small .25-caliber Browning automatic," says one article, which breathlessly describes the clothing and lifestyle of this dealer as if he were a high-society playboy.

Disco, of course, ushered in a whole new panoply of black looks, from the wine-colored suit to the extra-wide flares. The first men to teeter around in the ultra-high, lace-up platform shoes that became so much a symbol of the disco scene certainly were not the Bee Gees.

By the end of the seventies, black street style was showing up in the oddest of places. For instance, one navy ad that profiled a black pilot began with the headline: "They call him 'SUPER BAD.' " And at the bottom of the ad, the navy used a funked-up slogan: "The Navy's not just sayin' it, they're doin' it!" Yo, bro, slap me five and pass the ammunition.

TV AND THE ABSENT FATHER

In the movies, black dudes murdered, pimped, fought for the revolution, ran from the cops, made love, died. But the powerful black man never made it into the more conservative medium of TV. Witness the failure of *Shaft*: the black dick who sassed off to police lieutenant Rossi became, on the tube, a namby-pamby PI who sucked up to white authority figures.

More often than not, TV's black male wasn't just a wimp, he was not there at all. In sitcoms like "That's My Mamma" and "What's Happening!!," an obese matriarch presided over the black family, and the only males around were young enough (like Raj and J.J.) to still be under their mammas' thumb. "Why do the mothers . . . always seem to be fat? (The famous black matriarchy? Some residual white image of Mammy? Of Aunt Jemima?)," asks a 1978 essay in *Time*. "Why are there no strong, intelligent black father figures on TV?" Clearly, white society was not deemed ready to see any black male who wasn't, like George Jefferson or Fred Sanford, a ridiculous, strutting update of Stepin Fetchit.

With black fathers banished from the TV world and even mothers deserting their families (as Florida did on "Good Times"), who would raise black kids? Why, *white* fathers, of course.

The seventies saw the creation of one of the strangest new genres on TV: the black-boys-adopted-by-white-man show. It seemed that black people kept dying off and leaving their kids to their white friends—at least that was the premise of both "Diff'rent Strokes" and, later, "Webster" (1983). Or ghetto youths who bonded with their coach ("The White Shadow") and came to him with their problems. Gary Coleman of "Diff'rent Strokes," unnaturally dwarfish because of kidney problems, turned blackness into a metaphor for arrested childhood.

What about blacks in drama? Except miniseries, no long-running drama addressed black life. According to *Ebony* in 1980, "Black America, a thirty-minute sitcom worth a few twitters of canned laughter, is an urban Oz peopled with fat women, juvenile men and precocious brats, none of whom can be taken too seriously." In the seventies, black faces became a familiar sight on TV, but only in sitcoms, leading many to accuse the industry of reviving the minstrelsy of pre–civil rights fare like "Amos and Andy."

Revelation

Every cop show and bad detective movie of the seventies had a chase scene set in a parking garage. That way you could show Gran Torinos with profiles like sharks and black-windowed Eldorados screeching around corners at five miles per hour. People *liked* to see cars moving slowly back then. Think of low-riders, those Latino luxury cars so decked out with chrome, airbrushed art, and fuzzy seat covers that they could barely move. Think of vans, those shag-carpeted wombs that crawled along the highway. People appreciated big, ponderous cars because during the height of the energy crisis, they saw them as works of art rather than as speed machines. Thus, the inevitable scene in the underground parking garage—where the vehicles "chased" each other at a crawl—allowed our eyes to linger lovingly over the last of the giant cars.

81

"Gene, Gene, The Dancing Machine."

DO THE HUSTLE

With the seventies came big-business rock. FM stations started to resemble their bubblegum AM brethren as station managers bought playlists from consultants hired to suss out just what music would yield the juiciest audience. The result was the proliferation of album-oriented rock stations (alias classic rock), designed to please young white males. The AOR audience didn't want to hear Sly Stone, Parliament, or Barry White. They wanted metal in all its guises, from Zep to Styx to Aerosmith.

But as teenagers crowded into stadiums to see mass-marketed bands, something very different was happening in the nightclubs of New York and San Francisco. Gays, Latins, and blacks went out to dance to "party music"—high-intensity, shake-your-booty jams created by club deejays who mixed together soul and Motown songs. Because record companies and radio stations showed little interest in the new sound, the deejays formed their own networks through which they could find out about the latest Kool and the Gang or Hues Corporation songs.

Disco was the product of a commingling of styles, from the European slickness of producer Giorgio Moroder to the funk of Sly Stone, a groove as far-removed as could be from the white-boy album rock that ruled the airwaves. "Disco is predominantly a black sound, the best disco being an extension of the old Motown sound, and the best white group, KC and the Sunshine Band, sounding as black as the Righteous Brothers," Albert Goldman wrote in *Esquire* in 1977.

While the record companies had been busy foisting bands like Rush and REO Speedwagon on teenage boys, a genuine musical revolution had been going on. A lot of people didn't want to go to a stadium to watch tiny, faraway figures prance around on stage; they wanted to participate in the show or, better yet, to be at the center of attention on the dance floor. Disco songs—like "The Hustle," "Le Freak," "Disco Lady," "Dancing Queen," and "Boogie Oogie Oogie"—celebrated the dancers themselves. It was the perfect soundtrack for the me decade.

The music caught on despite the record companies and radio stations. Disco had been labeled "black," and it was shunned by big business as a fringe movement with little commercial potential.

"Curiously, nobody has been more surprised by the disco take-over than the major record-company executives. Until recently, they viewed the disco beat as a passing fancy, as dance music by black singers with limited appeal to the white, mainstream pop audience," *Newsweek* commented in 1979.

All of that changed after the release of *Saturday Night Fever*. The soundtrack by the Bee Gees—three apparently straight, white guys—turned disco into mainstream music. From then on, there was no stopping it. Everything had become discoized: radio stations, TV dance shows, newsletters, roller rinks, weddings, even murder (two men were driven into a jealous frenzy after they watched their girlfriends do Le Freak with other guys).

At the peak of the craze, it was hard to imagine a world without disco—it seemed that the slick, coked-laced beat would be around forever. In 1979, *The Disco Handbook* predicted what boogying would be like in the far future: "In the disco of the 1990s you would have the possibility of altering the appearance of your environment almost ad infinitum." The book envisioned walls covered with giant video images of exotic locations, so it would look like the dancers were doing the hustle on the Alaskan tundra or in the African veldt.

HISPANICS: THE "OTHER" MINORITY

Whether it was a "Kiss Me, I'm Irish" button or an "Italian Stallion" T-shirt, flaunting your ethnicity was an essential part of seventies fashion. If blacks could be proud of their history, then whites could, too—though "white" no longer sufficed to describe many people's identities. "Class ties based on common economic interest have been weakened. So too have faith and pride in national destiny," *Time* clucked in 1975. "The sense of identity and common purpose each was once able to supply—being a worker, being an American—is now more readily supplied for many people by an ethnic or racial or cultural bond."

Ethnic humor—updated, hip, and streetwise—became mandatory in urban sitcoms. Think of "Welcome Back, Kotter." (I do. All the time.) Each "sweathog" was a pastiche of ethnic clichés—especially Epstein, whose mixed Jewish and Puerto Rican heritage made him a laughtrack double whammy. He was lazy and conniving and even

Amazing Fact

Freddie Prinze, who mused about his death prior to killing himself, said he wanted Paul Williams to be one of his pallbearers.

smelly! Remember all those notes signed by "Epstein's mother"? Remember the jokes about fumes from Epstein's locker?

Hispanics, a militant group with its own underground style and slang, became the "new blacks" in pop culture—both a subject of fascination and the butt of the worst racist humor. "Chico and The Man" may have become an immediate number-one show when it hit TV in 1974 because it comforted whites. Chico ("boy") wasn't one of those scary Chicanos who glared at you as you drove through the barrio; instead, this self-deprecating Hispanic wanted nothing more than to enslave himself to The Man—in this case Ed, the grumpy owner of a run-down garage. The show angered Mexican-Americans for a number of other reasons, too, like the racist jabs ("Get out of here and take your flies with you," quips Ed) and the fact that Freddie Prinze, a Hungarian–Puerto Rican, played a Chicano.

The producers cleaned up the show and the charismatic Prinze became a superstar—especially when, months before Elvis, he died with all the flash and lurid drama of a true seventies idol. High on quaaludes, he blew his brains out.

Prinze's popularity was part of a wave of interest in Hispanic style—from Tony Orlando to Freddy Fender to the Latin beat of disco to low-riders. The latter epitomized Chicano cool. The low-rider subculture sprang up as a reaction to a California law prohibiting any part of a car's body from protruding below the wheel rim. Since this hampered the creativity of Mexican-American car customizers, they came up with a unique solution: they installed hydraulic lifts so that—at the glimpse of a cop—they could pump their car up to legal height. After a while, bouncing up and down became the whole point; after all, what could be more menacing than a huge old Impala lurching high in the air? In the car-obsessed and excessive seventies, the mainstream became fascinated with low-riders—so much so that War's song about the phenomenon ("Low-ride-der drives a little slower") became a hit.

But as Freddie Prinze proved, a lot of sudden attention can be dangerous. A mid-seventies episode of "Kojak" showed the lollipop-sucking detective battling Puerto Rican terrorists who belong to an organization called El Comite. The trouble was, the show had stolen that name from a real-life Puerto Rican group, one committed to socialism, not to assassination and terror. But the "Kojak" version of reality won out: soon after the episode appeared on TV, the FBI raided the houses of the Puerto Rican socialists.

Blacks, all too familiar with the political dangers of being stereotyped as Stepin Fetchit, Uncle Tom, or Superspade, had begun to wrest some control of pop culture, to participate in the creation of African-American characters. For other groups, newly visible on TV screens, the fight had just begun.

Charlie's Angels in yet
another predicament.
(LEFT TO RIGHT:
Jacqueline Smith, Farrah
Fawcett [Majors had
been dropped by this
time], and Kate Jackson.)
(UPI/BETTMAN)

WOMEN

R esentment brewed for years among women in the civil rights movement. Many had begun to appreciate a certain irony: even while they fought for black equality, they found themselves riding in the back of the bus; their male comrades in the movement expected them to cook, clean, type, have sex on demand, and stay out of the decision-making processes. In the mid-sixties, when women in the Student Nonviolent Coordinating Committee (SNCC) had compared their position in the organization to that of a "token Negro hired in a corporation," many of the men greeted their protest with ridicule. "The only position for women in SNCC," quipped Stokely Carmichael, "is prone."

But the fledgling feminists reached their boiling point in 1967, at a leftist convention in Chicago. When speaker Shulamith Firestone tried to take the podium to talk about women's demands, the chairman of the convention patted her on the head. "Move on, little girl," he said. "We have more important issues to talk about here than women's liberation." Little did he know it, but he had just patted one of the founders of radical feminism.

87

How appropriate that a pat on the head, a gesture of such intimate humiliation—rather than a shot, kick, shove, or stab—should be the blow that sent the women's movement spinning off from the male-dominated Left. While blacks and other groups tended to suffer in public, women's oppression centered around the private world of sexual relations, gay versus straight identity, reproductive rights, and dissatisfaction with domesticity.

For women, political transformation tended to be a much more private matter—it meant not just retelling the story of women as a group but retelling one's own story, often with wrenchingly personal consequences. For instance, Jane Alpert (who went underground as an antiwar activist and came out of hiding a feminist) could express her anger at the patriarchy only by revealing the most intimate details of her life. What particularly rankled her was her relationship with activist Sam Melville, who later was killed in the Attica prison riots. The unraveling of their love affair in many ways mirrored the loss of love between women and the male Left. Alpert revealed in a 1973 essay for *Ms.*:

> Sam began a secret affair with a woman friend of ours whom I hadn't seen in some time. He also at least hinted to her that the sabotage of military and corporate buildings around the city was the work of himself and friends. . . . To this day I don't know how many other dangerous, possibly fatal, violations of security his masculinist need to boast led him to commit. . . . How strange it is that not only the man I lived with but one of the most brilliant and sophisticated black militants of the 1960s should turn out to have [such] crass ignorance about women. And so, my sisters in Weatherman, *you* fast and organize and demonstrate for Attica. . . . Don't tell me how much those deaths moved you. I will mourn the loss of 42 male supremacists no longer.

Alpert had not been converted to feminism while Melville cheated on her, nor while she helped to bomb buildings in Manhattan, nor when she decided to go underground, but—like so many other women—had found feminism in the homey atmosphere of a consciousness-raising group. These groups, which combined therapylike discussion and political theory, became enormously popular during the seventies—a social fad and political movement all rolled into one. In fact, a 1974 TV movie made women's unhappiness the disease of the week: in *Tell Me Where It Hurts*, Maureen Stapleton plays a working-class housewife who organizes a consciousness-raising group with her friends and finds out why mopping the floor makes her so miserable.

If feminism revolutionized the kaffeeklatsch, it also turned the crafts-and-recipes magazine into a war zone. In 1970, a group of women staged a sit-in at *Ladies' Home Journal*, where they demanded a female editor in chief, a day-care center, and the elimination of all offensive advertising. Two years later, *Ms.* began publication. The magazine became the de facto voice of feminism, making moderate Gloria Steinem far more familiar to the average American than radicals like Firestone. Because the women's movement snuck into the popular consciousness through pop culture, it was only natural that the moderates of the movement should become its spokeswomen.

LOOKING OUT FOR NUMBER ONE

Why did the women's movement flourish during the seventies while black power, pacifism, and even ecology failed to hold the mainstream's attention? More than its moderate tone or pop-speak rhetoric, feminism's emphasis on the self was especially suited to the mood of the me decade.

Traditionally, leftists tended to pooh-pooh middle-class activists who showed too much interest in their own lives: when third worlders didn't have enough to eat, it seemed frivolous to worry about one's own misery in the sterile palaces of suburbia. So when feminism proposed that suburban angst was real and political, it created a heretical new form of politics—one that put as much emphasis on feelings as on material wealth. In her *Ms.* essay, Jane Alpert, for instance, describes her conversion to feminism as a journey through inner space: "The struggle to define oneself for oneself ultimately takes place in a realm of the mind in which one is always alone and unsupported."

Alpert was hardly the only one intent on discovering inner realms. In the wake of the extroverted postwar years, people longed to turn inward. Rather than revolution, therapy seemed like the answer and personal hang-ups, rather than capitalism or racism, the root of all evil. For instance, Thomas A. Harris, whose *I'm OK—You're OK* became a number-one bestseller, believed that a new age of peace and harmony would dawn if only everyone in the world hunkered down for a mass group therapy session.

The self had become, instead of a hard nugget inside, a fluid set of hobbies and feelings. It had become a *project.* "After the political turmoil of the sixties, Americans have retreated to purely personal preoccupations," complains Christopher Lasch in *The Culture of Narcissism* (1979). "Having no hope of improving their lives in any of the ways that matter, people have convinced themselves that what matters is psychic self-improvement: getting in touch with their feelings, eating health food, taking lessons in ballet or belly-dancing, . . . jogging, learning how to 'relate.' "

"Gee, your hair smells terrific!"

Underneath all of this energetic cultivation of hobbies, a great fear gripped Americans. If you could create any self you wanted, then who were you, really? Beneath the jogging and the beer making and the macrame, was there anything that endured? According to Alvin Toffler, the average American hardly felt settled in his new, constructed personality: "And one day the question hits him like a splash of cold water in a sleep-sodden face: 'What remains?' What is there of 'self' or 'personality' in the sense of a continuous, durable internal structure?"

Patty Hearst may have become a media darling precisely because she embodied this question. Kept in a closet, blindfolded, and made to intone SLA dogma, the mild-mannered Patty turned into gun-totin' Tanya. If Patty could be so easily brainwashed, her self erased, then what about the rest of us? It was becoming clear that once you were stripped of friends and family, you also lost your "self"—that is, the cultivation of a continuous identity could happen only in the midst of a supportive community. In the rootless, placeless world of 1970s America, we were all in danger of becoming Patty Hearst.

But within the framework of feminism, women could look inward without getting mired in me decade self-absorption—the movement gave women both a community and a set of practical political goals. Joining the revolution meant fighting for legislation from *Roe v. Wade* to no-fault divorce to the Equal Rights Amendment.

Even for those who never really joined the movement—never stepped inside a "womyn's safe space" or decked out in lavender for a woman-identified-women's coffeehouse—things changed rapidly. A shift in women's expectations occurred with the furious intensity of few other social movements in our history. In 1968, about 30 percent of young white women planned to have life-long careers. Five years later, nearly twice as many expected to keep working. (The shift among black women, many of whom *had* to work, was less dramatic.)

But the movement's strength—its emphasis on the self—also proved to be a weakness as the decade wore on. If feminism talked about sexuality, self-esteem, "beauty," body image, and buying power, so did commercials. TV shows and ads interpreted "woman power" as the power to consume.

By the late seventies, according to popular wisdom, the struggle for women's equality had been won. You'd come a long way, baby, and now it was time to get what you deserved: a corporate job. The way to get it was with a suit—not a civil rights suit but a business suit, worn with a feminine fedora and one of those floppy, bow-tie scarves. *The Woman's Dress for Success Book*, first published in 1977, became a best-seller as would-be execs tried to decide whether they should wear brown pumps or white sandals for their climb to the top.

Author John T. Molloy is all in favor of women wearing the pants. "I always found women in pants ultrasexy. But so many people told me otherwise that I was starting to think I might be a little weird. I'm happy to report that our research shows I'm normal and that my reaction is standard. Most men find women in pants very sexy."

As the women's movement became a pop phenomenon, the emphasis shifted away from finding your self to finding whatever self would make the most money. Unfortunately, that meant that many women ceased to see themselves as belonging to a larger political group, one whose interests were not the same as corporate America's.

MONEY, HONEY

The truth was, by 1980, women had both won and lost the fight. While an upheaval in family structure allowed females to become independent of men and marriage, it also had became easier for women—especially single women with children—to slip through the cracks. As social theorist Michael Harrington noted at the end of the decade, the face of poverty had become increasingly feminine because of the steep rise in families headed by women.

Despite all the hoopla about new opportunities, the bottom line

was that, financially, things had never been worse for women. Not since the depression had women's salaries, as compared to men's, been so low: throughout much of the seventies, women earned less than sixty cents for each man's dollar.

In an ill-conceived bid to celebrate feminist history, the U.S. Treasury released its Susan B. Anthony dollar in 1979. The dollars looked so much like quarters that people jammed them into vending machines and cashiers gave the wrong change. Soon after she appeared, Susan B. had to be shelved. How appropriate, in the decade when women's earnings fell so far below men's, that the woman's dollar should so often be mistaken for twenty-five cents.

BRA BURNERS

As real-life women changed their roles, so, too, did women on TV and in movies. Instead of blissful Donna Reeds and June Cleavers, housewives in the seventies tended to be depicted as robotic (*The Stepford Wives*), on the brink (*Diary of a Mad Housewife*), or spaced-out ("Mary Hartman, Mary Hartman"). While in the early sixties single, career women like Sally on "The Dick Van Dyke Show" were objects of pity—dowdy, lonely, desperate—ten years later, it was housewives who were saddled with unflattering stereotypes. Now TV shows and movies portrayed single women as adventurers (Princess Leia, Mary Richards, Jill Clayburgh's Erica in *An Unmarried Woman*).

Feminist writer Susan Faludi sees the 1970s as a sort of golden age, a time when the media finally treated women with respect. For instance, she notes, in 1973 Revlon came up with Charlie (both an imaginary character and a perfume), who appears in ads as "a confident and single working woman who signs her own checks, pops into nightclubs on her own, and even asks men to dance."

Faludi certainly has a point. Nonetheless, pop culture's "sympathetic" treatment of women in the seventies was often disingenuous. Picture the seventies feminist: a tough-talking go-getter in an Annie Hall suit (or perhaps gauchos and a man's jacket) with short-cropped hair and a cigarette hanging from her lips—she is as much a stereotyped figure as the fifties housewife. While some real-life feminists could only be called strident (like Valerie Solanas, who proposes castration as the final solution in her *Scum Manifesto*), the pissed-off woman who demonstrated her hatred for the patriarchy by torching her bra was entirely a media invention. "Bra burner" became a common pejorative synonym for "feminist," even though there's no evidence that underwear of any kind was ever set aflame. True, in 1968, demonstrators at the Miss America Pageant threw bras, girdles, and *Ladies' Home Journals* into a symbolic trash can. True, the demonstrators attempted to set fire to these instruments of oppression, but they were prevented from doing so by a city ordinance. So it's hard to say how this incident became transformed by the media into a "bra-burning" fest. (The other unresolved issue, of course, is whether bras made of seventies fabric like Qiana, Lurex, and assorted polyesters would even burn at all—perhaps a more appropriate term would have been "bra melting.")

Nonetheless, the media chose to focus on this image of female anger—as if women cared less about freeing themselves from on-the-job discrimination than they did about unleashing their breasts from confining straps and stays. "Bra burner" became a popular term because it perfectly expresses the media's ambivalence toward the new woman; she was both an unfettered sex object and a shrew; both a jiggling free-love kitten and a burn-baby-burn zealot whose unsupported breasts were now going to droop in all kinds of unflattering ways. While women voiced their frustrations through their mouths, national attention focused on a lower portion of the female anatomy.

HAVING A FEMALE BODY DOESN'T MAKE YOU FEMININE

For the media, the liberated woman represented both a hero and a troublemaker. For advertisers, she represented pure profit. The strong woman—engaged in the difficult task of adopting "masculine" jobs and sexual behavior—was a new kind of consumer, one who might feel especially insecure about losing her femininity. That's where advertisers stepped in, providing all sorts of concoctions—spray, shampoo, ointment, lotion—to help women wash away the masculine musk of freedom.

For instance, the print ad for FDS, a "feminine hygiene deodorant spray," says it all. "Having a female body doesn't make you femi-

"Just the right amount of freshness."

nine," the copy warns. One would think that if having a woman's body didn't make you feminine, spraying stuff on your crotch wouldn't do much good, either.

Weirder still were the ads that took the credit for women's liberation. According to one cigar maker, it was not the civil rights movement but the company's own advertising campaign that inspired women to fight for liberation. "It began 10 years ago when we asked, 'Should a gentleman offer a Tiparillo to a lady?'" boasts the cigar ad. "A lot's happened since then. Today, a gentleman not only offers a Tiparillo to a lady, but the lady is taking up the offer. Yes, times have changed.... Curvaceous young women are jockeys. Co-ed dorms are part of the education," the ad muses. And at the bottom of the page, a logo reads, "Tiparillo: Maybe we started something."

Another ad shows a woman wearing a flowing headband and a revolutionary-style armband. Over her head is emblazoned the word *Liberation*. Is she a follower of Che Guevara? No, she's a secretary, granted "new freedoms" by a more convenient dispenser of Liquid Paper.

BLOODY MAMAS

How were physically powerful, even dangerous, women treated in the pop culture of the seventies? How about women who were strong not in the standard she's-a-gutsy-divorced-mother mode of "One Day at a Time" but instead in the she's-got-bulging-muscles-and-an-M16-and-she's-mad-at-society vein?

It was the decade in which women suddenly had bodies—not figures molded by torpedo-shaped bra cups but unfettered bodies that sweated and moved. Billie Jean King took on Bobby Riggs and won. Female joggers became a common sight; and even grandmothers who didn't plan to run anywhere wore "designer" velour sweat suits to the mall. It was also the decade in which women became dangerous. Patty Hearst, Jane Alpert, Squeaky Fromme, and Diana Oughton wielded shotguns, planted bombs, and conspired against the government.

More important, it was the decade during which graphic depiction of sex and violence moved out of the margins and into the mainstream, giving rise to new pop-culture genres that were lavishly and

unapologetically tasteless: blaxploitation, disaster movies, slasher films, and "jiggle" TV shows.

The movies and TV shows that put women in their most active and powerful roles also tended to be the most exploitative—because when women became action-adventure heroes, the intended audience was usually male. "Charlie's Angels," for instance, was not a show intended to inspire young girls to pursue a career in detective work.

Black women—who more often get stereotyped as wildly sexual and physical beings—were the first bawdy superheroines of the seventies. Of course, during the blaxploitation craze of 1971 to 1974, both black women and black men broke out of subservient roles to hustle, pimp, jive, and posture their way through movies that turned the ghetto into a comic book world.

Blaxploitation films are about revenge—the moment when a member of the underclass finally gets sweet comeuppance against the oppressor. It was only natural that black women, doubly oppressed, should become the heroes in many of these movies. In fact, an entire subgenre of blaxploitation—what I'll call "bitchsploitation" movies—centered around the exploits of various voluptuous-yet-muscular actresses. The most beloved of these female cult figures was Pam Grier (see sidebar).

Grier emerged as a star in 1973's *Coffy*. Nurse by day and lingerie-clad vigilante by night, she fights the drug syndicate to avenge the death of her sister. Her tactics include blowing away junkies as they shoot up and hiding razor blades in her 'fro.

But *Coffy* saves the most violent revenge for the man who's done her wrong. When her boyfriend cheats on her, she takes a big ol' rifle, aims right between his legs, and fires. In bitchsploitation movies, women triumph not only over the white power structure but over men of all races.

According to Grier, American International Pictures (foremost of the sleaze-movie companies) tried to make *Coffy* as one-dimensional as possible. AIP found the first cut of the movie "too depressing, the character was too strong and too serious," Grier told *Ms.* magazine in 1975. "So they cut it up—taking out most important parts, like tender scenes between me and my sister. So all you see is *bang, bang, bang*, shoot 'em up tits and ass."

Foxy Brown (1974) is even more cartoony. Once again, Grier takes on drug pushers—but this time the leader of the syndicate is a

The Pam Grier Story

In the late sixties, Pam Grier—an aspiring actress who was part white, part black, part Native American, and part Asian—landed a job as a switchboard operator at American International Pictures. AIP churned out sleazy B movies and Grier was determined to act in one of them. "I started listening in on the calls and I got to know a lot about what was going on," she told *Ms.* magazine in 1975. "I got to know who was doing what, where they were doing it, and how long it would take. Everything went click, click, click in my head." Soon after, she used her savvy to land a bit part in *The Big Doll House*, about a prison guarded by sexy, sadistic females.

Her big break came when she costarred in another women-in-prison movie, *Black Mama, White Mama* (1973). In *Coffy* (1973), Grier no longer had to share the bill with a white woman. She was becoming as big a blaxploitation celebrity as her male counterparts—and she played, as they did, a lone seeker of justice up against a white man's conspiracy.

However, what's most radical about the Pam Grier ▶

films is Grier herself. With sarcastic delivery, she transmits to the audience her utter disdain for the terrible dialogue, the ugly yellow jumpsuits, the ridiculous plot. Grier screams out lines like "This is the end of your life, you motherfuckin' drug pusher" with such campy glee that her films become elaborate farces.

¶ Off-screen, too, Grier made fun of the AIP movies, calling them "jerk jobs." A real-life dynamo, she started a production company so that she could make her own films. Unfortunately, her Brown Sun Productions never made it. Still, the cult queen sought to wrest control of the camera and break out of her stilted scripts.

white woman who smokes slim cigars (the ultimate caricature of a seventies feminist). She barks orders at her henchmen, and they answer with an obedient "Yes, Miss Katherine" or "No, Miss Katherine."

Foxy Brown's eventual revenge against Miss Katherine could have been thought up only by a man—in this case, director and screenwriter Jack Hill. "It's a picture I don't even like to think about today, to tell you the truth. I mean it's so gross," Hill recalls in a 1992 interview with *Psychotronic* magazine. "The ending of the picture I tossed off as a joke and they grabbed onto it and thought that was just a really great idea."

What happens? Foxy tracks down Miss Katherine's boyfriend, strips off his pants, takes out a big knife and, well, you can guess the rest. In the final scene, she presents Miss Katherine with a pickle jar filled with the bloody lump of flesh. Weirdly, Miss Katherine immediately recognizes the contents as belonging to her man.

Of course, the bitchsploitation movies can hardly be called feminist, especially since—with lesbian bar brawls, cat fights, and torture scenes—they were designed for male titillation. According to black culture historian Donald Bogle, Pam Grier enjoyed a "lopsided type of stardom." He claims that "because the films never placed her in a realistic, everyday type of situation, black women found it hard to identify with her." Nonetheless, Grier's charisma, power, and sense of humor shine through, even when she has to model a skimpy halter top for her pimp. And while the bitchsploitation stars hardly seemed real, many black women may have found them inspiring—more so than Bogle realizes. In *Ms.*, Margaret Edmondson Sloan, founder of the National Black Feminist Organization, reported a certain lingering pleasure after watching *Cleopatra Jones*. She was not alone; after the movie, according to Sloan, the woman sitting behind her in the theater spontaneously exclaimed, "Damn. That movie felt good."

FOXY TV

Mid-seventies TV shows tried to cash in on the blaxploitation craze, presenting viewers with a prime-time version of baaaadness. In 1973, "Shaft" came to TV, airing on irregular Tuesday nights, and flopped—probably because it lacked all the sleaze, soul, and 'sploitation of the movie. Who would dare show a sassy black *dude* on the tube? In

1974, ABC aired the first regular weekly series inspired by the black film sensibility. Interestingly, the series starred a female hero. The prospect of a jive-talkin', ass-kickin' black *woman* must have seemed much less threatening to a mostly white audience.

"Get Christie Love" had a lot more character than did the TV version of *Shaft*—at least "Christie" tried to have soul, even if it was a campy white fantasy of what soul should be. Nonetheless, the show was doomed from the beginning.

Actress Teresa Graves was a devout Jehovah's Witness. (From a 1974 profile of Graves in *Ebony*: " 'I believe the world will be destroyed,' she says.... Moments later she hurried from the Universal Studios lot, headed for a religious meeting.") The actress refused to let her character kill anyone or even tell a lie, which somewhat cramped Christie's prowess as a death-dealing force of one. Stripped of any serious weaponry, Christie relied on her fists, holding off gangs of men with her karate chops—while still managing to flirt with them! As she slipped on the handcuffs she'd say, "You're under arrest, sugar."

Even deadlier than her fists was her wardrobe. As an undercover cop, Christie constantly had to change her outfit. One minute she masqueraded as a prostitute in a miniskirt and rabbit-fur jacket; the next minute, she made the scene in a studded denim pantsuit. Her hair also ran the gamut from an Angela Davis 'fro to Chaka Khan curls.

Many elements of the show were unabashedly white—for instance, sleazy guest stars like Arte Johnson and Bobby Riggs, who seemed to have nowhere else to go because "The Gong Show" hadn't been invented yet. But "Get Christie Love" was inspired primarily by the bitchsploitation movies—those action-adventure films that doubled as soft-core porn. Back in 1973 (when the series was first conceived), where else but in black action pictures did one see a street-smart amazon so dangerous that she could hold off several thugs at once? Where else were women allowed to be not only outlandishly sexual but chillingly vengeful, a harpie and temptress rolled into one? "Christie," of course, served up a much blander version of the blaxploitation goddess. Still, the show is landmark in that it brought the gun-toting mama into mainstream white culture.

A few months before "Christie" aired—in short, right at the tail end of the blaxploitation trend—Patty Hearst helped the SLA hold up a San Francisco bank. Patty waved a machine gun and yelled, "Get down or I'll blow your motherfucking heads off." It was a performance

worthy of Foxy Brown. One can only wonder if SLA leader Cinque, who scripted Patty's performances, had been inspired by movies like *Superfly*, *Coffy*, and *Shaft*. Patty was the first and only white girl to star in a blaxploitation movie.

BLACK MAMA, WHITE MAMA

There is a long tradition of portraying white and black women as opposites, rather than as sisters under the skin. Think of *Gone with the Wind*, which paired Scarlett with sidekick Mammy. Scarlett is too willful and rebellious to be a good mother, while the hymn-humming Mammy seems the very embodiment of life. Scarlett throws tantrums; the ever-philosophical Mammy keeps her under control. How different is this from the updated black-white duo of "Maude"? Maude is merely a suburban Scarlett, rebellious and ridiculous (she denounces the patriarchy from the comfortable perch of her Tuckahoe, New York, living room). Her maid Florida, on the other hand, is the soul of practicality, using her deadpan jibes to make fun of Maude's highfalutin politics.

Even those schooled in the feminist–civil rights movement tended to think of black women as earthy and white women as out of touch. According to historian Sara Evans, "Having broken with traditional culture, young white women welcomed the alternative [that black women] represented. For them these black women became 'mamas' in the sense of being substitute mother figures, new models of womanhood."

Not surprisingly, the early-seventies genre that made white women most dangerous—gun-moll movies—usually used the word *Mama* in their titles, as if to make the white stars seem blacker. Films like *Bloody Mama* (1970), *Big Bad Mama* (1974), and *Crazy Mama* (1975) portrayed their antiheroines as old-timey gangsters riding around in jalopies. In *Bloody Mama*, Shelley Winters plays Ma Barker as the quivering-chinned, ruthless mother to a brood of backwoods killers. In *Big Bad Mama*, Angie Dickinson is a sex-starved bank robber who hooks up with foppish gambler William Shatner (!). All of these films are set in a remote past and tell stories about women who kill only because they're so trashy and insane that they don't know any better. Unlike their black sisters, the white mamas did not fight injustice, nor did they live in the here and now.

On TV, white women kicked even less ass. For instance, you'd think a gal whose body has been wired full of machinery would become a whirling Shiva of destruction. Not so Jaime Sommers, the Bionic Woman. Remember the episodes of "The Six Million Dollar Man" that introduce us to Jaime? Sure she makes the same "dee-dee-dee-dee" sound that Steve Austin does when she jumps. Sure she makes that "thwack-thwack-thwack" sound when she throws boulders. But underneath all the technology, Jaime proves to be an old-fashioned gal, more interested in planning her wedding to Steve than cracking a crime ring. No wonder her body starts to reject its bionic parts, causing her to run around like a woman with horrible PMS, smashing a table and ripping the handle off a door.

Still, with her male name and her loose-fitting jogging suit, Jaime is curiously androgynous. She never does marry the Six Million Dollar Man. A fit of amnesia causes her to lose her feelings for Steve, and so she leaves him for her own spin-off, where she leads a spinsterish life as a schoolteacher. Occasionally she and Steve get together on missions, like when they team up to battle bigfoot, but the bionics must have taken away Jaime's sex drive, because the only serious man in her life is Max, the bionic dog. Like her TV sister Wonder Woman, the Bionic Woman seems to maintain her power only as long as she remains virginal.

It was as if TV execs didn't quite know how to show a superwoman carrying on a relationship with a man—and so they didn't. Perhaps, also, a hot-to-trot bionic woman just seemed too suggestive and offensive for prime-time programming. After all, we had yet to enter the era of jiggle TV shows.

ANGELS IN CHAINS

"Charlie's Angels" (1976) forever changed how powerful women would be portrayed by pop culture. The show stole many of its ideas from schlock movies and soft-core porn, repackaging them for mainstream consumption. The result was female characters who—although they often found themselves clad in bikinis—could shoot, kick, flirt, drive, and run their way out of any situation. "Charlie's Angels" made women into superdetectives as all-powerful, independent, and sexually liberated as Kojak or Shaft. When the situation called for it (and the situation always did), the angels could wield near-magical

How Charlie Got His Angels

What sociopolitical forces led to the first, full-fledged jiggle show—an oeuvre that would forever change TV's emphasis from traditional story lines to a moment-by-moment aggregation of car ▶

chases and low-cut blouses? Why three women instead of one? Why Charlie and why Bosley? To trace these ideas back to their source, the student of "Charlie's Angels" must begin with a strange, marginal character named Ted V. Mikels.

¶ This B-movie maker lived in a Hollywood "castle" with a floating population of "castle ladies," a harem of women who had agreed to be faithful only to him. The castle ladies doubled as his camera crew, scriptwriters, and actresses—so it is no surprise that Mikels hit on the idea of creating a band of female vigilantes to star in his 1973 movie *The Doll Squad*.

¶ Here's the gist of it: when government officials discover that a madman is threatening to destroy the space program, they turn to a computer for advice. The computer analyzes the problem and spits out its solution—a band of *women* must be called on the job to catch the wrongdoer. (Has there ever been a flimsier excuse to squeeze women into tight black jumpsuits and give them guns?) The bureaucrats hire a professional named Sabrina to do the job. She leads a team

powers. For instance, in one episode, Jaclyn Smith gets on a motorcycle and jumps (Evel Knievel–style) over a huge hurdle. These lovely ladies carry guns, but their preferred method of bagging the bad guy is a karate-style kick or a good shove—though they use some techniques that "Kung Fu"'s Kwai Chang Caine never thought of, like affecting a southern accent to make your opponent think you're dumb or pretending to fix your hair before you throw a punch.

"Charlie's Angels" is perhaps the most important TV show of the seventies—nay, it is perhaps the most important product of modern Western civilization. Over centuries, our culture has used the narrative form to make meaning. "Charlie's Angels," on the other hand, unabashedly dispensed with plot in favor of fashion, so much so that it used models instead of actresses.

Media critic Neil Postman explains, in a 1991 *Harper's*,

> I came to understand Charlie's Angels when I realized that the entire show was about *hair*. Do you remember that at the end of the show there was a two-minute segment in which the disembodied voice of Charlie explained to the angels *what the entire show had been about*. I imagine that the show was written by a bunch of former English majors. And I see them confounded by the fact that they have just written a show that is basically about hair. . . . So in the end, they shoehorn in a vestigial narrative.

Of course, porn movies had long ago dispensed with narrative in favor of moment-by-moment thrills. The genius of "Charlie's Angels" was to bring the sensibility of porn to prime time. In fact, the concept for the series was blatantly ripped off from a sexploitation movie called *The Doll Squad* (see sidebar). Many episodes of "Charlie's Angels" also lifted ideas from a variety of sexploitation genres, including the women-in-prison movie.

In a fan magazine called *Videooze*, Walter O'Hara defines several key elements of this cheesy genre: for a true women-in-prison movie, you need a sadistic warden, a bull dyke guard, and of course a shower scene. When the angels go undercover as prison inmates (in an episode called "Angels in Chains"), they discover all of this and more in a corrupt women's prison down South.

Upon arriving at the prison, they are met by a statuesque female guard named Max who looks and talks just like Tim Curry as Frank N. Furter in *The Rocky Horror Picture Show*. She ushers them off to the showers, where—yes—they soap down together in a stall without dividers. After their shower, Max makes them open their towels so she can hose them down with disinfectant and then tells them to "drop the towels" and get into prison uniform.

Soon the angels find themselves in the midst of a prostitution ring, being sold off to smarmy businessmen. Things are no better when they escape. Chained together at the arms, they flee through a swamp from redneck cops who have threatened to rape them. It's a twist that owes much to the 1972 *Black Mama, White Mama*, a movie in which Pam Grier plays an escaped con chained to a white girl. However, since "Charlie's Angels" dispenses with the obligatory cat-fight (why else show chained-together women if not for the catfight?), it should perhaps be hailed as a model of restraint and propriety.

It's interesting that so many of the strong female characters doubled as sex objects. Action-adventure movies and TV shows were still created for men, by men, which may help to explain why female superheroes came not just from the pages of comic books (like *Wonder Woman*) but also from soft-porn films.

Meanwhile, women had begun to wrest power on other cultural fronts, particularly the sitcom. "The Mary Tyler Moore Show," "Fay," and "Phyllis" realistically and sympathetically portrayed their heroines. Female scriptwriters flocked to such shows and generally were welcomed by producers eager to appeal to a female audience; the trend was so marked that female writers cleaned up at the 1974 Emmy Award ceremony. But it was nearly impossible for women to have much influence outside the domestic worlds of sitcoms and dramas. For instance, when one veteran writer asked to do an episode of "Emergency," she was rebuffed by producers who claimed that the writers had to sleep at a fire station to collect material—and they didn't want a woman doing that.

Whereas the action-adventure movies and shows of the eighties would tend to be aimed at a coed audience—that is, *Aliens*, "Cagney and Lacey"—this was less the case in the seventies. The result was that for a generation of women raised on shows like "Charlie's Angels," our most powerful role models did more than just fight—they also mud wrestled, acted dumb, went braless, and slapped each other.

of talented female spies, kills hordes of men with her machine gun, and even murders an ex-lover in hand-to-hand combat. She does answer to a male bureaucracy, but, Charlie-style, these men serve only to give Sabrina her assignment. It's she who calls the shots in the field.

"Charlie's Angels" was a blatant rip-off of Mikels's low-budget buns-and-guns movie, copying not just the structure of the work but also many of its details. For instance, in both the movie and the TV show, the brainy brunette (the "smart one," as we used to say in high school) is named Sabrina. And in *The Doll Squad*, Sabrina's deadliest weapon is a powder that makes her enemies erupt into fiery explosions. The "Charlie's Angels" logo, with the outlines of bell-bottomed babes against a similar explosion, may well have been inspired by the endless use of fireballs in the movie.

A friend of mine remembers playing "Charlie's Angels" as a kid. She and two other girls would sit in front of the mirror teasing their hair in preparation for a day of adventure. But usually they never even made it outside. Faces smeared with makeup, hair sticking up on end, they'd begin arguing about who was pretty enough to be Jill or worrying that they looked too fat or flat to wear their angel outfits.

We who grew up in the "postfeminist" late seventies learned that women could be powerful, but only if they dressed the part. We believed that women had achieved equal rights, but it somehow seemed that we could lose those rights if we looked too frumpy or too sexy. By the late seventies, real feminism had gone underground and become a subculture with its own music and literature. What we were left with was the cigarette ads, the perfume jingles, the cop shows, and the fashion magazines. They spelled out their own agenda for our future.

SEX AND FAMILY

ROOMMATES

If you watched seventies sitcoms to learn about the American family, you might conclude that people didn't mate for life, they *roommated* for life. Think of "The Odd Couple," "Mork and Mindy," "Laverne and Shirley," "Blansky's Beauties," "Three's Company," and, in 1980, "Bosom Buddies." The characters in these sitcoms seem forever stuck in the limbo of their blandly decorated TV apartments, the in-between stage of a singles lifestyle—perhaps only to find a mate when the show starts to fail and the producers will try any plot twist to get the ratings up. And think of all those "work buddy" sitcoms ("The Mary Tyler Moore Show," "Taxi," "Alice," "WKRP in Cincinnati") whose characters spend major holidays with their coworkers instead of with relatives.

The sitcoms of the seventies reflected a new truth: America was becoming a nation of singles. The marriage rate fell 10 percent between 1972 and 1976, and during the decade, the number of people living alone rose by 60 percent. Partly the singles explosion could be attributed to the proliferation of baby boomers, who were

103

now young adults. In 1971, *Newsweek* observed that one-third of the country's population growth would take place in the twenty-five-to-thirty-four-year-old age group. The magazine quotes a pundit who predicted that the seventies would be "a period of young families and of great interest in elementary-school enrollment."

But this generation was not like its parents. In no hurry to marry, these young adults created an America not so much of elementary schools as of discos, pick-up bars, porno movies, canned meals that came in single-serving sizes, personal ads, self-help gurus, Walkman stereos, hot pants, people talking to their plants. And as divorce skyrocketed, older singles began emulating the habits of the young.

TV reflected this loose, disconnected style of living, this weakening of traditional bonds as people looked to their peers for support. The difference between "All in the Family" (1971) and "Archie Bunker's Place" (1979) pretty much summed it up: in the earlier show, the family hung together despite the generation gap. The scenes took place almost exclusively inside the house, because (like so many TV fathers before him) when Archie went off to work, he disappeared. Eight years later, the show got rid of the "Family" in its title and named itself after Archie's workplace. This time most of the action happened in his bar and stresses the relationships among friends and employees (a sort of proto-"Cheers" situation). Mike and Gloria split for California, Edith died, and Archie ended up with one of those unconvincing late-seventies TV families: he was raising two nieces. Not only did Archie mellow from a virulent racist into a normal TV character, he actually began *dating*.

Of course, it is hardly as if families disappeared from TV. In fact, the travails of large clans became a favorite topic for dramas and sitcoms. As life became increasingly atomized—singles dining on frozen dinners in their efficiency apartments as they watch individual-size TVs—people became fascinated with togetherness. America's fantasy family had changed drastically since the fifties.

Because of shrinking family size, real-life children in the seventies had few siblings. In sharp contrast, TV couples produced huge broods: for instance, the Bradys, the Partridges, the "Eight Is Enough" and "Family" tribes, and the grown-up siblings who vied with one another on "Dallas." On TV, being part of a close-knit family often meant you were close to nature, too. Think of "The Waltons" and "Apple's Way": both shows championed old-fashioned values, blue-jean overalls, and living off the land.

Of course, the most important TV family of the seventies never budged from the 'burbs of Southern California, except when they vacationed at the Grand Canyon or in Hawaii. I'm talking Brady. I'm talking the family whose surname became an adjective (as in *A Very Brady Christmas*) and a synonym for, well . . . Bradyness, that particular brand of hokey togetherness that soothed like nothing else. Those of us who watched the show at a certain tender age lived in a "Brady Bunch" of the mind. Our own lives seemed like pale imitations of the show, and we tried our best to mold our inadequate families into Bradylike bunches. I, for instance, insisted that my family call me Marcia, but it never took. A friend of mine tried to arrange Brady-style family meetings. He passed notes to his sisters and parents that said, "Family meeting in the den, seven o'clock," but he was the only one who ever showed up.

We still look to the Bradys for a sense of belonging, since watching the show is one of the few experiences our generation has shared. "It comes as a great shock to me that advertisers have failed to tap the one genuine icon of [our generation]—the Brady Bunch—as spokespeople," says Douglas Coupland, author of *Generation X*. "I would buy dirt if Maureen McCormick endorsed it."

Had seventies TV changed to help buffer us from the decay of the family or had TV culture actually contributed to our alienation? You couldn't help wondering that after watching PBS's *An American Family* (1973). Subjected to three hundred hours of filming by a documentary crew, the Louds (a supposed "real-life" typical family) fall apart—the parents decide to divorce, right there in front of the TV cameras. As pretentious French guy Jean Baudrillard points out (with uncharacteristic clarity), the documentary doomed its subjects because it turned them into symbols. Instead of an individual family with its own particular quirks, the Louds became *the family*, their troubles symbolizing America's problems. They had become TV characters: "It is TV which is the Louds' truth, it is [TV] which is true, it is [TV] which renders true," says Baudrillard. "It is to this kind of truth that the Loud family is subjected by the TV medium, and in this sense it really amounts to a death sentence."

We were all the Loud family. TV and mass culture invaded our lives in the seventies as thoroughly as it did theirs. Privacy—in the sense of a secret culture created by the family, one impervious to media and politics—had become nearly impossible.

Pat Loud wants a divorce: "I have no sex life; I'm too young for that. I'm too old for women's lib but I'm too young for that." Son Lance—who shocks his Southern California parents by wearing red nail polish—disappears to hang out in gay New York and Europe.

The show presents the fundamental domestic drama of the seventies: the new freedom for adults to "find themselves"—to define themselves through political movements and peer subcultures—also means that it has become difficult for them to live within a traditional family structure.

DESTROY YOUR HIGH SCHOOL

It also meant that adults belonged more firmly to one world and children to another. *Over the Edge*, a 1979 movie (Matt Dillon's first), brilliantly depicted the split consciousness of the suburbs. The film's New Granada, a dusty wasteland of lower- and middle-class prefab housing, makes Levittown seem cozy by comparison. The kids barely ever go home; instead they hang in packs, riding around on banana-seat bikes and dealing drugs to one another. The film shows seventies childhood in all its seedy grandeur: shooting BB guns, drawing marijuana leaves on the blackboard before the teacher comes into class, listening to Cheap Trick at ear-damaging levels on headphones, hustling tickets for a Kiss concert, wearing a comb with a big handle in your back pocket. It captures that seventies feeling, too, that everything's falling apart—from the junior high where the letters that spell out the name of the school have been ripped off the face of the building to the girls' greasy hair that limply emulates the Farrah flip.

The adults, meanwhile, glide through the squalor in their cars, seemingly oblivious to the drugs-and-down-vests subculture of their kids. The fathers in this movie are salesmen; their goal is "growth." "A community with a juvenile problem is not a community with a high resale value," worries one of the men at a parents' meeting.

But what gets the kids down is not their elders so much as deadening boredom. Shown a cheesy movie about the dangers of vandalism, the junior high schoolers cheer at the image of a crowbar breaking glass. They meander through the streets complaining that there's nothing to do—until they find a gun.

Like *Rock 'n' Roll High School*, another 1979 movie, *Over the Edge* ends with the kids blowing up their own school. In *Rock 'n' Roll High School*, the destruction is a joyful act of riot led by the Ramones— a rebellion against teachers and parents who prevent the kids from head banging. In *Over the Edge*, the havoc is an act of desperation. The preteens lock their parents inside the school and then begin shooting cars to make them explode in fireballs that look like mushroom clouds. Both movies present the moment of destruction as a release from authority, but mostly as a relief from crushing boredom.

I can identify. Everything felt so *developed* (as in housing developments, industrial parks, malls, bad TV, mainstream disco), you just wanted to smash it, or at the very least, listen to the Clash on your Walkman as you walked through it. We suburban kids watched TV, played video games, or got dropped off at the mall until we felt stupefied by all the time we wasted. Just invoking the names of stores that used to be in the Montgomery Mall makes me feel progressively deadened: Foxmoor Casuals, Parklane Hosiery, Lerners, Ups 'n Downs, the Earring Tree, Fashion Bug, Thom McAn, Kay Jewelers, Orange Julius, Fanny Farmer. Every one is another nail in the coffin of a misspent seventies youth.

Going to the mall was like watching TV, only it was real. We went there because we were bored, but it only made us more bored, which is why it helped to take some acid in the Muzak-filled, fluorescent-lit shopping paradise.

Of course, teenagers' most popular respite from suburban ennui was sex, preferably the kind that required lots of lying to parents, borrowing of vans, and shoplifting of birth control (see the TV drama "James at 15" for more details). But it was adults who really got it on. The numbing blandness of mall culture helped to inspire a full-blown sexmania in middle America.

SEX COMES TO SUBURBIA

By the seventies, the sexual revolution had migrated from college campuses to the mainstream. Now becoming liberated did not necessarily entail joining a commune or quoting Fourier. Instead you might

Mall in the Family

Throughout the recessions of the seventies, malls represented one of the few safe investments, as mall developers like the Rouse Company consistently turned profits. By 1977, half of all retail business went on in temperature-controlled complexes with names like Westford Hills (which evokes a folksy, back-to-nature atmosphere) and Le Arcade (upscale, chic).

During the seventies, the mall came into its own, not just as a sound investment but as an art form. What started in the sixties as a glorified park-'n'-shop center had evolved into a consumer Disneyland by 1980.

In its earliest, Mesozoic period, the mall had a low-key, rec room look to it. With faux-brick walls, metal bannisters, and linoleum floors, it resembled a suburban basement. The stores tended to be local and nonpretentious—say, a yarn shop, a unisex haircutting place, a card store where you could buy little statuettes that said, "I wuv you this much." I still have fond memories of the Little Falls Mall, a rambling brick affair that dated back to the sixties. As kids we used ▶

to walk there, leaving our dog outside, so we could finger the puzzles and glass animals in the Hallmark gift store. Eventually someone would let the dog in and she'd run barking, skidding on the slick floors, toward us. This is the kind of nutty, down-home thing that could happen only in an old-fashioned neighborhood mall.

¶ By the early seventies, malls were built on a grander scale: the mall had entered its Paleolithic era. Now, huge "anchor" stores—such as Sears and Hecht's—stood like monoliths at either end of the complex, dwarfing the aimless consumer. The decorative details still seemed to be borrowed from a suburban home, but now they were more upscale, modular, Brady-esque. I'm talking imitation tile work—each tile the rich, reddish color of fake leather, fading to a dark brown border. I'm talking old-timey fake gas lamps. I'm talking ferns. It was in this era that the mall became an environment—an enclosed ecosystem, layered with mezzanines and useless balconies from which one could glimpse endless stacks of stores.

find your thrills at a barbecue in a suburban backyard where the guests, inspired by too many Harvey Wallbangers and Sloe Comfortable Screws and Sex on the Beaches, fooled around with each other's spouses.

A lot has been said of the decade's divorce epidemic. But the nature of marriage itself also changed for many people; having affairs became socially acceptable, even hip. Why, swinging could improve your marriage—at least that was what some sex researchers were claiming.

The celebrity scientists of the seventies weren't those nerdy guys delving into particle physics; they were sexologists like Dr. Joyce Brothers (a judge on "The Gong Show"), Shere Hite (proponent of the clitoral orgasm), and the old standbys Masters and Johnson. Most titillating of the sex studies had to be the one conducted by a husband-and-wife team, the Bartells, that examined the mating habits of suburban swingers. "Extra towels are laid out, for there is a constant traffic into and out of the bathtub and shower (swingers are fanatics about personal cleanliness)," *Time* reported in 1971, summing up the study. The Bartells concluded that about a million Americans had experimented with group sex—most of them white, middle-class denizens of suburbia. What prompted these respectable people to swing? The researchers noted that Eskimos, too, were wife swappers, and so perhaps it was cold, sterile environments—like the frozen tundra or suburbia—that drove people to promiscuity.

Trading spouses had become so much of an obsession that it even served as the premise for a sitcom, the short-lived "Bob & Carol & Ted & Alice" (1973) that spun off from the movie. Around the same time, two pitchers for the New York Yankees, Fritz Peterson and Mike Kekich, moved in with each other's wives, a sports page scandal that read like a real-life version of the sitcom.

But by the late seventies, spouse swapping would seem as pathetically outdated as tie-dyeing. Swinging no longer had to be clandestine, a secret weekend adventure for couples who would return to their humdrum lives on Monday. Now you could go to the disco any night of the week and rub your body up against a stranger's out in the public space of a dance floor.

Later in the decade, sexual fulfillment became a solitary quest. Sex clubs no longer operated as a suburban underground—they had become big business (there were several open to the public in New

York), which made swinging an anonymous pursuit. If you were a woman, you could go into Plato's Retreat alone and leave alone. You needed a partner only to get into the orgy room.

In 1978, *Time* described the revels at Plato's as affectless and flat:

> Oddly enough, there is less sexual electricity in the air than at a Rotary Club party. All the trappings of the normal sexual dance—talk, gestures and clothing—are stripped away as unessential, and emotions are under tight control. . . . Many patrons seem bored. A pleasant young woman with a distressing overbite is staring aimlessly into middle distance. "I don't know why I'm here," she says. "I'm only nude because there's nothing to do here with your clothes on."

Orgy-going had been reduced to an activity as solitary and blank as watching TV.

SELLING IT

In the early seventies, two new cartoon characters became wildly popular; they showed up in the funny papers and on T-shirts, glasses, jewelry, towels. But these characters were fundamentally different from Snoopy or Bugs Bunny; the cutesy critters in Kim Grove's "Love Is . . ." syndicated cartoon were a man and a woman—both naked. Granted, the couple's nakedness was about as sexy as Daffy Duck's. The man, with big eyes, black hair, and sideburns, had a belly button and behind but lacked any other equipment. His wife had huge eyelashes, long hair, and pin-prick breasts. Although they went everywhere in the buff (donning only a bow tie or apron now and then), the cartoon championed old-fashioned, prefeminist values.

What is love, according to artiste Kim Grove? Love is . . . staying quiet while he watches the news on TV. Love is . . . letting him mess up your kitchen . . . taking her to the top of a hill to watch the sunset . . . paying for her weekly visits to the beauty shop . . . sending a package to him in Vietnam . . . letting her have hen sessions on the phone . . .

These malls had outgrown human scale, so they poured on the "friendly" details. One innovation was mall art—primarily the bronze people. These were life-size, extremely realistic statues of people whom you'd ordinarily see at the mall—an old man sitting on a bench, a woman and a child, a mime. You might even mistake them for real people, if not for the fact that they were made of brown metal and never moved. Ostensibly the statues were a sort of "fun" sight gag. But at a deeper level, the bronze people both glorified and threatened shoppers. On the one hand, they turned ordinary shoppers into art; even as we fought our way into Foxmoor Casuals to buy a tube top, they suggested, we were also living out the beautiful dance of the universe. On the other hand, they stood like vague threats about what might happen to us if we failed as consumers. These bronze people were ur-shoppers; we were only their imitations. They were real and we were the shadows.

The Paleolithic mall also spawned a new kind of restaurant, equally determined to make shoppers have "fun." These ▶

places had names like J. C. Dillingham's or B. D. Hartlington's and billed themselves as "an uncommon eating establishment" or "a fine foods emporium." The interiors were aggressively cozy, with faux-Victorian cut-glass dividers, low ceilings, pictures of Gibson girls, brass bar rails The menus gave every dish an elaborately cute name, like the "Humongous Avocado Sprout Sandwich" or "Curiously Delicious Potato Skins."

¶ At the end of the seventies, developers began creating a new type of mall, the kind we're still pretty much stuck with today. These enormous complexes, with their slick white facades and acres of glass, no longer imitated the suburban home. No, they were cold Taj Mahals with white marble walls, the buildings connected by "crystal walkways"—glass tubes that looked like see-thru-plastic Habitrail gerbil tunnels. (The popularity of Habitrail pet cages may have had a lot to do with the fact that teens wanted to give their gerbils an environment that was as much like a mall as possible.)

¶ Anticipating the lavish Trump style of the eighties,

110

drinking hot chocolate by firelight . . . buying her a warm maxidress for winter . . . being very happy though not liberated.

The "Love Is . . ." cartoon typified the new openness about sex. Rob and Laura Petrie of "The Dick Van Dyke Show" had separate beds; but in the early seventies, Mike and Carol Brady slept together—and when a scene ended with Carol reaching over her husband's body to turn out the light, we knew what would happen next. "Love Is . . ." not only acknowledged sex, it made naked people cute—in the mish-mash of pop culture, this sexiness easily coexisted with old-fashioned values. On the surface, the cartoon couple personified childlike inno-cence; they were as winsomely big-eyed as the Keene kids. But if you could ignore the sickly sentimentality of the captions, "Love Is . . ." resembled nothing so much as soft-core porn or a sex how-to book. A woman doing housework in nothing but an apron? A naked couple spooning on the couch? A woman greeting her husband at the door, au naturel, with a cocktail in hand? The images contained a sexual power made safe by their domestic setting.

But increasingly pop culture presented an image of sex freed from the bonds of marriage and no longer linked to procreation. As authors John D'Emilio and Estelle B. Freedman point out in *Intimate Matters: A History of Sexuality in America*, "from the mid-1960s to the 1980s, as the liberal consensus disintegrated, the nation experienced perhaps the greatest transformation in sexuality it had ever witnessed." The most obvious result of this revolution was the mass marketing of sex. When mainstream Americans came to accept sex outside of commitment or social ties, then it could be sold as never before. *The Joy of Sex* (1972) served as the manifesto of this new sensibility. Sex was like food, the book's title suggested, and the upscale consumer would demand the very best: gourmet sex.

It was in the seventies that porn came aboveground—hip young adults weren't embarrassed to admit they'd seen *Beyond the Green Door*, and psychologists and film professors discussed the artistic merit of *Deep Throat*. But even mainstream culture became sexual-ized, as if some secret committee had suddenly changed the rating from G to PG. (For instance, the hit movies of the decade—like *Star Wars, Smokey and the Bandit, The Sting*—always seemed to be rated PG.) What the hell had happened to America? You could only shake your head and wonder after Grace Jones showed up on prime-time TV singing "I Need a Man" and tickling Merv Griffin with her whip.

Advertising especially made use of outrageous innuendo. For instance, one toothpaste company went so far as to steal a pick-up line for its slogan. In the TV ad, a young woman smiles as a man's voice says to her, "Ultrabright toothpaste wants to proposition you."

What's this? Is the voice issuing from a giant tube of toothpaste that has come to life and is standing just out of our sight, wearing a low-buttoned shirt with gold chains? Whatever's going on, the woman doesn't seem to mind. In fact, she's all compliance. "That's the best proposition I've had all year. . . . Well, almost," she smiles back. Thus, advertisers associated women's newfound sexual freedom with women's power as consumers—implying that products were men, objects that women could "pick up" in the same way they might cruise a guy in a bar.

As consumption began to mimic the mating ritual, it's no surprise that the reverse happened, too—that people "advertised" themselves in order to get laid. The most obvious example, of course, was the personals—a new dating phenomenon that even inspired a hit song. In "The Piña Colada Song," a guy sings about his turn-ons and turn-offs, which he has listed in a personal ad.

Weirder and perhaps more embarrassing were the T-shirts. You know the ones I mean. You could order them from ads in the back of *Seventeen* magazine, skintight "French designer shirts" that told the world you were "Kool," "Foxy," "Good & Plenty," "Indescribably Delicious," "Available," "Crème de la Crème," or a "Community Chest." With a T-shirt slogan, you could signal not only your willingness to be picked up but also hint at the nature of your sexual proclivities—for example, whether you were a "Princess" or a "Bitch."

The sexy T-shirt fad may have been inspired by a gay subculture in which earrings, bandannas, and keychains all became codes for desire. After all, it was gay culture—coming aboveground for the first time during the decade—that provided a new model of sexuality for straight America.

IT STARTED WITH STONEWALL

The seventies began and ended with dramatic clashes between the gay community and the police. In 1969, cops attempting a routine bust on a Greenwich Village gay bar, the Stonewall Inn, found them-

the late-seventies malls practically screamed, I dare you to shop. No Sears here. Instead the anchor stores were upscale chains like Bloomingdales ("Bloomies," in seventies parlance). One went to these malls to feel glitzy and swank, to live out a consumerist fantasy. At such a mall, you could pretend to be "Dallas" 's fabulously wealthy Sue Ellen, stopping to buy a shoulder pad–heavy dress on your way home to Southfork.

In the late seventies, everyone I knew in suburban Maryland was buzzing about a new mall that had a Bloomies and a Lordies and, most important, a *glass elevator*. Très chic. Suddenly all of the other malls seemed as lumpy, brown, and pathetically unfashionable as five-year-old Earth shoes.

You could point to every item in the Sears catalogue and somebody, somewhere, wants to sleep with it.
—Detective Arthur Dietrich on "Barney Miller"

Farrah Fawcett Majors, Karen Carpenter, Andy Gibb, and Jesus Christ are classic seventies "superstars"—that is, celebrities who no longer did anything except exude an aura of fame. A 1976 book called *John Travolta: Super Sensation of the '70s* asks the question, "What has made John Travolta a superstar? Most folks agree it's a combination of good looks, talent, charisma and hard work." In fact, the book is wrong. Travolta's superstardom had nothing to do with his talent or charisma and everything to do with his having been photographed so many times that he had lost his soul and become a bundle of cultural symbols masquerading as a human being.

¶ Along with the superstar, the seventies saw the evolution of another type of celebrity, only this kind was never talked about, never given a name. These stars were the bottom feeders in the ocean of fame—those who weren't too proud to appear in the scummiest game shows and TV movies. You may have no idea how these people became celebrities, but for some

112

selves hit by a hail of coins and bottles thrown by lesbians and gay men. In the highly politicized late sixties, the bar brawl—and the riot that ensued—was enough to start a new movement. The first gay power groups formed soon after Stonewall.

Almost ten years later, life had changed drastically for urban gays: once battling for the right simply to congregate, they had become a highly visible subculture in big cities. *Business Week* noted in 1979 that gays were America's most affluent minority (one study attributed 19 percent of spendable income to them) and that the savviest businesses weren't too prejudiced to advertise in the *Advocate*.

Meanwhile, the gay community had become so accepted in San Francisco that by 1978 it had its own district and its own city supervisor. So accepted, in fact, that this time, antigay violence came not from the establishment but from a lone nut who felt he represented a powerless minority: straight working-class whites. The aptly named Dan White—a former cop and former city supervisor who had failed to regain his seat—lashed back at the liberals by shooting Mayor George Moscone and gay city supervisor Harvey Milk. The death of San Francisco's foremost gay leader was bad enough, but when White got off with a mere eight-year prison sentence, protesters erupted in rage, burning cop cars and smashing windows. The jurors had let White off easy on the flimsiest of excuses: they decided he had been mentally unstable at the time of the shooting because he'd eaten too much junk food (the infamous "Twinkie defense").

PURE, NATURAL ORANGE JUICE FROM FLORIDA?

Harvey Milk's death seemed to dramatize how fragile the gay gains of the seventies were—especially since, in the late decade, homosexuals had became the favorite target of a new coalition of evangelists and ultraright leaders. Among this parade of backlash figures, the weirdest had to be Anita Bryant. Her attacks against gays ran the gamut from the offensive (calling homosexuals "human garbage") to the ridiculous (insisting that if God had wanted men to love each other, he would have put Adam and Bruce together in the Garden of Eden). The trouble was, you couldn't laugh her off: Bryant's Save Our Children crusade in Dade County, Florida, had succeeded in overturning a civil rights ordinance that protected gays. Bryant and her Moral Majority backers had convinced voters that gays should be banned from teaching jobs because they would use their positions to "recruit" kids—so if you sent little Johnny off to the wrong kindergarten, he might come home with, say, a new curiosity about the relationship between Batman and Robin. In cities like St. Paul and Wichita, the Moral Majority won similar civil rights repeals, often by using the same "recruiting" argument to block gays from jobs.

How did the crusade against gays in the seventies resemble earlier hate movements? Examine the fears surrounding black men and those surrounding gay men and you can hardly miss the common thread: reproduction. After the Civil War (which brought threatening social reforms to the South), the black man was stereotyped as a wildly sexual being, one with a rapacious hunger for white women—the ultimate fear was of the interracial children he might produce. The phobias surrounding the black man stemmed from his ability to "pollute" white "blood." Since people who had even the most remote black ancestry were considered black, any miscegenation would quickly lead to the "elimination" of the white race.

Likewise, the Moral Majority of the seventies imagined gay men to be insatiably sexual and "polluters" of the straight population. Gay men were thought to destroy the heterosexual world not by fathering children but by stealing children away from straights, or even by inducting full-grown men and women into their ranks. "Please remember," raved Jerry Falwell, "homosexuals do not reproduce! They recruit!"

No wonder Anita Bryant prayed so fervently. If gay men could seduce straight guys over to their side, then even her icky husband, Bob Green, might forsake his blow-dried hair and double-knit suits for a pair of Levis with a bandanna in the back pocket.

GLOBAL VILLAGE PEOPLE

Homosexuals posed another threat to the "family values" crowd. What Elvis's gyrating hips were to the fifties, the bathhouse and the disco were to the seventies: symbols of a new kind of sexuality.

Marshall McLuhan theorized in his groundbreaking essay "The

reason, you still recognize their names. They are the opposite of superstars—they are the substars.

Many substars propped up sagging careers by appearing on "The Gong Show" or "Match Game '75." Others kept showing up on TV movies. Still others made the variety show rounds, filling in when "The David Frost Revue" or "The John Davidson Show" couldn't get a real star like, say, Michael Landon.

A brief list of substars: Jaye P. Morgan, Foster Brooks, Rich Little, Arte Johnson, Charles Nelson Reilly, Rosey Grier, Rip Taylor, Lyle Waggoner, Paul Williams, Marty Ingels, Elaine Joyce, Gene Rayburn, Brett Somers, Fannie Flag, Paul Lynde, Dr. Joyce Brothers, Vicki Lawrence (what was she famous for—looking like Carol Burnett?), Charo, Red Buttons.

In retrospect, the substars are more emblematic of the seventies than are the much-talked-about superstars. They form the filler material of countless disaster movies—the most interest you can muster in them is to wonder whether they'll die off before or after Shelley Winters. They are the ▶

113

Future of Sex" that just like media, sex could be classified as either "hot" or "cool," and he predicted that the seventies would be the decade of cool sex. A cocktail napkin with a cartoon depicting a man leering at a large-breasted woman might epitomize hot sex; unisex clothing and haircuts epitomized cool sex.

What gay culture helped to introduce—and straight culture quickly adopted—was the coolest of cool sex. Getting laid became nothing more than a new form of entertainment, a diversion, a night out, for both gays and straights.

Gay journalist Dennis Altman sardonically noted in 1974 that New York's Continental Baths had become overrun by heteros. "It is my guess that the co-option of the gay world's surface hedonism by straight swingers, via institutions like the Continental . . . is not accidental," wrote Altman. "Increasingly, modes of behavior once stigmatized as part of the 'psychopathology' of homosexuality, and described by such loaded terms as promiscuity or inability to form meaningful relationships, are becoming part of the heterosexual norm for at least a section of those who would be 'with it.'"

Out of necessity, homosexuals had created their own underground culture, which at its most hormone-drenched fringes included net shirts, quick pickups, and pulsing music. In a time when sex was just becoming a full-blown mainstream industry, this rich subculture couldn't remain secret for long. Warner Brothers, for instance, hired a gay promoter to oversee its huge, new investment in disco music. Even the U.S. military got into the act of co-opting gay culture: apparently, navy officials thought about using a film of the Village People gyrating to their song "In the Navy" as an enticement for men to join up. Is this what Jerry Falwell meant when he warned that homosexuals recruit?

Straights also copied less-commercial details of the gay lifestyle. Homosexual relationships offered a new model for post–sexual revolution living. While men and women were still arguing about who would take out the trash, some gays were pioneering partnerships that were free of gender role playing. In addition, gays—many of whom were estranged from relatives—tended to cobble together impromptu "families" made up of friends and coworkers, a new kind of community that we see singles exploring on "The Mary Tyler Moore Show" and "Taxi," too.

But as Altman implied, straights often failed to notice how closely homosexual relationships paralleled or even prefigured their own, and they tended to stereotype gay sexual habits as particularly debauched.

ONLY HER HAIRDRESSER KNOWS

From disco to high camp, gay influences were everywhere in seventies pop culture—but only apparent to those in the know. For instance, homosexual characters rarely walked into the living rooms we saw on TV shows, except for the occasional issue-laden guest appearance. Those shows that did try to introduce regular gay characters found themselves in the middle of a cultural battle. Even before "Soap" debuted in 1977, with Billy Crystal playing the flamboyant Jodie Dallas, letters of protest poured in from people who didn't want to see gays or extramarital sex on TV. Meanwhile, gays pushed for better portrayal of a homosexual couple on the sitcom "Hot L Baltimore" and pressured NBC to can an episode of "Policewoman" that featured, à la *Basic Instinct*, three murderous lesbians.

Gays may have been all but banned from TV, but that hardly put a damper on the antigay jokes. Middle America was caught between two contradictory desires: an unwillingness to be confronted by homosexuality and a lust for ever-more-titillating humor. This led to one of the most unique cultural forms of the seventies: the movie or TV show in which a heterosexual pretends to be gay.

The first example of this genre that I've been able to identify is *Shampoo* (1975). In this sexual comedy of errors, the main character, George, works as a hairdresser and diddles his (female) clients on the side. When George needs a loan, he goes to see a mogul named Lester, even though he's sleeping with Lester's wife, daughter, and mistress. Lester, who assumes that the hairdresser must be gay, over-looks the most compromising situations (for instance, his mistress locked in a steamy bathroom with a hair dryer–equipped stud). The film uses George's presumed homosexuality to add an atmosphere of way-out swingerdom and tolerant sophistication—without having to bring in truly gay characters.

The same dynamic was clearly at work in a hit sitcom of the late seventies. I'm talking "Three's Company," of course. The premise of the show went like this: two single, beautiful gals are looking for a roommate. They can't find another woman, but one day after a party,

they discover this hunky guy in their bathtub. Knowing a good situation when he sees one (nudge, nudge, wink, wink), he convinces them he's gay so he can shack up with them. But when he moves in, boy, do they find out he's straight! Hubba, hubba, wouldn't you like to trade places with Jack Tripper?

Actually, Jack's situation is hardly enviable. Though he keeps hitting on his roommates, he never gets it on with them; and to convince the suspicious landlord that there is no hanky-panky going on, he has to pretend to be gay whenever Mr. Roper walks in—the TV version of gay, as in limp-wrist jokes. (Reality never intrudes in this sitcom. What late-seventies landlord would approve of a gay tenant but draw the line at male and female heteros rooming together?)

Like George, Jack Tripper can "pass" for gay because of his "effeminate" job: he's in cooking school. Like George the hairdresser, Jack pretends to be gay in order to get chicks. But unlike George, the ever-horny Jack rarely scores with his dates, usually because Mr. Roper walks in at just the wrong moment.

The crux of "Three's Company," the fulcrum on which it balanced, was that even though all of the characters are ready and willing, no one gets laid. Not Jack. Not the man-hungry Janet, so often the victim of flat-boob jokes. Not the idiotic Chrissie, wholesome daughter of a preacher. Certainly not Mrs. Roper, who's always trying to coax her husband into bed. And not the impotent Mr. Roper. (Nor did the new, "swinger" landlord played by Don Knotts in 1979. By then the swinger had become so much of an outlandish, outdated character that Knotts could play him as a combination of Barney Fife and a Wild and Crazy Guy from "Saturday Night Live.")

"Three's Company" may have been a hit because it comforted its audience into believing that all of those young people who seemed to be having sex weren't. The show let Middle Americans—shell-shocked from the rapid social changes of the decade—tune in to find out that even when young men and women lived together, they weren't having premarital sex, and that even when people seemed to be openly gay, they weren't really gay; they were just *pretending* to be homosexual so they could get better housing.

As offensive as "Three's Company" could be, it had nothing on the 1980 movie *Cruising* (not to be confused with the Village People album "Cruisin'"). In it, Al Pacino plays a cop who's sent undercover to investigate murders taking place in the leather-clad demimonde of the gay hard-core fringe. We see men tying each other up, stabbing each other, fisting, and wearing bondage paraphernalia, but never once treating each other kindly. The one sympathetic gay character ends up being hacked to pieces by his lover—who isn't even supposed to be the murderer! It's as if to say that stepping into a gay bar amounts to a death sentence.

And as always, the central character is a straight guy who's only masquerading as gay. To remind us that he really is straight, we get a lot of scenes between him and his girlfriend, including one truly bizarre shot of them having sex while the sounds of the gay bars echo through his head. The movie treats the cop's foray into New York's gay subculture as a sort of descent into hell. For him, homosexuality becomes a waking nightmare, one that threatens to degrade his soul.

Cruising was the movie version of the New Right's paranoia. Anita Bryant described what she thought went on in gay bars (as quoted in a *Playboy* article): "Many married men with children who don't have a happy marriage are going into the homosexual bars for satisfaction." *Cruising* took this fantasy one step farther. The straight man is *forced* to go into the gay bar and even to pick up guys. However, the film assures us that after melding with the homosexual community, he can emerge untarnished.

This, then, was what *Cruising* was really all about. Heterosexual America harbored the fear that gays could brainwash straight people in the same way that the Moonies were brainwashing teenagers and convincing them to run away from home. No wonder the straight-man-who-pretends-to-be-gay genre suddenly became popular: it showed men coming as close as possible to "converting" without ever losing their straight identities.

For Maximum Pulling Power...
Develop A Headline
To Interest The Reader

NOSTALGIA

I n 1970, *Newsweek* noted that the country seemed to be gripped by contradictory impulses—judging from its best-selling jigsaw puzzles, anyway. Three were Norman Rockwells and four were *Playboy* center-folds. "The pure and simple Rockwell portraits, which depict a runaway boy chatting with an understanding policeman and a rancher sending his son off to college and a kindly doctor preparing to inoculate the bare behind of a young lad, underscore the nostalgic fascination with 'the good old days,'" according to *Newsweek*. Meanwhile, the *Playboy* puzzles "seem to say little about the times except that sex sells."

MANUFACTURED MEMORY

That sex did sell so well in the seventies actually says a lot about the times. Why, in the swingingest era ever (that brief interlude between the legalization of abortion and the discovery of AIDS), did people need so much pornography? Why did they also need so much nostal-

"Lookin' goood."

gia, so many hyperwholesome Rockwell paintings? I submit that the answer to both is the same: alienation. As the family fell apart, people often succeeded in improvising communities made up of coworkers, favorite relatives, step-siblings, neighbors, ex-boyfriends and ex-girlfriends, roommates, and so on. But in the brave new world of single-serving sizes, many found themselves cut off from others, living alone and watching TV alone.

Whereas the housewife had been the ur-consumer of the post-war era, in the seventies, corporations courted the single person. That is, when the family fell apart, the market stepped in, offering us ready-made communities and prepackaged intimacies. The mall, the rise of TV, therapy, cults, discos, senior retirement villages—all bespoke a consumer culture rushing in to fill the vacuum where private life had once been.

What is porn but a company selling you ersatz intimacy? Instead of the mess and fuss of dealing with a real person, you get the convenience of a manufactured fantasy. A friend of mine remembers how quickly the porn of the seventies escalated from stylized soft core to readily available hard core. In 1972, when he was ten, all he could get ahold of were *Playboys* in a friend's attic—arty, soft-focus pictures. By the time he was fifteen, he and his friends knew which convenience stores would illegally sell them the harder stuff, *Club International* and *Hustler*. The boys who rode their Stingrays from store to store in search of the raunchiest photo spreads learned to consume sex like cigarettes.

Media became more than the message in the seventies, it became a substitute for human contact. Which is why a Norman Rockwell painting of a kindly policeman in an old-fashioned diner may not be so different from a photo of a topless playmate. What pornography is to sex, commercialized nostalgia is to history: a way to substitute media images for real contact with our past and with the people who remember it. The rise of the nostalgia industry (from "Happy Days" to ads for granola that showed the ingredients spilling out of old-timey burlap sacks) coincided with a cooling of relations among people of different ages. By the seventies, the generation gap had widened into a gulf: old people had moved to "retirement villages" while young adults lived within their own rock and roll culture. Manufactured nostalgia stepped in to give us a sense of continuity and connection with the past—for every real grandma who had moved to Florida, there was a doe-eyed, bespectacled TV grandma praising some brand of oatmeal cookies with old-fashioned warmth 'n' wisdom in her voice.

TV helped to break down our sense of history; in its place, we got a chopped-up collage of outdated styles. Tail fins and jukeboxes are the tits and ass of the nostalgia industry. The past has been turned into a theme park.

In looking back at the seventies—because we are products of the nostalgia-crazy seventies—it is tempting to turn the decade into sound bytes: happy-face buttons, bell-bottoms, mood rings. Even to use the term *decade* is somehow false, since it implies that each ten-year period has nothing to do with the one that came before it or the one that followed.

How do we get out of this trap (our past, made into a ten-night miniseries or a ten-CD set and sold back to us)? We study the seventies not to escape into our fantasy version of that time but to become more aware of how the present got to be like it is. We never lose sight of the fact that many of the guys who brought us Watergate, Vietnam, and Three Mile Island still run our country. We never forget that the seventies are our future.

Don Knotts (LEFT) worrying
about an argument that
his "Three's Company"
costars John Ritter and
Joyce DeWitt are having.
(THE BETTMAN ARCHIVE)

APPENDIXES

FORBIDDEN SEVENTIES   Phil Milstein

Now, I don't want to go starting any conspiracy theories here, but doesn't it strike you as very suspicious that while you can catch "The Love Boat" practically any time you turn on the TV—can hardly *avoid* it, in fact—"Fantasy Island" is not available on videotape, cable, or anywhere else? The message is clear: the dregs of our seventies culture are being force-fed to us in trendy little Scooby Doo vitamin–size morsels, and we seem to have no choice but to take what *they* want to dish out. Our collective seventies memory is fading rapidly, and it is high time for us to take decisive action so that future generations will know of the truly neglected trash of our childhood. It is my assignment to help rectify this tragic situation by putting back into the public record some of the keener items, articles, and entities that have been overlooked in the recent flurry of obvious seventies nostalgia. We *must* crush the Klassic Hits Konspiracy now, before it is too late.

Willie Aames.   The least annoying of Dick Van Patten's three sons in "Eight is Enough," Aames is less remembered for roles in two other mid-seventies family dramas, each of which preceded that esteemed program: "We'll Get By," with Paul Sorvino as the father, and "Swiss Family Robinson," an Irwin Allen production starring Martin Milner as the dad.

Aames spent much of the eighties working in a most fitting summation of seventies mediocrity, playing a bumbling second banana to Scott Baio in "Charles in Charge."

"An American Family."   A twelve-part PBS series from 1973 that captured in riveting cinema verité the gradual dissolution of the Loud family of Santa Barbara, California. The Louds were good looking, talented, intelligent, and moneyed, and so the programmers deliberately avoided calling them *the* American family. At the outset of the series, they seemed like the *perfect* American family, privileged enough to make you barf. But the perpetual intrusion of a full camera crew into their daily lives exacerbated problems that apparently had been lying dormant for some time, and a huge audience watched in rapt attention and with not a little glee as each week the Loud family unit came more and more unglued. Did we even address the nature of our own voyeurism as we watched Lance Loud come out of the closet to his mom or the Loud parents initiate divorce proceedings on national TV?

The fallout of the show lasted well past its twelve weeks. Lance went on to lead the New York new wave group the Mumps, who were perhaps the worst band to have come out of that scene. Albert Brooks' first feature film, *Real Life*, was a brutal lampoon of "An American Family."

Idi Amin Dada.   Uganda's now-exiled "president for life," and one of the most bizarre raving-maniac fascist dictators of our time, with a corruptness of the soul like we've hardly seen since. He's still out there somewhere, most likely living in the lap of luxury, probably even dining on a few Ugandan babies every now and then—nothing very dada about that.

"Annie's Song"/"Danny's Song."   John Denver versus Anne Murray. (Now that's an episode of "American Gladiators" *I'd* pay to see.) Hell might very well be these two songs played in alternation for all eternity. (Was his song an answer to hers?)

Susan Anton; Susan B. Anthony Dollar.   Isn't it curious that the careers of both went into the toilet at right around the same time?

Ayds.   Popular dietetic candy that packed its bags and quietly disappeared in the night when the Center for Disease Control adopted a soundalike name in the early eighties as a virulent new viral strain was being discovered.

Rona Barrett.   A nasally little peroxided creature from Brooklyn who dominated the gossip profession throughout the 1970s. At the peak of her fame and power she had syndicated TV and radio spots, had her own magazine, and occasionally would appear as herself in motion pictures—she was the Howard Cosell of the gossip game. The parodists of the day would regularly take a poke at Rona Barrett, and not just because her name could be so easily translated into Rhonda Blabitt. It's been so long since I've even heard either name mentioned that she seems to have disappeared off the face of the earth.

Robby Benson; Glynnis O'Connor.   The Tracy and Hepburn of the seventies teen set. He was one of the most annoying actors of the era; she was one of the most hot-cha. He had open-heart surgery before he was thirty; she has not been seen or heard from in about ten years. He found huge major career resurgence as the voice of the Beast in Disney's *Beauty and* . . . (they had to electronically deepen his thin, reedy voice); she—?

Barbi Benton.   "Hee Haw" was her *most* legit job in show business.

"The Bill Cosby Show."   As hip as his eighties sitcom was mawkish. In this one, "Cool Cos" (as he was called by *Junior Scholastics* magazine) played high school gym teacher Chet Kincaid. Great theme song, written by Quincy Jones and grunted by Cosby himself.

Bonefone.   The strangest portable radio ever invented, the Bonefone was a semiflexible, snake-shaped thingie that was meant to be draped around the neck and down the upper arms. The amazing part of it is that its signal was not heard, but felt! The thing operated on the principle that human bone is an excellent conductor of sound waves, and so instead of pumping them into the air, the signal from the Bonefone would vibrate the arm bones (humerus?) and the body would in turn send the signal up those bones, through the collarbone, and all the way on up into the middle ear. Ostensibly, the signal was every bit as clear as from an ordinary pocket radio. The Bonefone was advertised heavily in such mainstream publications as *Rolling Stone* and *Playboy* but somehow failed to catch on. The only one I ever saw was on some kid skateboarding at UMass in 1979, and he was too preoccupied for me to question him about it.

Earl Butz.   Gerald Ford's agriculture secretary was forced to resign when he was caught uttering a racial wisecrack so obscene we cannot print it here. In fact, one broad-minded periodical whose name escapes me published a table cross-referencing the euphemisms other news reports used for each segment of the tripartite slur. Ford's cabinet was a notoriously ill-mannered one—a famous photo of the day showed his vice president, Nelson Rockefeller, rabidly giving some heckler the finger.

Candypants.   Edible underwear, "the underwear that's fun to wear." By the time I was old enough for a taste test, they were gone.

Richard Castellano.   Excellent character actor. Was on the verge of big things (*The Godfather*; Oscar nomination for *Lovers and Other Strangers*; he even had two short-lived sitcoms in the seventies), but Burt Young (Rocky Balboa's brother-in-law) came on the scene and copped Castellano's style without half his presence and rode it to much greater success.

Catchphrases.   Match the once-popular catch-phrase with the character who most made it famous:

"Sit on it."	Gabe Kotter
"Kiss my grits."	Arthur Fonzarelli
"Up your nose with a rubber hose."	Fred Sanford
"What choo talkin' about, Willis?"	Ralph Malph
"How you like one 'cross your lip?"	Flo Castleberry
"Eet's not my yob."	Geraldine Jones

"Aaayyh."   Chico Rodriguez
"The devil made me do it."   Arnold Jackson
"Baby, you're the greatest."   Sorry, wrong decade

Cerrone.   The poor man's Giorgio Moroder.

Choppers.   Made famous by *Easy Rider*, these diagonal low-riders of the biker world remained popular for a few years after that, then quickly went out of style for no apparent reason. Overripe for a big comeback.

Cigarette Commercials.   Best jingle: "Taste me, taste me, c'mon and taste me, take a puff and let me do my stuff." Congress should consider allowing these back on the air again. Banned in 1970.

Odia Coates.   That's all. Just ... Odia Coates.

Colt .45 Malt Liquor Commercial.   The drink is still alive and kickin'— and *kickin'*—but their remarkable commercial starring Redd Foxx is, like the man himself, long dead and gone. We open with a shot of Foxx seated at a table in a sparsely furnished apartment, a glass of Colt. 45 before him. The camera slowly tracks out of the window and away from the building to reveal a cutaway view of a dilapidated tenement, with Foxx's apartment on the second floor. The building has no front to it. Foxx takes a drink just as a wrecking ball plows into one side of the building. Cut to a shot of a pile of rubble. Foxx, still sitting at the table, takes another gulp and announces, "That's urban renewal for ya."

     Development for the nineties: mint-flavored malt liquor. *That's* urban renewal for ya?

Suzanne Crough.   The littlest Partridge, and just about the only seventies TV kid who has not gone public with a (circle one): drinking/drugging/beaten-by-parent/sex maniac/all-of-above horror story. She was also probably the most dour little girl to ever act in any sitcom—a smile from her was about as uncommon a seventies event as a full-count strike from Mike Torrez or a pleasing emission from Sally Struthers. Perhaps she released all of her demons through her acting.

     This is as good a time as any to remind you that "The Partridge

Lindsay Wagner in "The Bionic Woman."
(THE BETTMAN ARCHIVE)

127

Family" is to "The Brady Bunch" as "The Addams Family" is to "The Munsters." Say what you will, but the appeal of "The Brady Bunch" is clearly predicated on camp value, while "The Partridge Family" is well written, well acted, and genuinely pretty funny. Unlike its antecedent "The Monkees," however, the musical portions are generally awful, and seeing one of their decent songs is like finding . . . um, a pleasing emission from Sally Struthers.

Mac Davis.   It's mystifying why he has yet to be clasped bosomward by the X generation. Few stars of the seventies so successfully combined kitsch ("Baby, Don't Get Hooked on Me," "Stop and Smell the Roses," "I Believe in Music") with quality (writer of "In the Ghetto" and "Somethin's Burnin' "). And let's not overlook his fine acting career, highlighted by a starring role as an NFL jock, second-billed under Nick Nolte, in *North Dallas Forty*.

Denim Everything.   In the seventies, we had denim car upholstery, denim parkas, denim book bags, denim shoes, denim lunch boxes . . . I'll bet someone in the seventies even tried to sell denim food.

Joyce DeWitt; The Joyce Who Was in Dawn.   Suzanne Somers is a big TV star and John Ritter is a big something or other. Telma Hopkins is a big TV star and Tony Orlando is probably hanging in there playing the oldies, dinner theater, and summer stock circuits. But where is Joyce?

Douchebag.   Favored curse among Jersey youth. Could actually be given any of a dozen or so different inflections, the most common one featuring the accent on *bag*. I absolutely could not believe it the first time I learned there was a real thing called a douchebag, though I still have never met any woman who would admit to having used one.

Downers.   Reds, 'ludes, and so on. Taking reds and listening to southern boogie-rock was considered a big night in my hometown. I could never understand the appeal of a drug that made you as stupid as these ones did.

Dune Buggies.   Like much of the American culture of the 1970s, dune buggies were both totally cool and completely stupid at the same time. Perhaps it's the delicate tension between those two extremes that makes the era so fascinating.

"Dusty's Trail."   Bob Denver starred in this short-lived syndicated sit-com, which might just as well have been called "Gilligan Goes West." It was virtually a note-for-note knockoff of the castaways, only this time the Magnificent Seven were doomed to roam the Wild West in a wagon train. Replacing the Skipper was Forrest Tucker (Sgt. O'Rourke from "F Troop") as Callahan the wagon master, and both Lulu (Ginger) and Betsy (Mary Ann) were portrayed by "Petticoat Junction" rene-gades. For the record, the Howells became the Brookhavens and the Professor became a guy named Andy. (A sixties aside: did you know that on "Gilligan's Island," the Skipper's full name was Jonas Grumby and the Professor was Roy Hinkley?)

Dynaflex.   A new record-pressing process that left an album so flexi-ble that the ends of the record could be bent almost as far as touching each other without damaging the grooves. Dynaflex records were cheaper and less breakable than standard ones, yet they failed to catch on. RCA, Motown, and Fantasy were among the major users, and Dynaflex records still turn up frequently in used record bins.

Ecology.   What we now call "the environment." Besides being easier to say, I really miss the ecology flag, with that kicky little logo based on the Greek letter theta, though I suppose in twenty years, today's recycling arrows will seem just as cute.

Anne Eickelberg.   For *the* most dead-on and evocative depiction of 1970s teen culture, read her hilarious, true diary excerpts published in issue number seven of *Bananafish* magazine (write Tedium House, Box 424762, San Francisco, CA 94142 for ordering information). Here are a few free samples:

"Barry Gibb A GAY? Oh my Lord, my stomach feels like I swal-lowed shit. I'm practically crying. HOW CAN PEOPLE SAY THINGS LIKE THAT???? I swear, I will never (if I can help it) call anyone gay—even that @*!!?&:*@+!?* Shaun Cassidy, Kiss, Bay City, etc." ...

"Rod Stewart's new song freaks me out! It (naturally) reminds me

of Jim, in a way. The 'just reach out and touch me, come on sugar let me know' is him perfectly." ...

"When we went to Cedar Rapids we went into Strawberry Starship to look at waterbeds and the one that Jim wants was there. Oh, *man!!* It is *beautiful!'*

Elephant's Memory.   John Lennon's post–Plastic Ono backup band. Pretty decent group, though I've never heard any of their non-Lennon material.

Yvonne Elliman.   Remembered mostly for playing Mary M. in *Jesus Christ Superstar* and for her soundtrack hit "I Don't Know How to Love Him." She had a number of other moderately successful recordings, collaborating with Eric Clapton, The Who, and the Bee Gees, but has never been heard from since.

"Fantasy Island."   Every time you turn on the damn tube, it seems you run head-on into an episode of "The Love Boat," and to make matters worse, nine times out of ten, it's a Vicki episode, with Ted McKinley and those awful Mermaids (the future Clair Huxtable among them). I'm starting to believe that Vicki was giving free toot to Julie so she could get her job. But just try to find *one* episode of "Fantasy Island"—just try! So what's the story here?

Clearly, "Fantasy Island" was a so much cooler show than "Love Boat." Christ, Mr. Roarke could take Merrill Stubing with one hand tied behind his back, and you know that Tattoo could fend off Julie, Adam, Isaac, and Rep. Gopher (R-Iowa) all by his little self, just so long as that behemoth Vicki didn't join the fray. The disappearance of "Fantasy Island" from our airwaves is one of the great mysteries of seventies culture.

Herve Villechaize, RIP.

Charles O. Finley.   The man and the mule. The owner of the Oakland As (he officially changed their name from the decades-old Athletics, though it was changed back again after his reign of terror had ended) would never become quite as evil as George Steinbrenner or Marge Schott, but he was as bad as it got for a long time. Best idea: orange baseballs.

5 Stairsteps.   Protegees of Curtis Mayfield, this singing group of soulful young siblings had a number of hits on the R and B charts in the late sixties and early seventies and certainly were poised for more lasting mainstream appeal when the Jackson 5 and then the Osmonds appeared out of nowhere and blew them out of the water. It seems there was room for only two preteen brother acts on the charts at any one time back then.

I know this will sound like reverse-popularity snobbism, but one listen to the best of the 5 Stairsteps will clearly show that as great as the Jacksons were, the Burke family was even greater, less slick and more soulful. Some of their album tracks feature three-year-old Cubie on lead vocals, and he can barely even pronounce the words let alone carry a tune! They did manage to get in one pop hit, the lovely "Ooh Child," before fading from sight.

Curt Flood.   The name of Andy Messersmith will be forever linked to the Supreme Court decision that finally unlocked the shackles of baseball's reserve clause, but this former Cardinal all-star centerfielder was the first to bring the argument to court. He lost, and he paid a great personal price for his insolence, but the players of today should be eternally grateful to Flood, for it was clearly his losing effort that paved the way for Messersmith's successful one.

Larry Flynt.   *Hustler* magazine is still around, but nobody ever mentions its publisher's name anymore. For a time in the 1970s, he was as famous as Hugh Hefner. Flynt was a major warrior on the battlegrounds of the First Amendment (certainly not a *completely* altruistic act on his part, huh?); he got born again by Jimmy Carter's evangelist sister Ruth yet continued to publish *Hustler*; and he got shot and paralyzed for life in a still-unsolved assassination attempt. One of the most interesting total sleazeballs of the era.

Fanne Foxe; Elizabeth Ray.   The Donna Rice and Gennifer Flowers of their day, only much wilder and much funnier. Also, the guys they brought down were not hot-panted young bucks but were among the power elite of old-time Capitol Hill. Both episodes occurred in the middle part of the decade.

Rep. Wilbur Mills of Arkansas was virtually unrepentant in his pathetic drunken downfall when he was first arrested flopping around in Washington's Potomac Tidal Basin with Foxe, a stripper known as the Argentinian Firecracker, then caught red-handed dancing with her on-stage in Boston's Combat Zone. Rep. Wayne Hays of Ohio was forced to resign when he was nailed keeping the busty blondshell Ray on his payroll as a secretary, even though she didn't know how to type. She went on to do a nude layout for *Playboy*.

Frings.   Jack in the Box for a very short while featured a strange side-order combining french fries and onion rings—a natural, right? Frings were my first step into the forbidden adult world of onion eating, and I've never looked back, but I never did see them again anywhere, nor has anyone I've asked ever even heard of them. I guess I was just a test-market baby and didn't know it.

Frogurt.   Before there was frozen yogurt there was Frogurt, a trade-marked concoction that never did catch on. Perhaps the formula was changed or maybe it was just going with the less *blecchh* name, but after a hiatus of a few years, the product was reintroduced and has sold like . . . uh, hotcakes ever since.

The Fuzz.   I can't understand why officers of the law got so bent out of shape over this rather innocuous epithet. The term wormed its way into common usage, even lending itself to a Burt Reynolds–Raquel Welch vehicle and to a Barbara Eden made-for-TV job (dig this fabulous cast for *The Feminist and the Fuzz*: (I dream of) Jeannie, Lucas Tanner, Jill Munroe, Jo Anne Worley from "Laugh-In," Col. Potter, the original Catwoman, and Laverne De Fazio!) before harmlessly fading into the twilight of quaint and moldy vernacular phraseology.

Oscar Gamble.   Many are they who insist that the only aspect of major league baseball worth watching throughout the 1970s were the remarkable Afros worn by this journeyman outfielder. In its more extreme incarnations you had no choice but to wonder how he could keep his hats and helmets on his head—bobby pins?

Leif Garrett.   Did you know that Dawn Lyn, the obnoxious little girl who played Dodie (Steve Douglas's stepdaughter) in the later episodes of "My Three Sons," was Leif Garrett's *sister*? 'Tis a fact.

Uri Geller. Professional spoon bender from Israel who, like the Amazing Kreskin, did not have the guts to say it was all just a trick. I remember a New York newscast that followed Geller around as he went into clock shops around the city causing broken timepieces to run again by the sheer power of his presence. Last seen curing cancer for rich suckers.

Lisa Gerritsen; Pamelyn Ferdin. Two cool teen TV actresses of the early seventies. Gerritsen was the more successful, with continuing roles in "Mary Tyler Moore" (as Phyllis's daughter) and "My World and Welcome To It," but the long, thin Ferdin was the greater talent. She even got to play Paul Lynde's daughter for a year.

Karen Lynn Gorney. Two nights ago, I saw *Saturday Night Fever* for the very first time. One of the things that struck me most about it, besides the great music and Travolta's decent James-Dean-in-platforms performance, was the fact that I've never heard of almost any other actor or actress in the film. Apart from Travolta and Donna Pescow, whose main source of income for years has been from playing in obscure syndicated sitcoms, not one of *Saturday Night Fever*'s top-billed names—immortals such as Barry Miller, Joseph Cali, Paul Pape, and Julie Bovasso—went on to any fame whatsoever. But it is Gorney's noncareer that is the most perplexing. In *Saturday Night Fever*, she offers an interesting performance as the downtown girl trying to pass for uptown, but other than this film and an obnoxious appearance as herself on "America 2-Night" (Harry Shearer wins a contest to be Gorney's blind date), we've heard not a peep from her. Perhaps she's still out there in Bay Ridge, dancing her weekends away at 2001 Odyssey.

Halter Tops. The single greatest article of clothing ever invented by man to be worn by woman.

Mark Hamill. Imagine *being* Mark Hamill. Believing everything everyone tells you about how big a star you're gonna be, so don't rush things; take only the choicest *quality* acting assignments ... *thud!* It's fear of being Mark Hamill that causes people to become Valerie Bertinelli or Jim Belushi instead.

A blindfolded Lynette "Squeaky" Fromme being carried into the Sacramento courthouse by a federal marshal. Squeaky refused to participate in her trial on a charge of attempting to murder then-President Gerald Ford. She chose to watch the proceedings on closed-circuit television in a holding cell.
(UPI/BETTMANN)

Harvey Wallbanger.   First mixed drink recipe to be immortalized on a T-shirt: "Into a tall glass filled with ice pour one ounce vodka. Fill glass with orange juice and stir. Float one-half ounce Galliano on top." Drink two without breathing in-between and puke your insides out.

"Hello, Larry."   Sitcom, ostensibly based on the life of Larry King, in which McLean Stevenson—NBC president Fred Silverman's fuck you to the nation—worries about keeping his job as late-night radio talk-master while trying to raise two horny teenage daughters. The younger girl was played by Kim Richards, the cute kid sister Prudence from "Nanny and the Professor."

"I Am Woman."   OK, people talk about it all the time, but when was the last time you actually *heard* it?

Clifford Irving.   Glomming onto the decaying bones of the still-alive Howard Hughes was a major growth industry in the 1970s. Hughes's bogus will leaving everything to service station attendant Melvin Dummar is well rememberd today, if only for its sympathetic portrayal in Jonathan Demme's film *Melvin and Howard*, but Irving's biography of Hughes, ostensibly written with its subject's cooperation, is not. The book was aborted by its publisher before it ever came out when it was revealed to be a total scam. The fuss and hoopla—McGraw-Hill and *Life* magazine were among those left with mud in their eye—was enough to bring Hughes out of hiding briefly to denounce the hoax, and Irving even did some time in the big house for fraud.

Jesus Freaks.   Along with the Vietnam War and the singer-songwriter movement, the Jesus freak movement (and *movement* is a most appropriate word here) was the scariest thing going for American youth in the early 1970s. Jesus freaks were ex-acidheads "who found Gawd at the bottom of a purple cap-syule" and decided that their salvation should be yours, too. They'd stalk the halls of the high school, still sporting acid regalia and hippie haircuts so as to better infiltrate their marks, and walk up to anyone they deemed needy of the Word, whip out their tattered pocket Bible, and spout chapter and verse right in their face! Thank the good Lord this trend didn't last very long.

Jobriath.   The most successful of the several Bowie knockoffs. PBS did a documentary about the making and packaging of his career, which quietly faded from sight shortly after the program aired.

"Junior's Farm."   Paul McCartney got on a real hot streak around the mid-seventies, what with this song, "Jet," and "Band on the Run." David Sugarman had me convinced that it was written as a condemnation of President Ford, though except maybe for Ford being Junior, I never could figure out how.

Kekich and Peterson.   This tale of wife swapping among Yankee pitchers pretty much killed off the free-love era all by itself. Mike Kekich and Fritz Peterson didn't just throw the keys on the table for one night, however—they permanently traded wives, kids, and houses, right down to the family dogs. The story broke in spring training of 1973, and both were pitching for Cleveland before the year was out—a fitting conclusion to this now-forgotten morality tale of big league sin.

Happy Kyne.   Other than the aforementioned diary of Anne Eickelberg, Nick at Nite's reruns of "Fernwood 2-Night" and its successor "America 2-Night" (both created by Norman Lear and produced by Alan Thicke) are the most complete and concise time capsules we have of the wondrous silliness of seventies American culture, and bandleader Happy Kyne is one of the main reasons why. Scrawny, deadpan, crag-featured and ever-aggravated, Kyne's frequent appearances on Barth Gimble's couch by themselves practically justify the cost of being wired for cable, and that's not even taking into account some of his unforgettable musical showcases. Such as, how does a syncopated, accordion-led version of "Boogie Fever," featuring a harmonica solo by Hap, grab ya? Not wild enough? Then take a look at Happy's one-man Mexican band routine, playing maracas, claves, cowbells, gourd scraper (attached to a helmet), and bass drum (with the drum stick on a long pole attached to his ass) all at once. Indescribably delicious.

Kyne's band the Mirthmakers included some of the top LA session musicians, usually playing just slightly out of tune, off-key, or off-time. Happy himself was played by Frank DeVol, veteran actor, bandleader, and arranger with a résumé that could blow the hair clean off your head, as it did his. It includes: bandleader for variety shows starring Betty White, Rosemary Clooney, Dinah Shore, and George Gobel; actor in "I'm Dickens—He's Fenster," "Camp Runa-muck," and "The Betty White Show"; writer of incidental music for "F Troop" and theme songs to "The Brady Bunch," "Family Affair," "My Three Sons," and at least one of the Matt Helm movies; arranger for Tony Bennett and many others.

Laetrile.   A supposed cure for cancer that was derived from the pit of a peach. It was never approved by the Food and Drug Administra-tion, and so those who had run out of options that *were* legal were forced to flee to Mexico as outlaws to try it. But laetrile proved to be just another snake oil, and so the U.S. government was not long in making fugitives out of the terminally ill.

Lenny and Squiggy.   Even with the twenty-twenty hindsight of con-stant reruns, I still think Lenny and Squiggy fully justify the existence of "Laverne and Shirley," more than compensating for the inadequacies of the title characters and other losers like the Big Ragu. In 1978, I drove a hundred miles to see Lenny and the Squigtones, Lander and McKean's cash-in stage show, and it was easily worth it. Even got Michael McKean's guitar pick—does that also qualify as a Spinal Tap artifact?

Little Cigars.   Basically just cigarettes wrapped in brown paper in-stead of white, lending the losers who smoked them a faux-sophistico cachet. Among the leading brands were More and Fridays, whose motto was "T.G.I.F."

Sacheen Littlefeather.   Marlon Brando's Native American girlfriend, who stood in for the big guy when he declined his *Last Tango* Oscar. Decked out in full war dance regalia, she delivered a brief speech for him condemning Hollywood and the U.S. government for their mistreatment of the American Indian. It later came to light, however, that Miss Littlefeather was in reality a struggling actress named Maria Cruz who previously had been Miss Vampire of 1970.

Guru Maharaj Ji.   "The 13-Year-Old Perfect Master," he was popular enough to sell out the Houston Astrodome for a personal appearance.

Lost much of his following when his playboy lifestyle became public knowledge.

Terence Malick.   Movie director who seemed to come out of nowhere in 1973 by debuting with the already-accomplished *Badlands*, an interesting and lushly filmed depiction of the Charlie Starkweather murder-spree case. A few years later, he made *Days of Heaven* in much the same vein, and he looked set for a long career as a successful Hollywood filmmaker. Instead he then seemed to vaporize back into the same wherever as he came out of (actually, before his film career, he had been deeply involved in intellectual circles, including a stint as a philosophy professor at MIT), and he hasn't made a single picture since.

Don Meredith.   The "Monday Night Football" announcer so affable that even Howard Cosell was made tolerable by his presence in the booth—alongside anyone else, Cosell was never even remotely listenable. Meredith's easygoing sense of humor best exposed itself one night in the late minutes of a dull, lopsided game. Panning a section of empty seats, the camera found one last fan sitting out there. Sensing a momentary national forum, the lonely spectator quickly shot the middle finger, to which the ever-composed Meredith quipped, "That just means 'We're number one,' Howard." Cosell, for once in his life, had nothing to add.

Metric System.   A rare breeze of logic swept through the U.S. legislative branch in the mid-1970s when it was decreed that this country would be gradually switching itself over to the weight and measurement standards used by most of the rest of the world. Nobody over the age of twelve took too kindly to this news—we all agreed that the metric system made *sense*, true, but we were just so used to the old way, which always seemed to work perfectly well.

As part of the gradual process, measurements would be given in both units until the inch-and-foot standard was eventually phased out. New road signs were made giving distances in miles and kilometers, baseball fences were repainted to display home run clouts in feet and meters, and digital public clocks were reprogrammed to include the temperature in both Fahrenheit and centigrade. An unhappy but logical population girded itself for the inevitable. But something happened—no one even today seems quite sure what—and the metric movement died out as gradually as it was supposed to be phased in. Not a single American mourned its passing. Today about its only residual effect is that nobody bothered to reprogram the public clocks to get rid of the centigrade (or is it Celsius?) display, and so those degrees in "C" continue to flash out their reminders of what might have been.

Mexican Jumping Beans.   Not, strictly speaking, a seventies phenomenon, but I remember them from the seventies part of my childhood and have not heard from them since. Is the species extinct?

M Movie Rating.   "M" stood for "mature audiences only." This became GP, which became PG, which became PG-13, sort of.

National Faith in Authority.   It's kind of a cliché to say it began to crumble with Watergate, but it sure does seem that way. Prior to that, most of us readily fell for every line we were fed by science, government, historians, and other experts, existing in a perhaps willfully induced stupor of naivete. But the first consummated fall from grace by an American president precipitated twenty years of debunkings of our cherished half-truths, and I don't think we can ever go back again, Reagan-Bush notwithstanding. Not that I'm in mourning over this ever-growing cynicism, mind you—I think we'd all be much better off being surrounded by even fewer saps, rubes, and dupes.

Neutron Bomb.   The perfect capitalist war tool—a bomb that would destroy life but not property. Plans for their production by the United States were squashed by that human rights do-gooder Jimmy Carter.

New Journalism.   The New Journalism was a style of hard-hitting, investigative reporting that differed from traditional journalism in that it was now deemed OK to dispense with the pretense of objectivity. In other words, the reporter would go about finding and reporting his or her facts same as always but with a very personal interpretation or analysis that in the best of hands (i.e., Hunter Thompson, Tom Wolfe) could be as exciting as great fiction writing. Today a lot of people seem to think of *All the President's Men* as having been an example of New Journalism, but it wasn't really the same thing.

Nolo Contendere.   Latin for "no contest." In legal terms, this is an acceptance of a conviction without an admission of guilt, and it was the tricky maneuver Vice President Spiro Agnew pulled, in the midst of Nixon's Watergate mess, to avoid prison for income tax evasion. It was Agnew's resignation of his office that led to the nomination of Gerald Ford, which in turn led to the total pardon of Nixon.

OK, now, quick: Spiro Agnew, dead or alive?

"No No Song."   Ringo Starr's totally forgotten hit from 1975, written by the son of the composer of "Heartbreak Hotel." Easily the worst song any Beatle has ever been involved with, with the possible exception of the McCartney catalogue.

Oliver.   A male given name that came into some kind of perverse popularity in the 1970s. Lessee, there was *Oliver's Story*, the sequel to *Love Story*; the obnoxious little brat cousin on "The Brady Bunch"; and Oliver, the unbelievably fey singer who had hits with "Jean" and "Good Morning, Starshine." Perhaps the single best thing about the 1970s was that the threat of continued stardom by Oliver never came to pass. (Also Eddie Albert's character on "Green Acres.")

1-2-3.   A dessert treat that kids could kind of half-make themselves from premixed ingredients. I remember that it involved a lot of shaking—I mean a *lot* of shaking—and that the treat would eventually settle into three sedimentary layers: Jell-O, imitation whipped cream, and imitation pudding. Nobody I've ever mentioned 1-2-3 to could remember it, which leads me to conclude that either northern New Jersey must have been a test market for the product or else it just shows the power of selective recall.

Paraquat.   The federales plot to mass annihilate the nation's pot smokers. The plan was to spray this potentially lethal solution on marijuana fields south of the border, but public outcry forced them to cut the program before it ever got off the ground.

Peignot Bold.   *The* typeface of the seventies—you'll recognize it as the font used for the credits of "The Mary Tyler Moore Show." Type design of the day favored wide, rounded letterforms. Other defining fonts of the decade include Dom Casual, Brush, Bauhaus, Avant Garde (still popular today, this font was first designed as the logo face for *Avant Garde* magazine, a great postsixties art mag published by Ralph Ginzburg. In fact, this is what you're reading right now), Cooper Black, Harry Obese, Hobo, and the ever-popular Ronda.

Valerie Perrine.   I had always thought of her as just one more actress who fucked her way to the top, but a closer exam of her career shows that maybe she wasn't entirely talentless after all. Most of her parts— such as those in *Slaughterhouse Five*, the first *Superman*, and a PBS take on Sartre's *The End* called *Steambath*—called for her to be little more than a dumb bunny with perky tits, but the job she did in the demanding role as Honey Bruce in Bob Fosse's *Lenny* was quite remarkably good, garnering her an Oscar nomination. Still, she never did display the kind of talent that would age well, and maybe she was smart enough to simply grab it while she was still young.

Pieing.   What passed for terrorism after all of the post-SDS dangerous hombres and hombrettes had finally been captured or blowed themselves up was throwing pies at public figures. Aron Kay, a New York Yippie, was responsible for most of the good ones, and his hits included William F. Buckley and Daniel Patrick Moynihan, Phyllis Schlafly and New York mayor Abe Beame, and Studio 54 owner Steve Rubell. Of the latter, Kay said he was protesting discos as being "meaningless, decadent and lobotomizing." Yeah, so?

A friend of mind found herself in the pokey at one point during the run of this fad for attempting to hit aging tennis brat Bobby Riggs— the shaving-cream monstrosity landed limply at his feet—as he innocently cut the ribbon to open a new mall in Hadley, Massachusetts.

Plymouth Duster.   Not the only car to ever have a cartoon as its official logo, just the coolest.

"Punky Reggae Party."   Bob Marley's 1977 single sympathizing with the British punk movement. The record came and went pretty quickly but stands today as an interesting little cross-cultural curiosity.

Quadrophonic.   Surround-sound is a noble pursuit, I suppose, but— correct me if I'm wrong—since we have only two ears, isn't stereo going to be just about the most accurate sound reproduction we can perceive?

Leo Sayer.   The poor man's Elton John.

Debralee Scott.   Befanged TV character actress who was forever playing the horny kid sister or the bad-girl best friend. Credits include "Hotsie" Totzie on "Welcome Back, Kotter"; Mary Hartman's younger sister Cathy; Donna Pescow's sister on "Angie"; numerous made-for-TV movies; and more appearances on "The Love Boat" than anyone except Charo.

Donald Segretti.   Of the entire stupefying litany of not-so-discreet operatives working for the Committee to Re-Elect the President (appropriately pronounced "creep," this was Nixon's 1972 reelection committee) who were in one way or another involved in the Watergate debacle, Segretti stands out as one of the more amusing. A weasely, baby-faced little guy, his job was to think up and execute small-time "dirty tricks," political hijinks that would get the Democratic candidates attacking each other instead of Nixon or generally would disrupt the individual campaigns themselves. Among typical operations attributed to Segretti was a pamphlet ostensibly originated by the McGovern campaign blaming the war on Humphrey, a supposed Muskie flier accusing Humphrey and Henry Jackson of sex crimes, and random late-night calls to New Hampshire voters by the "Harlem for Muskie Committee," urging votes for Muskie "because he'd been so good for the black man." Segretti's activities were known around CRP as "ratfucking."

Sensurround.   I lived through a real earthquake and thought it was Sensurround.

It was late 1979, just under the wire for qualification as a true seventies event. I recently had moved to San Francisco and my companions and I decided to visit the city's multimedia tourist promotion, *The San Francisco Experience*. The big attraction was that the 1906 earthquake was depicted in Sensurround, the movie theater quake-simulating device invented for Irwin Allen's disaster hit *Earthquake*. Never having seen that film (I know, I know—*for shame*), I had no idea what to expect, but I didn't expect much. About a half hour into the showing of the *Experience*, as they were doing a little bit about San Francisco's gay community, we felt the earth and the seats beneath our buns rumble mightily for fifteen or twenty seconds. I thought that this was the Sensurround and that it had been started up before the 1906 segment to surprise the audience and segue into that portion, and that it was a pretty well-done simulation. But the rumbling ended and the narrator was still going on about the gay community, so I figured that maybe the kid running the projector had hit the Sensurround button too early.

Ten minutes later, they finally came to the 1906 earthquake, and at that time, the bass on the audio was turned all the way up for the entirety of the brief segment and then turned down again as the show moved on to another topic. *That* was Sensurround, and for all its hype, it turned out to be the lamest movie gimmick I've ever heard of, let alone experienced. When the show ended and we went back outside, we learned that a real quake—a 5.5er—had hit the area while we were watching the *Experience*, but we inside had thought that it was just the magic of Sensurround.

William Shatner. I've never even seen "Star Trek" (so sue me!), yet I consider myself a pretty big Shatner idolater nonetheless. He came out of Canada in the late fifties with a reputation as a hot new turk of serious drama, and the critical success clearly went to his head. He tried to make his every role into a Shakespearean tour de force, and maybe it washed when he was getting some meatier parts, but after Capt. Kirk he began getting lesser and lesser assignments yet continued to give each of them everything he had, and then some.

With the success of "Star Trek," he was able to make a few recordings, specializing in bizarrely literal recitations of pop hits of the sixties and seventies. Highlighted by the album *The Transformed Man*, which includes his interpretations of "Mr. Tambourine Man," "Lucy in the Sky with Diamonds," "It Was a Very Good Year," and the source material of his entire dramatic ouvre, Hamlet's soliloquy itself, these pieces weave deliriously around the border area of "is he serious or is he joking?" In an appearance on a science fiction awards TV program around 1973, Shatner offered a mind-bending tripartite take on Bernie Taupin's lyrics for "Rocket Man," a performance that lives on today in ever-hazier bootlegged videos passed on feverishly from generation to generation.

Anyone out there have a copy of the Shat's version of "Taxi"?

Skylab; Kahoutek. Two objects that came out of the sky with a whimper and not a bang.

Abe Vigoda. Also known as the Lord himself. "Fish," currently being rerun on superstation WWOR, holds up as a pretty decent little sitcom. Some of the kids on the show were really great, too—among them was the precrack Todd Bridges. By the way, do you suppose there was a single square inch on Vigoda's body *not* covered by hair? And were Jerry Tarkanian and Abe V. separated at birth?

"What's Happening!!" Better than "The Jeffersons," not as good as "Good Times," but certainly the black sitcom most obviously put together by white people. The peak of weekly hilarity—to judge by the laugh track, at least—is when Dwayne would bound into the room and wittily announce, "Hi hi hi." And isn't there something vaguely racist about naming a character in a ghetto sitcom Rerun? A few levying points to the show's credit: Rerun was played by the rotund Fred Berry, who was a member of the Lockers, the seventies LA street dance group that invented breakdancing; Henry Mancini wrote the title theme (not one of his most memorable, however); Roger's little sister Dee was played by Danielle Spencer.

Whip Inflation Now. Gerald Ford's flaccid slogan, which was somehow supposed to magically dissolve the malevolent clouds of doom from the recessed economy of the mid-seventies. That rascally little power of positive thought didn't quite do the do this time, however.

White House Kids. Forgotten today are all of the Carter kids except for Amy and all of the Ford kids, period.

Willard. Because of its love-song-to-a-rat anthem, *Ben* is the one remembered today, but this was the original and the scarier of the two.

Demond Wilson; Flip Wilson. Where they be at now, you wonder? It ain't very pretty.

Demond W. (TV son to Redd Foxx) got himself involved with the archetypal low-life theatrical sleazeball Roy Radin in the early 1980s and was apparently one of the last people (other than the killers, of course) to see Radin alive before he disappeared. It was months before Radin's disfigured, mummified body was discovered in the California desert. Demond is now a traveling preacher.

Flip W. has done a little better for himself. It's hard to recall just how big he was in the early seventies, when his comedy-variety show ranked at the top of the Nielsen ratings for several years (for a cryptic reminder, see the earlier "Catchphrases" entry). He reappeared on the tube a few years back, playing opposite Gladys Knight in a short-lived domestic sitcom. He is now in semiretirement, apparently well-off enough to enjoy hot-air ballooning, long ocean cruises, and Gibran.

"A Year at the Top." A surreal concept: David Letterman's fave toady, Paul Shaffer, starring in a Norman Lear sitcom in which he sold his so-called soul to the devil (played by Gabe Dell, one of the original Bowery Boys—or perhaps you remember him for his early-seventies sitcom "The Corner Bar") in exchange for one year as a pop superstar. This bizarre program lasted only five weeks—not quite long enough to see Shaffer roast in Satan's pizza oven. Ironically, the music director of the show was Don Kirschner, whom Shaffer would gain his biggest early flash of real fame imitating on "Saturday Night Live."

Zodiac Everything. In the seventies we had zodiac watches, zodiac belt buckles, zodiac key chains, zodiac wallpaper, zodiac air fresheners, zodiac glow-in-the-dark Kama Sutra posters . . . I'll bet someone in the seventies even tried to sell zodiac food.

ZPG. "Zero population growth," a no-more-kids movement that rode sidesaddle astride the ecology thing until those selfish yuppies started acting as if they'd never heard, the term *birth control*.

P-FUNK   Scot Hacker

For the religiously inclined, P-Funk[1] offered up an entire array of minor gods, an intangible and omnipotent metaphysical reality (the funk itself), and a whole flotilla of ministers (actually a loose-fitting assemblage of crack musicians and crackpots dedicated to the administration of an entire cosmology[2]). The roots of this church lay deep in the African polyrhythmic pantheon; its disciples ("Maggot Brains" or "Funkateers") consisted of anyone who sought a quasi-cohesive view of a universe that included a god who *danced* and who knew that having a loose booty to shake was as crucial to the keeping of the faith as the rosary was for the Catholic.

While their ministers were many—a constantly evolving lineup guaranteed the elasticity of the band—it is undeniable that high pope George Clinton wore the miter. From the cryptic, ridiculously bent versifying of the liner notes to the album sleeve art production (which narrated the genesis and mission of the band in a series of ongoing, albeit disjointed, cartoons) to the inception and direction of the outrageous stage production—a black sci-fi extravaganza/space party that could cost upwards of $350,000[3]—Clinton wielded the scepter of Funkentelechy and wore the righteous robes of the Afronaut (actually Holiday Inn bedsheets covered with Crayola scribbles).

But what was the aim of this religion without proscriptions? To what heaven, to what nirvana, did it aim? Like good gnostic bacchanalians, P-Funk had the good epistemological taste not to define their vision of the great beyond too specifically. With commandments like "Shit! Goddam! Get off your ass and jam!" you knew that whatever and wherever "the beyond" was, it was going to be funky.

You knew very well what was going to take you there: the same vehicle from which George descended out of a massive blue denim cap and down to the stage in bad-ass righteousness: the Mothership.

---

[1] P-Funk is shorthand for one group that recorded under two names: Parliament and Funkadelic. To generalize crudely in distinguishing them, Parliament's music focused more or less on the dance floor, while Funkadelic had more of a psychedelic aspect. In general, Funkadelic was more serious than Parliament, but since most of the members were the same, there was a lot of crossover in style and message.

[2] See "The P-Funk Cosmology-in-a-Nutshell," page 155.

[3] P-Funk's stage shows were actually written by Clinton, costumed by Larry Gatsby (who was also haberdasher to The Who, Patti LaBelle, and *The Wiz*), and designed by Jules Fischer (who also created sets for the Stones, David Bowie, and Kiss).

PLATFORMS

Just as protestants distinguish between the icon of the Messiah and the true, ineffable spirit, we knew that George's silver saucer was but a model—a mechanical and ideological messiah figure represented in the terms of the day, as the glory of UFO contact for a generation reared on honky "Star Trek" and honky *Close Encounters of the Third Kind*. But it didn't matter whether the Mothership was a prop[4], because the hallmark of a myth is that you don't go peering around behind the curtain—you simply *believe*. As usual, P-Funk co-opted the pop mythology, made it black, and made it intergalactic—in this case, the mythos of (*funky*) contact.

And so shows began with the descent, and ended with the subsequent assumption, of what was at once a symbol and a reality: Clinton's arrival on the scene in his glorious ship through backlit fog and the incantations of the crowd: "The Mothership connection is *here!*" Disciples held aloft the Mothership mudra in invitation: index and pinky fingers extended upward, the rest of the fist curled. Was this an extrapolation on the black power fist, that is, black power plus archetypal twin steeples toward God? Perhaps, but this mudra goes farther back than that. In yoga, this posture of the fingers is held in stillness to channel chi into the body through the arms and into the chakras. Tibetan art and sculpture sometimes depicts goddesses with one hundred arms in a vertical fan arrayed around the body, each hand signaling the imminence of the Mothership.

In the sign language of the deaf, the same hand symbol means "I love you," and it also is seen depicted on bumper stickers for the deaf (ostensibly as a signal to cops and emergency vehicles that the driver may not hear the sirens). But more likely the bumper sticker signifies membership in the society of riders of the everlasting funk wave—to demonstrate that deaf people are cosmic love surfers. Funk doesn't have to be *heard* because the aural music is only a physical manifestation of the yet deeper, noumenal galactic vibe, which is always *felt* by one whose receptors are tuned to Channel One.

If the Mothership beckoned us aboard, where would it go? Certainly not to Palm Beach, Florida, to see Tony Orlando and Dawn. Not to Vegas to watch Tom Jones, although he's funky, too, in the same way that Velveeta is funky because it's mucilaginous. Let's suppose for

---

[4]These days, it's not uncommon for the crowd to shout out, "Props! Props!" at P-Funk shows.

146

a moment that the Mothership returns metaphorically to the motherland, to Africa. Maggot Brains didn't come to America on the Nina, the Pinta, or the Santa Maria, and they ain't going back on them, neither. When Cap'n George is at the helm, you know you're going to ride in outrageous style to your repatriation. The Mothership takes off in the middle of a concert in Detroit and lands in the middle of a Yoruba fertility dance. The scenery changes *ever* so slightly, but the song remains the same.

This repatriation theme dovetails nicely with a semiotic breakdown of the dual meaning of *funk*. The musical definition is apparent: it is that which moves, irresistible, an ineluctable conclusion of motion ("dedicated to the preservation of the motion of hips"), and of course it's always on The One. The other usage of the term refers to the *smell* of funk—earthy musk, the purple smell of global vagina, the source of jazz in sweat, saxophone jism, the smell of spontaneity and origination, funk giving birth to funk, the fertile rhythms of the song cycle life and death, conception and birth in dirt and secretions, the visceral funk of sweat and sex, pussy rotation, the stank thang, the glory of juices in vapor reacting at base level in the gut, gut bass thumping spleen . . . in all fertility awareness the funk figures as smell, cosmic progenation, funk of dame nature in labor harmonizing with funk of loose booty boarding the Mothership, the smell that leaves us "standing on the verge of gettin' it on."

So when I say that the Mothership represented a vehicle of repatriation, I don't mean that P-Funk were Zionists. Quite the opposite—they took all the cheese America had to offer and ran with it, taking the fashions and technology of the day to their ultimate, preposterous conclusions, amplifying the aesthetics of the seventies into a throbbing, fish-eyed cartoon of itself, and in so doing glorified American culture and their role in its continuing evolution.

Thus, as platform shoes were becoming merely popular, P-Funk was giving us the amplified version, wearing knee-high silver boots with nine-inch heels ("hoofs decked out for atomic toe-jam action") back when Gene Simmons was still playing air guitar in his mother's bathroom mirror. When the revitalizing puissance of pyramid power began to take hold in the collective consciousness, P-Funk gave us a stage show that included a Claes Oldenberg–like floppy pyramid (what could be funkier than a soft monolith?). When *A Clockwork Orange* brought the codpiece to our attention, Clinton had to wear one the size of a loaf of Wonder bread, covered in rabbit fur, natch. When the boxy virility of the Cadillac trickled down to the working class as a symbol of status and cool, George Clinton began arriving on stage in a likewise soft-'n'-floppy silver lamé roadster, the engine compartment of which opened like coffin doors to reveal George in full Funkateer regalia, dripping in feathers and ermine, ready to rise from the dead and do it to you in your earhole.

No, it was not a question of repatriation. P-Funk's brand of black freedom was not Malcolm X's. Returning P-Funk to Africa would have been like returning Ling-Ling the Panda to China. The Mothership, as a symbol of the P-Funk gestalt, took Funkateers out of the disco-dominated dance scene, which smelled clean and felt rigid, and returned them to the belly of the cosmos, where it smells skanky and feels rubbery. The Mothership symbolized the possibility of a spiritual, not a physical, return to blood and to roots, to the swirling gasses and dust of galactic conception, to the smell of freshly plucked wild yams, amorphous and still covered in the funk of the earth; of a return to a cut-loose, stink-up-the-place, get-your-ya-yas-out, freak-on-down-the-road domain where "funk is its own reward."

P-Funk seemed to believe that music wasn't so much something that you *made* with your instruments as it was something that you *caught* with them, as if funk was out *there* in the form of an ambient residual energy left over from the big bang. It was as if their basses and horns were finely tuned, specialized antennae dialing into cosmic leftovers. Funk became a unifying presence—the godhead as manifest to anyone willing to laugh and boogie at the same time.

Despite all of their self-inflatulatory bravadaccio, P-Funk were nevertheless unflaggingly humble before the great unnameable face of the big cookie. Such humility is a necessary underpinning to any sincere encounter with or metaphysical proclamation on the nature of mind-universe. Without it they would come off as self-serious charlatans, wielders of the scepter of pompousness. But their cosmology combines the best of the principles of the world's great gnosticisms. The sense of undifferentiated cosmic unity inherent in Buddhism, the paradox, humor, and dance of Sufism, the ecological implications of quantum mechanics via the implicit order of the universe's interconnectedness, and the surrealism of psychedelic awareness.

148

Everything is on The One y'all, can you get to that?

When The One comes down, and bulbs of sweat pop from Star Child's brow, and the bass thumpasaurus slaps its cosmic tail against a lighted dance floor, every boo-tay in the house meets its neighbor as hineys mash together in plush synchronicity. Being "on The One" means never having to call your choreographer, because he would only mess things up. The unity of the dance is given unto the dancers … it is not their responsibility to keep in step but their priviledge to have "The One" channeled through the band's antennae and onto the dance floor. Even if you have no intention of dancing, your protons are going to go ahead without you. It can't be helped.

But "The One" is of course also the cosmic one, the unified field of awareness, or in Hindu terminology, Shiva, the dance itself. Funk is like the carrier wave that is channeled through the eye of the floppy pyramid, through Clinton's multicolored dreads and through sunglasses that could shame Elton John. Throwing down on The One with every coil of DNA at their disposal, flopping plasma braids, flopping groove lines like fish out of water funking on deck, they did for togetherness what disco could only dream of doing. P-Funk was the "us" to disco's "me." The ego wasn't the thing … the thing was the funk. To strut *and* to partake, not just to strut. The "partaking of" was the reason that P-Funk had the essence of religion while disco did not. It was a "participation-in," and the crowd could be as bad-ass as the band. By coming to jam along, you were taking sacrament, not stage. There were no John Travoltas, because Travolta had the moves but none of the soul. P-Funk was all soul, although even they couldn't begin to tell you what soul *was*. "What is soul? I don't know! Soul is a hamhock in your cornflakes. . . . Soul is a joint rolled in toilet paper. . . ." But whatever it is, they had it, because they *were* it, and they were it because they *partook* of it.

And this is why disco was so often soulless: it didn't stink! Disco has no smell because it is clean, a product of the deodorant movement, revelling in crystal clear white polyester, cocaine, and mirrored balls, in perfumes that mask and repress the funk in its carnal primality. Sure there is sex in disco, but it is nude, not naked, without clothes but never exposed. It relies on the veneer of soaps on the body as much as it relies musically on the whitewashed veneer of danceability. Beats

149

without The Beat. The sweat is not integral to the music as it is in funk, in jazz.

Colonel Tom wiped Elvis's forehead after each song; the sweat was there because Elvis *worked*, to be sure, but its presence was denied in the classic Victorian tradition by way of its immediate elimination from the stage. For P-Funk, sweat was the nectar of the scene, was the oil that lubed the gears of the galactic funk machine; funk *is* "Cosmic Slop." Rather than deny its grip, P-Funk wallowed in the aroma, celebrated it, acknowledged its putrefying stupefaction quotient as part of the equation. Witness this celebratory testimonial to the deep and effervescent mojo of a (presumably) just-danced-in pair of panties from the grind/groove "Funky Woman": "She threw them in the air (*funky woman*) the air said this ain't fair!" While these accolades may sound at first more like insults, the ineluctable wisdom of Star Child scripture must be perpetually borne in mind: "And all that is good—is *funky*."

Let's illuminate the point further with an analogy to biker consciousness. To deodorize the funk would have been tantamount to stripping the Harley-Davidson of its characteristic irregular heartbeat. Harleys appeal to some bikers for just this reason: they are machines that rumble in a time zone of noneuclidean geometry, whose engines sound like free-jazz drummers. Hondas are efficient, but they lack that stochastic quality; the rhythm of their internal combustions can be predicted. Disco and funk have a similarly parallel relationship. Disco sacrifices the pulse of the earth, a pulse that stinks of life, in exchange for the efficiency of the drum machine or the metronomic drummer. Because it is *of* the earth, funk's wave is not predictable like disco's or house music's—it is elastic, organic, unpredictable, and gooey. Funky music smells funky because it is a *secretion* and not a form of *logic*.

So P-Funk has returned to claim the secret of the pyramids, partyin' on the Mothership, gettin' down in 3-D, to save a dyin' world from its funkless fate. How was P-Funk accorded this special privilege? According to the liner notes from *Standing on the Verge of Getting It On*,

> On the Eighth Day, the Cosmic Strumpet of Mother Nature was spawned to envelope this Third Planet in FUNKADELICAL VIBRATIONS. And she birthed Apostles Ra, Hendrix, Stone, and CLINTON to preserve all funkiness of man unto eternity. . . . But! Fraudulent

forces of obnoxious JIVATION grew; Sun Ra strobed back to Saturn to await his next Reincarnation, Jimi was forced back into his basic atoms; Sly was co-opted into a jester monolith and ... only seedling GEORGE remained! As it came to be, he did indeed begat FUNKADELIC to restore Order Within the Universe. And, nourished from the pamgrierian mammaristic melonpaps of Mother Nature, the followers of FUNKADELIA multiplied incessantly!

Mother Nature gave us the funk because she loves us, and here is where Clinton and Nietzsche rub booties. Compare: "What is done out of love always occurs beyond good and evil" (Nietzsche). "The concept of FUNKATIZATION was declared a Universal Law by Mother Nature, and therefore exempt from control by the Forces of Good, and those of Evil" (Clinton). So to be in love is to be in funk is to retain our natural state, that is, to remain beyond the possibility of valuation. But, alas, we live in a world far removed from the beneficence of perpetual love and funk—we live in a world where humans pit themselves over and above nature (see Pagan's section on how Nixon altered the structure of time) and thereby incur the bummer of the placebo syndrome. It is thus our responsibility to evangelize on behalf of nature, that is, to bring an awareness of the funk we were born in back to the world. The squirm of a rubbery bass line and the generous application of the Bop Gun's stroboscopic, pulchritudinous salve to the scabbed and placebo-pocked Nose Zone has the potential to bring us to a utopia of funk beyond what Nietzsche calls "valuation" and what Clinton calls "exploitive jivation."

Funkadelia is upon thee! ... Verily, those soulfulifically jaded swashbucklers of agitproptic burnbabydom have descended from the Original Galaxy Ghetto to cleanse thy wayward souls through music worthy of the immortals themselves! ... that what shall penetrate thine ears shall truly be a gas! ... For the truth is the way, and Funkadelic is verily the truth! Awake not, and earth remains as this solar system's space strumpet ... sour milk from the breast of Mother Nature! ... The ass thou pimpest shall be your own! Cease all manner of exploitive jivation!

—*Funkstrom Chronicles*

If Clinton sounds like some kind of intergalactic messenger, or a prophet sent to us from the beyond, or a reincarnated shaman, that's because he is. And he's not the first to visit upon us a similar wisdom. He considers himself to have been spawned by the Cosmic Strumpet, along with Jimi Hendrix, Sly Stone, and Sun Ra, in what must have been a furious blast of raw funk—the trans-African continuum rupturing at the seams, spewing these messengers in a single time cycle into our life stream for reasons outlined in Clinton's copious testament. Among his fellow emissaries, he seems to have the most in common with Sun Ra, although Ra has been more subtle in the delivery of his message (perhaps he was allowed this because he, for the most part, addressed the generation previous to Clinton's—a generation not already jaded by rock-and-roll bombast, machine-gun television, and the sociopolitics of LSD). Both Clinton and Ra prescribed "Cosmic Tones for Mental Therapy," both preached the origin of funk in the farthest recesses of the galaxy, both employed kinekaleidoscopic theater in their shows, fusing outrageous entertainment unabashedly with the most profound of philosophies or cosmologies. "Sun Ra? Yeah, he's out to lunch all right—same place I eat at!" Clinton has remarked.

As if raw funk wasn't enough, Clinton's lyrics and profuse liner notes also took on social, political, economic, and environmental issues. The core of his message paralleled hippie ideology (by the mid-seventies a dwindling phenomenon) but transcended it in virtue of its ability to laugh at itself. His style was simultaneously insane and right on.

The cover of *America Eats Its Young* is a good example of the manner in which P-Funk takes the material America has to offer and turns it inside out. The fold-out cover depicts a dollar bill, accurately rendered in most details. The significance of "One" at each of the dollar bill's four corners is not to be overlooked, and these are unaltered. However, the eagle in the great seal is clutching not branches of laurel and a fistful of arrows but a hypodermic needle and an apparently kwashiorkor-emaciated child.

In the center stands Miss Liberty herself, eyes bloodshot, vampire fangs gripping the bloody arm of one of the children she cradles. Another child has half of its skull lopped off. The brain has been removed, presumably cannibalized by our most esteemed icon. The very fact that the cover is laid out as a dollar bill invokes Funkadelic's feelings about money—that it can play the roles of both creator and destroyer ... but mostly destroyer.

A paean to the plight of the psychically brutalized veteran returning from Vietnam, "March to the Witch's Castle" describes the nightmare of readjustment after the happiest day in thirteen years (February 12, 1973—the day of the signing of the treaty that was supposed to have ended the war ... but didn't). "Father, help him to understand that when his loved one remarried, she truly believed that he was dead." A rare moment of dead seriousness in response to that which can bear no humor. America truly was the witch's castle to returning soldiers. This was not a hyperbolically extended metaphor but a direct and piercing picture of what was.

A somewhat more playful but no less disarming portrait of the psychic investment in war is heard in Funkadelic's own counterpart to "Revolution 9," a ten-minute, lyric-free sonic landscape called "Wars of Armageddon." Through the interplay of the long, slow-funk dirge, guitar screaming over the top, and an endless litany of disjointed sound effects (seemingly lifted right off one of those great sound effects records of the period), from lowing cows to groaning orgasms to cuckooing Swiss clocks, one can hear the collective psychosis, the furious dementia, and the crumbling of sensible structure that accompanies the approach of demise, personal or public (and aren't they one another's crutches?). As for what kind of Armageddon Clinton is invoking here we can only speculate. It could be Vietnam, or it could be our self-pimped biological demise.

What is protest but a bowl of lame-duck pudding without suggested alternatives? Chocolate City is full of them—namely, recommendations on how to take over Washington, D.C.: "Yeah, they're still calling it the White House, but that's a temporary condition too." If Funkateers were running Chocolate City, would Watergate and Vietnam never have happened?

Sadly, their message didn't always get through to the pundits and sometimes seemed to be swallowed up or obscured by the pageantry of the road show. In 1978, Bootsy Collins (master of the space bass) and Clinton were given a slap on the wrist by the Rod McGrew Scholarship Fund for Communicators with a Conscience, who apparently saw the group as a superficial glitter band, suggesting in no uncertain terms that the Funkateers do something more ambitious with their popularity.

Direct attacks on the political machinery of the seventies crop up throughout the annals of the voluminous material P-Funk laid upon the earth. Nested deep within Sir Lleb's "Funkstrom Chronicles of Orbitron,"[5] a war is waged against the slime of 1974's political landscape. In this prophetic account, Clinton eradicates Nixon, Agnew, and the entire Pentagon.

> And by the gods, the P.F.T. berserker machine descended to even lower depths to battle with blasphemous malodorfied legions of maggot-coloured honkiteers! Guarding their reeking nest, the PIT OF PENTAGON, the foam-flecked degenerates filled the air with watergate buggers and ensnarling webs of mysterian tape reels! But, before our strength ... their agnewesque attack vexed but their own destruction!

Naturally, the hero is awarded when "The Cosmic Strumpet of Funkadelia gazed uponst my sweaty bod with arduous satisfaction." However, in another display of final humility before the grace of trim in its eternal and universal manifestation (the funk), he admits, "I could handle it not!" Thus, able to take on the Pentagon but eternally humbled before the funk, the furthermucker (as critic Greg Tate calls Clinton) finds defeat in a penile shrivel before a yawning abyss of cosmic 'tang. As a result, he is returned to some kind of karmic holding tank, banished to live inside this mortal coil with only a booty to wave in salute toward The One: "I would wait in limbo for precious eons to become; HOT, NASTY, AND LOOSE!"

Although the mythology may sound at first like an overblown reel at an animation festival for phreaks, everything within it has its place in a coherent ideology. Sir Nose, Star Child, and Dr. Funkenstein are not just leftovers from *The Wiz* but a troupe of cosmic thespians who play out very definite roles in a more-or-less cohesive vision of what things are, in the face of what they could be. That is, they fulfill the same function as the villains and saviors in any religion or mythology. The only thing that prevents them from becoming a religion in the usual sense of the word is the same thing that divides other cults and religions: size. When a cult becomes large enough, it becomes a

[5]The ongoing, piecemeal, far-flung-yet-coherent narrative of P-Funk and its constituents' journeys, battles, and rank-yet-pneumatic sexual jamborees that is excerpted as if from nowhere and reproduced chunkwise in liner notes. Perhaps these chronicles exist in their entirety somewhere; perhaps they're the only remaining vestige of a long-forgotten transmission from Mothership Central—the Rosetta Stone of funk.

religion, or at least it takes on religious proportions. If enough people had really taken the P-Funk message seriously, there is no reason the movement wouldn't have grown from the status of a continually beleaguered fan club[6] and roving posse of fanatical Funkateers to a fully formed philosophy/pantheon/belief system that could have altered our spiritual landscape forever . . . or at the very least landed its own TV show.

THE P-FUNK COSMOLOGY-IN-A-NUTSHELL

Dig: the secret of funk was placed inside the pyramids five thousand years ago. If we had stayed tuned (to pyramid power? Connect this to the Chariots of the Gods milieu of the same era and the visiting spacemen theme of P-Funk) to The One, we wouldn't be in the mess we're in. It took the arrival of Dr. Funkenstein to unearth the funk and usher its viral spread over the defunkatized surface of the planet. The problem with Earth is that it is devoid of funk,—Earth is the "Unfunky UFO"—due to the unfunky operations of the White House, the Pentagon, Nixon, businessmen, and greed in general, and an overall lack of supergroovalisticprosifunkstication. The symbol for the collective greed-war mentality is embodied by Sir Nose, D'Void of Funk, who relentlessly pimpifies the people "By sucking their brains until their ability to think was amputated."

The ruthless whoring of Funkentelechy has brought mother nature to her knees, and we're pinned beneath them. In other words, we all have a bad case of the "Placebo Syndrome," having traded in "the real thing" for a civilization comprised of cheap imitations, which is now crumbling around us. The "Placebo Syndrome" has given the body politic weak knees, which are doomed to give out from under us at any moment. We no longer feel the pulse or smell the deep draughts of the Cosmic Slop that generates the funk.

---

[6]The fan club, Uncle Jam's Army, asked in its solicitations whether members wanted to be "duplicated, xeroxed, multiplied or divided," a phrasing that seems ironically to admit the danger of rampant clonedom that lurks in organizing masses of people—that is, the potential pitfalls of religiousifications.

155

But hark! We do have booties and we do have boots, so let's move 'em! We have the strategic assistance of Star Child, who takes careful aim and shoots at Sir Nose (who inhabits the Nose Zone, or the Zone of Zero Funkativity) with his Bop Gun, funkatizing him in the luminescent sheen of its rays. In concert, guitarist Gary Shider flew over the crowd, wearing diapers of course, blasting at the crowd with a strobe light attached to a space-age rifle, "Chasing the noses away," which forces Sir Nose to give up the funk and dance. To gather the collective energies of the Funkateers into a mobilized force, Uncle Jam's Army was created to snuff out Sir Nose wherever he may lie.

PARTIAL DISCOGRAPHY

As Funkadelic
1970—*Free Your Mind and Your Ass Will Follow*
1971—*Funkadelic; Maggot Brain*
1972—*America Eats Its Young*
1973—*Cosmic Slop*
1974—*Standing on the Verge of Gettin' It On*
1975—*Let's Take It to the Stage*
1978—*One Nation Under a Groove*
1979—*Uncle Jam Wants You*
1980—*The Electric Spanking*

As Parliament
1970—*Rhemium*
1974—*Up for the Down Stroke*
1975—*Chocolate City; The Mothership Connection*
1976—*The Clones of Dr. Funkenstein*
1977—*Funkentelechy; P-Funk Earth Tour*
1978—*Motor Booty Affair*
1979—*Gloryhallastoopid*

VARIETY SHOWS   Phil Milstein

Without getting all misty over it, the 1970s were clearly the last golden age of the TV variety show. *Everybody* had to have one, and perhaps it was this concept of giving a variety show to any goose who claimed to be a singer, dancer, comedian, storyteller, mime, and/or mimic that killed the golden egg. A friend of mine noted at the time that as soon as singing stars got their own variety show, they pretty much stopped having hit records, so giving one to the most annoying of them might not be such a bad idea.

At any rate, I figure that since the facts of these shows pretty much speak for themselves, I'll not interject much in the way of comment. Also, I wasn't lucky enough to have seen too many of them. In fact, the factual information for this article has been garnered not from memory but from *The Complete Directory To Prime Time Network TV Shows, 1946–Present*, by Tim Brooks and Earle Marsh.

The symbol ☺ indicates "summer replacement." You will note that many of these programs fall into that "vast wasteland amidst the vast wasteland" netherworld, sort of an eighth circle of TV hell. Of course, the advantage of having a summer replacement series is that you can't really get cancelled.

By the way, if any readers know who the hell Billy Van is, please pass this information along—he seemed to turn up on an awful lot of these shows.

Andy Williams Presents Ray Stevens ☺
June 20, 1970–August 8, 1970
PBN: (Primary Broadcast Night) Saturday
Notable regulars: Lulu, Steve Martin, Mama Cass, Billy Van
Note: Andy Williams was not in this series—it was the summer replacement for his series.

The Andy Williams Show
July 3, 1958–July 17, 1971
PBN: Saturday
Notable seventies regulars: Osmond Brothers, Mike Post Orchestra, Jonathan Winters, Professor Irwin Corey, Ray Stevens, Lennon Sisters, Charlie Callas

157

The Barbara McNair Show
1969–71
PBN: syndicated

The Bobbie Gentry Show
June 5, 1974–June 26, 1974
PBN: Wednesday
Note: Also known as "Bobbie Gentry's Happiness."

The Bobby Darin Show
Jan. 19, 1973–April 27, 1973
PBN: Friday
Notable regular: Dick Bakalyan
Note: Regular features included sketches starring Bobby as Dusty John
   the hippie poet.

The Bobby Goldsboro Show
1972–75
PBN: syndicated

The Bobby Vinton Show
1975–78
PBN: syndicated
Notable regulars: Freeman King, Billy Van

The Brady Bunch Hour
Jan. 23, 1977–May 25, 1977
PBN: Sunday
Notable regulars: Water Follies Swimmers
Notes: Fake Jan; originally scheduled every fifth week, in the "Nancy
   Drew"/"Hardy Boys Mysteries" time slot.

The Burns & Schreiber Comedy Hour ☺
June 30, 1973–Sept. 1, 1973
PBN: Saturday
Notable regulars: Teri Garr and Fred Willard

The Carol Burnett Show
Sept. 11, 1967–Sept. 8, 1979
PBN: Saturday

Notable seventies regulars: Dick Van Dyke, Kenneth Mars, Tim Conway, Jim Nabors, Jim Connell, Lyle Waggoner, Vicki Lawrence, Harvey Korman, Ken Berry, Steve Lawrence

Cher

Feb. 16, 1975–Jan. 4, 1976
PBN: Sunday
Notable regulars: Anita Mann Dancers (*sic*), Steve Martin, Teri Garr, Chastity Bono

Cos

Sept. 19, 1976–Nov. 7, 1976
PBN: Sunday
Notable regulars: Jeff Altman, Buzzy Linhart, Willie Bobo

The David Steinberg Show ☺

July 19, 1972–Aug. 16, 1972
PBN: Wednesday

The Dean Martin Comedy World ☺

June 6, 1974–Aug. 15, 1974
PBN: Thursday
Hosts: Jackie Cooper, Nipsey Russell, Barbara Feldon
Note: Dean Martin was not in this series—it was the summer replacement for his series.

Dean Martin Presents ☺

June 20, 1968–Sept. 6, 1973
PBN: Thursday
Notable seventies regulars: Golddiggers, Tommy Tune, Charles Nelson Reilly, Bobby Darin, Marty Feldman, Rip Taylor, Steve Landesberg, Cathy Cahill, Dick Bakalyan, Schnecklegruber, Loretta Lynn, Lynn Anderson, Jerry Reed, Ray Stevens
Notes: Dean Martin was not in this series—it was the summer replacement for his series; each season's program had a different emphasis and different subtitle to it.

The Dean Martin Show

Sept. 16, 1965–May 24, 1974
PBN: Thursday

Notable seventies regulars: Golddiggers, Ding-a-Ling Sisters, Kay Medford, Lou Jacobi, Marian Mercer, Tom Bosley, Dom DeLuise, Nipsey Russell, Rodney Dangerfield

Notes: Dino's contract allowed him not to show up until the day of the taping; series of "Friars Club Celebrity Roasts" was spun off from occasional episodes (called "hepisodes" by the series' producers) of this program.

The Diahann Carroll Show ☺
August 14, 1976–September 3, 1976
PBN: Saturday

Dick Clark's Live Wednesday
Sept. 20, 1978–Dec. 27, 1978
PBN: Wednesday
Note: To maximize impact of broadcasting live, a death-defying stunt was performed (alas, not by Dick himself but by a professional daredevil) each week.

The Don Knotts Show
Sept. 15, 1970–July 6, 1971
PBN: Tuesday
Notable regulars: Elaine Joyce, Ken Mars, John Dehner, Gary Burghoff
Note: "The Front Porch" portion of each show featured Don and his guest star sitting in rocking chairs discussing their "philosophies."

Donny and Marie
Jan. 16, 1976–May 6, 1979
PBN: Friday
Notable regulars: Ice Vanities, Ice Angels, Disco Dozen, Jim Connell, Paul Lynde
Note: First season was produced by Sid and Marty Krofft.

Easy Does It . . . Starring Frankie Avalon
Aug. 25, 1976–Sept. 15, 1976
PBN: Wednesday
Notable regulars: Annette Funicello, War Babies (improvisational group)

The Engelbert Humperdinck Show
Jan. 21, 1970–Sept. 19, 1970
PBN: Wednesday
Note: Series was produced in London.

The Flip Wilson Show
Sept. 17, 1970–June 27, 1974
PBN: Thursday

The Funny Side
Sept. 14, 1971–Dec. 7, 1971
PBN: Tuesday
Host: Gene Kelly
Notable regulars: John Amos, Teresa Graves, Warren Berlinger, Pat Finley, Dick Clair, Jenna McMahon, Michael Lembeck, Cindy Williams, Burt Mustin, Queenie Smith
Note: Each show revolved around a current theme, which would be commented on in song and skit by the five sets of "married" couples.

The Glen Campbell Goodtime Hour
Jan. 29, 1969–June 13, 1972
PBN: Sunday
Notable seventies regulars: Jerry Reed, Mike Curb Congregation, Dom DeLuise, John Hartford

The Hanna-Barbera Happy Hour
April 13, 1978–May 4, 1978
PBN: Thursday
Notes: Hosted by life-size puppets Honey and Sis; included regular features entitled "The Disco of Life" and "The Truth Tub."

Happy Days ☺
June 25, 1970–Aug 27, 1970
PBN: Thursday
Host: Louis Nye
Notable regulars: Bob and Ray, Chuck McCann
Note: Program's entire contents were nostalgia-based.

161

The Hudson Brothers Show ☺
July 31, 1974–Aug. 28, 1974
PBN: Wednesday
Notable regulars: Gary Owens, Esquerita, Ronny Graham

Ice Palace
May 23, 1971–July 25, 1971
PBN: Sunday

The Jerry Reed When You're Hot You're Hot Hour ☺
June 20, 1972–July 25, 1972
PBN: Tuesday
Notable regulars: John Twomey (Chicago attorney who made music
    with his bare hands)

The Jim Nabors Hour
Sept. 25, 1969–May 20, 1971
PBN: Thursday
Notable seventies regulars: Frank Sutton, Ronnie Schell, Nabors Kids

The Jim Stafford Show ☺
July 30, 1975–Sept. 3, 1975
PBN: Wednesday
Notable regulars: Richard Stahl, Deborah Allen

Joey and Dad ☺
July 6, 1975–July 27, 1975
Hosts: Ray Heatherton, Joey Heatherton
PBN: Sunday
Notable regulars: Pat Paulsen, Henny Youngman, Bob Einstein
Notes: Ray Heatherton was TV's Merry Mailman in the 1950s; Bob Ein-
    stein is also known as Super Dave and is the brother of Albert Brooks.

The John Byner Comedy Hour ☺
Aug. 1, 1972–Aug. 29, 1972
PBN: Tuesday
Notable regulars: Patti Deutsch, Ray Charles Orchestra

The John Davidson Show ☺
May 30, 1969–June 14, 1976
PBN: Monday
Notable seventies regular: Pete Barbutti

Johnny Cash Presents the Everly Brothers Show ☺
July 8, 1970–Sept. 16, 1970
PBN: Wednesday
Note: Johnny Cash was not in this series—it was the summer replacement for his series.

The Johnny Cash Show ☺
June 1969–May 1971; Aug. 1976–Sept. 1976
PBN: (1976 show)
Notable seventies regulars: Statler Brothers, Carter family, Carl Perkins, Tennessee Three, Steve Martin, Jim Varney

Johnny Mann's Stand Up and Cheer
1971–73
PBN: syndicated
Note: One episode featured Milton Berle delivering a dramatic recitation of "Desiderata."

The Julie Andrews Hour
Sept. 13, 1972–April 28, 1973
Notable regulars: Rich Little, Alice Ghostley, Nelson Riddle Orchestra

The Keane Brothers Show ☺
Aug. 12, 1977–Sept. 2, 1977
PBN: Friday
Notable regulars: Anita Mann Dancers
Note: The Keane Brothers were twelve-year-old John and thirteen-year-old Tom.

Keep On Truckin' ☺
July 12, 1975–Aug. 2, 1975
PBN: Saturday
Notable regulars: Franklyn Ajaye, Didi Conn, Wayland Flowers, Jack Riley, Fred Travalena

Note: Rod Serling was originally going to be the host of this show, but he died two weeks before it went on the air.

The Kelly Monteith Show ☺
June 16, 1976–July 7, 1976
PBN: Wednesday

The Ken Berry "Wow" Show ☺
July 15, 1972–Aug. 12, 1972
PBN: Saturday
Notable regulars: Teri Garr, Steve Martin, Billy Van, Cheryl Stoppelmoor (Cheryl Ladd)

The Kraft Music Hall
Sept. 13, 1967–May 12, 1971
PBN: Wednesday
Note: Each week's program featured a different host and often was based on a particular theme; this program was the original home of the "Friars Club Roasts," which later were picked up by "The Dean Martin Show."

Kraft Music Hall Presents the Des O'Connor Show ☺
May 20, 1970–Sept. 1, 1971
PBN: Wednesday
Notable regulars: Connie Stevens
Note: Series was produced in London.

The Late Summer Early Fall Bert Convy Show ☺
Aug. 25, 1976–Sept. 15, 1976
PBN: Wednesday
Note: Don Knotts, appearing on just the first episode, was this series' only guest star.

The Mac Davis Show ☺
July 1974–Aug. 1974; Dec. 1974–May 1975; March 1976–June 1976
PBN: Thursday
(initial run)
Notable regulars: Shields and Yarnell, Strutt, Mike Post Orchestra

Note: Regular feature of the show had Davis improvising songs from titles suggested by audience members.

Manhattan Transfer ☺
Aug. 10, 1975–Aug. 31, 1975
PBN: Sunday
Note: Occasional comic bits featured a character named Doughie Duck.

The Marilyn McCoo and Billy Davis, Jr. Show ☺
June 15, 1977–July 20, 1977
PBN: Wednesday
Notable regulars: Jay Leno, Tim Reid

The Marty Feldman Comedy Machine
April 12, 1972–Aug. 16, 1972
PBN: Wednesday
Notable regulars: Barbara Feldon, Spike Milligan, Thelma Houston, Orson Welles
Note: Title sequence and animated interludes done by Terry Gilliam.

Mary
Sept. 24, 1978–Oct. 8, 1978
Host: Mary Tyler Moore
PBN: Sunday
Notable regulars: Dick Shawn, James Hampton, Swoosie Kurtz, David Letterman, Michael Keaton

The Melba Moore-Clifton Davis Show
June 7, 1972–July 5, 1972
PBN: Wednesday
Notable regulars: Ron Carey, Richard Libertini, Liz Torres

NBC Follies
Sept. 13, 1973–Dec. 27, 1973
PBN: Thursday
Notable regulars: Sammy Davis, Jr., Mickey Rooney

Nashville on the Road
1975–83
PBN: syndicated
Host: Jim Ed Brown (1975–81); Jim Stafford (1981–83)
Notable regulars: Jerry Clower, Cates Sisters

The New Bill Cosby Show
Sept. 11, 1972–May 7, 1973
PBN: Monday
Notable regulars: Lola Falana, Foster Brooks, Quincy Jones Orchestra, Pat McCormick, Ronny Graham

Pat Paulsen's Half a Comedy Hour
Jan. 22, 1970–April 16, 1970
PBN: Thursday
Notable regulars: Bob Einstein, Jean Byron
Note: One bit was called "Children's Letters to the Devil."

The Pearl Bailey Show
Jan. 23, 1971–May 8, 1971
PBN: Saturday
Notable regulars: Louis Bellson Orchestra

Presenting Susan Anton
April 26, 1979–May 17, 1979
PBN: Thursday
Note: According to *The Complete Directory*, the show included "a recurring sketch about the Disco Monks . . . three religious men attempting to modernize their order to make it more appealing to contemporary men."

Redd Foxx
Sept. 15, 1977–Jan. 26, 1978
PBN: Thursday
Notable regulars: Slappy White, Damita Jo, LaWanda Page
Note: Regular bit entitled "Redd's Corner" featured appearances by Foxx's performer friends from his chitlin circuit days.

The Rich Little Show
Feb. 2, 1976–July 19, 1976
PBN: Monday
Notable regulars: Charlotte Rae

The Richard Pryor Show
Sept. 13, 1977–Oct. 20, 1977
PBN: Tuesday
Notable regulars: Sandra Bernhard, Tim Reid, Marsha Warfield, Robin
    Williams

Sammy and Company
1975–77
PBN: syndicated
Notable regulars: William B. Williams, Avery Schreiber
Note: This was really a talk show, but I felt it deserved inclusion in this
    list anyway.

Saturday Night Live
October 11, 1975-present
PBN: duh
Notable seventies regulars (in addition to the Not Ready For Prime-
    Time Players): Albert Brooks, Gary Weis, Jim Henson's Muppets, Don
    Novello, Paul Shaffer, Al Franken, Tom Davis

Saturday Night Live with Howard Cosell
Sept. 20, 1975–Jan. 17, 1976
PBN: see above
Notes: First broadcast included American TV debut of Bay City Rollers;
    program began a few weeks before more lasting show with similar
    name; Cosell sang on one episode.

Shields and Yarnell ☺
June 1977–July 1977; Jan. 1978–March 1978
(initial run)
Notable regulars: Joanna Cassidy
Note: Hosts were a husband-wife mime team.

The Sonny and Cher Comedy Hour
Aug. 1971–May 1974; Feb. 1976–Aug. 1977
PBN: only nights *not* scheduled at some point were Tuesday and Thursday
Notable regulars: Murray Langston (the Unknown Comic from "The Gong Show"), Chastity Bono, Freeman King, Steve Martin, Teri Garr, Bob Einstein, Billy Van, Shields and Yarnell
Note: Shortly after Sonny and Cher's divorce in 1974, the team split professionally as well, and this program was cleaved in twain, begatting "Cher" and "The Sonny Comedy Revue." When those both bombed, the two opportunistically revived "The Sonny and Cher Comedy Hour," although the spark obviously had gone out.

The Sonny Comedy Revue
Sept. 22, 1974–Dec. 29, 1974
PBN: Sunday
Notable regulars: Freeman King, Murray Langston, Billy Van, Teri Garr

This Is Tom Jones
Feb. 7, 1969–Jan. 15, 1971
Notable seventies regulars: Ace Trucking Company
Note: Tapings were done both in Los Angeles and London.

The Tim Conway Comedy Hour
Sept. 20, 1970–Dec. 13, 1970
PBN: Sunday
Notable regulars: McLean Stevenson, Sally Struthers, Nelson Riddle Orchestra

Tony Orlando and Dawn ☺
July 3, 1974; Dec. 1974–Dec. 1976
PBN: Wednesday
(initial run)
Notable regulars: George Carlin, Edie McClurg
Notes: Initials of program name spell out TOAD; known in its final season as "The Tony Orlando and Dawn Rainbow Hour."

INSIDE THE SEVENTIES MUSEUM

Forget Graceland. Memphis's real monument to trash culture is the Shangri-La Seventies Museum.

You see, there are these guys, Sherm and Eric, who run one of the best record/CD stores I've ever seen out of this big old house. The Seventies Museum is their bathroom. Not *just* their bathroom—it's also open to the public during Shangri-La's business hours.

You walk in there and it's so crammed with Fonzie paraphernalia and such stuff that you can barely make it to the sink. But you must get over to the sink to scrub your hands. You must purify yourself before you dare to touch such holies of holies as the twelve-inch-high Cher doll in full "Half Breed" regalia.

Sherm and Eric are trying to get official recognition and federal funding for their museum—so far they haven't had much luck. But perhaps one day, when people begin to see the seventies as a bona fide historical period rather than a bad joke, money will pour in. Then the boys will finally be able to construct the Farrah wing they've been talking about. And seal those "Mork and Mindy" trading cards in a temperature-controlled viewing case to protect them from the ravages of time. And install that full-size diorama of Seventies Man sitting in a fern bar.

While the boys may not have federal funding yet, amazing contributions have been flooding in from friends all over the country. Below Sherm lists some of the best gifts to come their way.

Seven-inch Stacks.   Must see to believe! If you're considering a trip to Memphis, these shoes should tip the scales for you. More like clodhoppers than the "seven inch . . . leather heels" that Paul Stanley eulogized in "Do You Love Me," but we've received bids of two hundred dollars for these babies. No chance, sirs, donations are not for sale.

"All in the Family" Game.   Guess Archie's answers to a whole bunch of questions. "Is there a little bit of Archie in every one of us?" the cover asks. I hope not. Play while listening to the "All in the Family" LP. Edith looks like she's had too much of Archie's abuse in the group photo on the box cover—and she's already a junkie (and this was early in the show's run, 1972). Poor Edith. Poor Meathead. Poor us.

Proprietors Sherm and Eric outside their seventies museum.

169

Frampton Comes Alive! **Plaque.**   A thank you to WLYX from A&M records for "helping to establish Peter Frampton as a platinum recording artist." Nice photo. Shop class—quality workmanship.

"Welcome Back, Kotter" Books One, Two, and Three.   Three fine works by author William Johnston, chronicler of all things Sweathoglike. *The Sweathog Trail* and *The Sweathog Newshawks* depict the foibles of the Sweathogs' populist movements in the political and media arenas, respectively, with guidance from Mr. Kott-*aire* of course. Wild stuff. The third, *The Super Sweathogs*, is also quite mid-seventies activist as the boys fight for tenants' rights in the building Epstein's uncle super-intends, but this is a much more Scooby Doo meddling kids—esque thriller in plotting and pacing.

Epstein Doll.   The above books take on a new meaning when read with this fine-featured Puerto Rican fighter on one's desk. In the grand tradition of the best likeness dolls, this eight-inch doll looks nothing like Epstein. The box reads: "Signed Epstein's mother." Mattel did a fine job on this one, Epstein in acid wash, sporting a huge brown belt and a sizable Afro. The problem is, he looks more like Tom Jones. With a real cloth bandanna! (The Kotter doll comes with a briefcase. Horshack comes with a lunchbox. Washington comes with a basketball. Barbarino gets a comb.)

   Take a break from your serious Sweathog reading and doll admiring to peruse the "Welcome Back, Kotter" comic number one (and only?). Don't worry, it's not printed with their own blood, as the **Kiss comic book** was rumored to be. Imagine yourself abusing lots of black caffeine in the **Sweathogs coffee cup**, featuring fine photos of our favorite illiterates with a few of their witty put-downs on a blackboard behind them. I remember "Up your nose with a rubber hose," but "A hairy canary"? Those Sweathogs were just too cryptic.

Xaviera! and **Xaviera Meets Marylin Chambers.**   Yes, the seventies were a time of coked-up sexual experimentation. Did I meet you in the Studio 54 bathroom or was that your husband? Blockbusters like *Beyond the Green Door* got middle-class wanna-be hipsters out into the porno theaters en masse, and here we got the pulp product. In the name of sexual openness and understanding, Xaviera Hollander tells a couple of sexy stories about prostitution and answers questions from straight-but-willing-to-learn folks.

Famolare Skateboard. Yeah, I thought they only made shoes, too, but here it is, a prime promo double-kicktailed flexible number with Chicago trucks and open-bearing Power Paw—copy wheels. Imagine all of the skatekids today who have never, ever ridden a board like this one, never chased ball bearings down the street, never had their wheels stop on microscopic pebbles. A sticker on the tail of the board says, "I'm a Superstar. I Give Blood." And with fine equipment like this, I'm sure the previous owner gave a whole bunch.

Pet Rock Box with Training Manual. Well, whoever attempted to train the rock that used to reside in this box obviously did not read the manual carefully, because the thing escaped and is probably being tossed at cars by delinquent kids right now. This exquisite memento of one of the most stupid fads ever is testament to perhaps the most successful concept-packaging-advertising job ever.

Chrissy Puzzle. Imagine the suspense as, piece by piece, you put together the puzzle of Suzanne Somers falling out of her black bathing suit. Or just stare at the cover, like I do. But whatever you do, send her money and save the starving rain forests!

Kiss Puzzle. Probably recipient of the highest number of "I had that!" comments, this two-hundred-piece puzzle supposedly depicts our makeupped marvels as seen on the cover of the *Destroyer* album. It's restricted to ages six to fifteen, so I haven't been able to assemble it myself to make sure. Any preteens willing to donate a couple of hours a week to our museum in the name of research?

***Land of the Lost* (Little Golden Book).** Who did they get to do the art for these books? This is *awful*! No wonder kids were so confused in the seventies. Nothing in here looks like anything or anyone from the show.

Dawn: Portrait of a Teenage Runaway. From the publishers of the fine *Sarah T.: Portrait of a Teenage Alcoholic* comes another sensitive story about bell-bottomed youth in distress. Fans take note: Eve Plumb does not star in this written adaptation of the made-for-TV movie.

Grease **Fotonovel.**   In our minds, this is an essential companion to *Grease*, the movie. Here you get over 350 color stills from the film, lots of dialogue in cool cartoon bubbles with comic sound effects added, and the bonus of characters sharing their unexpressed thoughts via thought balloons. These inner ruminations add depth to many of the less-featured characters and make the motivations and aspirations of these no-gooders and do-gooders all the more pronounced.

Imagine wearing a **"May the Force Be with You" shirt** as you sip from your very own **Darth Vader coffee mug**! Fill this six-inch-high likeness of Luke's secret dad full of java and you can bet you'll feel mean.

David Cassidy Comic Number Six.   Full of ads (I especially liked "Make and wear luv beads like David does!"), this is ultra ultra no-effort comic making. Just plain *cheep*. An additional incongruous "humorous" short story about the coming computer age is one of the *worst* things I have ever read. I almost feel sorry for the true fans who owned this. Looks great in the museum's Partridge wing, though.

Pong.   Here it is, cyberkids, your past. Before Nintendo, Smash TV, Robotron, Pac Man, Crazy Climber, and Galaxian, before Atari home systems and even Space Invaders, Pong ruled the electronic-gaming universe. This is real fun, like playing Ping-Pong or tennis except you just sit there staring at the TV and you really can't control your racket very well. No wonder these things caught on.

To see all of these wonders and more, head on down to Shangri-La, 1916 Madison Avenue, Memphis.

WHY EIGHT-TRACK TECHNOLOGY RULES

People who own CD players scoff. How could anyone want to go back to the low-tech world of eight-track? Why forsake the sturdy CD for that chunky plastic cassette, with its flimsy strip of tape that has become notorious for the way it inevitably snaps in half, sometimes just days after you buy it? In this digital age, many people think of eight-track technology as some kind of bad joke. But don't join the scoffers; instead recognize the technology as one that tried to do too much too soon. Like Icarus flying too close to the sun, eight-track died because it attempted greatness.

Remember how frustrating it was back in the era of tape recorders, when you had to keep fast-forwarding or reversing to find your favorite song? Eight-track offered a different solution. Each eight-track tape had four different "programs" on it; by pushing the select button you switched among programs—this would get you *near* the song you wanted but not right to it. So if you think about it, eight-track technology was trying to offer people a humble version of the CD's ability to skip between songs.

Of course, you paid a price for the convenience of eight-tracks. They were very fussy. The tape tended to snap if you pulled it out of the player too vigorously; the various recordings on different programs tended to bleed into one another; and the rubber rollers inside of the tapes could melt down, filling the deck with black goo. (I was personally touched by this tragedy when my copy of Cream's *Wheels of Fire* began oozing black bile. When I pulled out the tape, the roller looked as lumpy and misshapen as a moon rock—it truly had become a wheel of fire.)

However, the eight-track had one cool feature that the CD player lacks. Inside the cassette shell, the tape was looped over itself in a figure-eight configuration (or infinity symbol, if you will). Once you shoved an eight-track into your stereo, it would play over and over and over until the tape snapped. (OK, you can put some CD players on an endless repeat cycle, but it's just not the same.)

And for true seventies enthusiasts, there's no substitute for that particular fuzzy eight-track audio quality. Would *Shades of Deep Purple* or Kiss's *Double Platinum* sound right in the airy, clean world of CD? No way. Albums like these should be cranked at full volume on a eight-track player with bad speakers built into a Chevy Malibu.

173

And while we're on the subject of car stereos, there's a really cool scene in *The Omega Man* where Charlton Heston, cruising the zombie-filled wasteland in a red sports car, pops in an eight-track of the Ventures. Weaving through the wreckage as he listens to "Telstar," Heston is the ultimate postapocalyptic playboy.

If you're still not convinced that eight-track rules, consider this: for ten bucks you'd be lucky to get one CD. But for that same price and some tireless thrift shopping, you probably could score an eight-track console and enough Montovani and Abba tapes to keep you busy for days. In fact, this author was able to buy about thirty eight-tracks plus a swank traveling case, all for ninety-nine cents at Amvets thrift store. Thank you, American veterans.

EIGHT-TRACK TAPES TO DIE FOR

Never Mind the Bollocks, Here's the Sex Pistols. Imagine listening to songs like "Anarcy in the U.K." with that "ka-thunk" sound in the middle as the tape switches tracks. Imagine having all of that raw, spontaneous anger repeating itself in a continual loop, like a hammer that never stops hitting your head.

According to connoisseur James Burnett, *Never Mind the Bollocks* is the Holy Grail, the pièce de résistance of rare eight-track tapes. It took him three years to find his copy. After some self-examination, he decided to put the tape on display at his record store, with a price tag of one hundred dollars to ward off potential buyers. Eternal vigilance is the price of freedom. He left town to visit his family and when he came back, the tape had been sold.

Disco Express. It's put out by TeeVee Records, so you know it's got to be good. "Boogie Oogie Oogie," "Keep on Dancin'," "Got To Be Real." This is the one to slip into your Panasonic portable (the eight-track player that looked like a dynamite detonator) and take to the roller disco.

Our Best to You: The Wonderful World of Reader's Digest Music. What Reader's Digest condensed books did for literature, this does for popular music. Three decades of music on one tape! "Sentimental Journey" is right next to "Up, Up and Away." The artists are a veritable laundry list of "and His Orchestras": David Whitaker and His Orchestra; Douglas Gamley and His Orchestra; Marty Paich, His Orchestra and Chorus. A cool logo informs the listener that the tape is "pleasure programmed."

Original Motion Picture Soundtrack: Car Wash. If not for one flaw—the inclusion of Richard Pryor's monologue from the movie, which becomes a torment by the fifth time the tape has gone around—this eight-track would be entirely perfect. Rose Royce gives you lots of laid-back, waa-waa-heavy movie scores—sort of like disco meets blaxploitation funk.

It was while making out and listening to a battered *Car Wash* eight-track that the author and her boyfriend became filled with a

175

druglike ecstasy that they can attribute only to hearing "Righteous Rhythm" twelve times in a row.

What is so sexy about eight-tracks? It's not just their aura of romantic tragedy (a failed and forgotten technology); it's that, unlike cassettes, records, and CDs, they never interrupt you in the throes of passion because they never end (until they break, that is).

Sonny and Cher: *Mama Was a Rock and Roll Singer, Papa Used To Write All Her Songs.* If *Car Wash* is the eight-track of luv, this is the eight-track of calumny, deceit, and shame. In 1973, when this came out, the twosome had a hit TV show ("The Sonny and Cher Comedy Hour"); the secret of the show's success was perhaps the sick pleasure that comes from watching a couple who hates each other pretend they don't on national TV.

Here's an excerpt from Sonny's diary that year: "I have a lover now, Connie. She's been a part of my life for several months. Don't ask me how everything is going. I don't know. Cher and I have a TV show, and the public still thinks we are married. We are both very involved in our careers. At home? Connie and I live together as husband and wife. We live in the same house with Cher and the baby. Cher has her boyfriend."

When the two signed off their show singing "I've Got You Babe" and cuddling Chastity between them, the sugary sweetness of this mod couple had an aftertaste of battery acid. By 1974, they had begun divorce proceedings.

The cover of *Mama Was a Rock and Roll Singer* pictures Sonny and Cher in a kid's bedroom—presumably Chastity's—surrounded by toys, as if to symbolize that the only thing that holds them together is their daughter.

Abba: Greatest Hits. It doesn't get any cleaner and more synthesized than this disco-influenced Swedish group. Songs like "Fernando" and "SOS" sound like they've already been made into Muzak versions of themselves.

All in the Family (2nd Album). The best part is the cover, of course, because who can bear to listen to a tape of TV dialogue more than once (if that)? Mike, Edith, Archie, and Gloria are arranged in a *tableau vivant*. Archie's in his chair, smoking his stogie; Gloria's leaning over

Auto TAPE DECK

and sticking out her butt in a pre–women's lib pose. The words *All in the Family* appear in that American-flag, red-white-and-blue typeface so popular before the bicentennial, and best of all, the plastic of the cassette is hot pink.

Boz Scaggs: *Silk Degrees.* The label shows Boz sitting on a park bench, brooding. At the very edge of the picture, you can see a woman's hand (with long, red nails). Presumably she's sitting at the end of the bench, trying to convince the Boz to give her some. He's turned away, contemplating his own hand through dark shades—too much the tortured artiste to have anything to do with her. Can any woman really understand the mind that created "Lowdown"?

Barry White: *I've Got So Much to Give.* I'll bet you do, Barry. Chill the Riunite and pop this tape into your waterbed's built-in eight-track system before you ask that special lady over. Barry was one of those smooooth, deep-voiced crooners of the seventies whose music seemed specially designed for intimate evenings. He's pictured on the cover with a relaxed Afro and a Fu Manchu mustache, wearing a playboy's leather coat and holding four tiny women in the palms of his hands. Patron saint of the swinger.

Peter Frampton: *Frampton Comes Alive!* Oooh, baby! I love your long Leif Garrett hair and your skinny, hairless Shaun Cassidy chest. I want you-ooo-ooo to show me the way.

If you think about it, Peter Frampton was the ur-idol. He never had his own TV show (as did the Monkees, David Cassidy, and Bobby Sherman), but he did have the golden tresses, low-cut shirts and emaciated body that became standard equipment for late-seventies teen idols.

And unlike some of those bubblegum sex symbols, Peter knew how to rock out. My copy of this album is especially awesome because the tape has become so stretched out and dirty that it sounds like Peter's playing his searing guitar solos underwater.

Together: *Today's Love Hits.* Love—or should I say luv?—went out of style when disco fever came in. Real romance was too *gooey*. What you wanted was the slick impersonality of a one-night stand, the thrill of seeing the object of your desire lit by little flecks from the disco ball.

177

Many of these "love hits" compiled by K-Tel celebrate lust instead, songs that are really just pick-up lines put to music—like Little River Band's "Lady" and Dr. Hook's "Sharing the Night Together."

20th Century Steel Band: *Warm Heart Cold Steel.* The band appears on the cover in matching white bell-bottom unitards. They do "Theme from Shaft," Caribbean-style.

Cheryl Ladd: *Dance Forever.* The model-turned-Charlie's-angel tries to look like a sort of disco cowgirl for her cover photo: she wears cowboy boots over knee-high legwarmers, baring her thighs up to her hotpants. Weird. Best song is "Rock and Roll Slave," in which she promises a prefeminist enslavement to her guy. But I thought rock and roll slaves wore tube tops, spandex pants, and platform shoes—what's with the cowgirl stuff?

Put the Hammer Down! This is a compilation of country songs about trucking put together by the people at Realistic (you know, the maker of fine audio equipment—did this tape come free with car stereo systems or something?). Of course, the compilation includes C. W. McCall's "Convoy" and Merle Haggard's "White Line Fever," but it also acquaints us with some trucker songs that are a little more esoteric. Like, for instance, Red Simpson's "I'm a Truck," a surrealistic narrative from the truck's point of view. On the cover, we get a beauteous bunch of pictures of the big rigs—flatbeds and snub-nosed eighteen-wheelers. Almost makes you want to be a truck.

READING IS FUNDAMENTAL

The following is a list of books and fanzines from which I've quoted—along with others I used as reference works and background resources.

Adam, Barry D. *The Rise of a Gay and Lesbian Movement*. Boston: Twayne Publishers, 1987.

Alley, Robert S., and Irby B. Brown. *Love Is All Around: The Making of The Mary Tyler Moore Show*. New York: Dell Publishing, 1989.

Altman, Dennis. *Coming Out in the Seventies*. Boston: Alyson Publications, 1981.

Andrews, Bart, with Brad Dunning. *The Worst TV Shows Ever*. New York: Dutton, 1980.

Barnouw, Erik. *The Sponsor: Notes on a Modern Potentate*. New York: Oxford University Press, 1978.

———. *Tube of Plenty: The Evolution of American Television*. New York: Oxford University Press, 1990.

Baudrillard, Jean. *Simulations*. New York: Semiotext(e), 1983.

Bogle, Donald. *Blacks in American Films and Television: An Illustrated Encyclopedia*. New York: Fireside, 1988.

————. *Toms, Coons, Mulattoes, Mammies & Bucks: An Interpretive History of Blacks in American Films.* New York: The Continuum Publishing Company, 1991.

Bono, Sonny. *And the Beat Goes On.* New York: Pocket Books, 1991.

Booker, Christopher. *The Seventies: The Decade That Changed the Future.* New York: Stein and Day, 1981.

Brooks, Tim, and Earle Marsh. *The Complete Directory to Prime Time Network TV Shows.* New York: Ballatine Books, 1992.

Brown, H. Rap. *Die Nigger Die!* New York: The Dial Press, 1969.

Carroll, Peter N. *It Seemed Like Nothing Happened: The Tragedy and Promise of America in the 1970s.* New York: Holt, Rinehart and Winston, 1982.

Castleman, Harry, and Walter J. Podrazik. *Harry and Wally's Favorite TV Shows.* New York: Prentice-Hall, 1989.

Crawford, Alan. *Thunder on the Right: The "New Right" and the Politics of Resentment.* New York: Pantheon Books, 1980.

Dates, Jannette L., and William Barlow, eds. *Split Image: African Americans in the Mass Media.* Washington, D.C.: Howard University Press, 1990.

D'Emilio, John, and Estelle B. Freedman. *Intimate Matters: A History of Sexuality in America.* New York: Harper & Row, 1988.

Diamond, Edwin, and Stephen Bates. *The Spot: The Rise of Political Advertising on Television.* Cambridge, Mass.: The MIT Press, 1984.

Echols, Alice. *Daring to Be BAD: Radical Feminism in America 1967–1975.* Minneapolis: University of Minnesota Press, 1989.

Edelstein, Andrew J., and Frank Lovece. *The Brady Bunch Book.* New York: Warner Books, 1990.

Edelstein, Andrew J., and Kevin McDonough. *The Seventies: From Hot Pants to Hot Tubs.* New York: Dutton, 1990.

Ehrenreich, Barbara. *Fear of Falling: The Inner Life of the Middle Class.* New York: Pantheon Books, 1989.

Evans, Sara. *Personal Politics: The Roots of Women's Liberation in the Civil Rights Movement and the New Left.* New York: Vintage Books, 1980.

Faludi, Susan. *Backlash: The Undeclared War Against American Women.* New York: Crown Publishers, 1991.

Grossman, Gary H. *Saturday Morning TV.* New York: Dell Publishing, 1981.

Grove, Kim. *More Love Is . . . .* New York: Signette, 1971.

Harrington, Michael. *Decade of Decision: The Crisis of the American System.* New York: Touchstone, 1980.

Hoffman, Abbie. *Steal This Book.* New York: Pirate Editions, 1971.

Jacobs, Jerry. *The Mall: An Attempted Escape from Everyday Life.* Prospect Heights, Ill.: Waveland Press, 1984.

Jacobs, Timothy. *Lemons: The World's Worst Cars.* Greenwich, Conn.: Dorset Press, 1991.

Key, Wilson Bryan. *Media Sexploitation.* Englewood Cliffs, N.J.: Prentice-Hall, 1976.

Lasch, Christopher. *The Culture of Narcissism: American Life in an Age of Diminishing Expectations.* New York: Warner Books, 1979.

Lifton, Robert Jay. *Home from the War: Learning from Vietnam Veterans.* Boston: Beacon Press, 1973.

Mailer, Norman. *Miami and the Siege of Chicago.* New York: Signet, 1968.

Marable, Manning. *From the Grassroots: Essays Toward Afro-American Liberation.* Boston: South End Press, 1980.

Marcus, Greil. *Mystery Train: Images of America in Rock 'n' Roll Music.* New York: Plume, 1990.

Marill, Alvin H. *Movies Made for Television: The Telefeature and the Mini-Series 1964–1979.* Westport, Conn.: Arlington House Publishers, 1980.

McCrohan, Donna. *Archie & Edith, Mike & Gloria: The Tumultuous History of All in the Family.* New York: Workman Publishing, 1987.

McGinniss, Joe. *The Selling of the President 1968.* New York: Trident Press, 1969.

Miezitis, Vita. *Nightdancin'.* New York: Ballantine Books, 1980.

Miller, Mark Crispin. *Boxed In: The Culture of TV.* Evanston, Ill.: Northwestern University Press, 1988.

Mitz, Rich. *The Great TV Sitcom Book.* New York: Perigee Books, 1980.

Molloy, John T. *The Woman's Dress for Success Book.* New York: Warner Books, 1977.

Parenti, Michael. *Democracy for the Few.* New York: St. Martin's Press, 1977.

Pollack, Bruce. *The Disco Handbook.* New York: Scholastic Book Services, 1979.

Price, Jerome. *The Antinuclear Movement.* Boston: Twayne Publishers, 1982.

Ribakove, Barbara, and Sy Ribakove. *The Happy Years.* New York: Award Books, 1974.

Schrank, Jeffrey. *Snap, Crackle and Popular Taste: The Illusion of Free Choice in America.* New York: Dell Publishing, 1977.

Schremp, Gerry. *Kitchen Culture: Fifty Years of Food Fads.* New York: Pharos Books, 1991.

Spear, Joseph C. *Presidents and the Press: The Nixon Legacy.* Cambridge, Mass.: The MIT Press, 1986.

Terp, Pop-Top, with Kenneth Patton. *Pop-Topping!* Radnor, Pa.: Chilton Book Company, 1975.

Toffler, Alvin. *Future Shock.* New York: Bantam Books, 1970.

Vale, V., and Andrea Juno, eds. *Incredibly Strange Films.* San Francisco: Re/Search Publications, 1986.

Van Peebles, Melvin, and Mario Van Peebles. *No Identity Crisis: A Father and Son's Own Story of Working Together.* New York: Simon & Schuster, 1990.

Ward, Ed, Geoffrey Stokes, and Ken Tucker. *Rock of Ages: The Rolling Stone History of Rock & Roll.* New York: Summit Books, 1986.

Weldon, Michael. *The Psychotronic Encyclopedia of Film.* New York: Ballantine Books, 1983.

Wolfe, Tom. *In Our Time.* New York: Farrar, Straus & Giroux, 1980.

Zaroulis, Nancy, and Gerald Sullivan. *Who Spoke Up?: American Protest Against the War in Vietnam 1963–1975.* New York: Holt, Rinehart and Winston, 1984.

Zinn, Howard, *The Twentieth Century: A People's History.* New York: Harper & Row, 1984.

MAGAZINES/FANZINES

8-Track Mind; 8-TM Publications; P.O. Box 90, East Detroit, MI 48021-0090

Flake: The Breakfast Nostalgia Magazine; Scott Bruce; P.O. Box 481, Cambridge, MA 02140

It's a Wonderful Lifestyle; Candi Strecker; 590 Lisbon, San Francisco, CA 94112

Psychotronic; Psychotronic Video; 151 First Avenue, Department PV, New York, NY 10003

Teenage Gang Debs; Erin and Don Smith; 5812 Midhill St., Bethesda, MD 20817